T0190029

Multiple Instance Learning

Francisco Herrera · Sebastián Ventura
Rafael Bello · Chris Cornelis
Amelia Zafra · Dánel Sánchez-Tarragó
Sarah Vluymans

Multiple Instance Learning

Foundations and Algorithms

 Springer

Francisco Herrera
Department of Computer Science
  and Artificial Intelligence
University of Granada
Granada
Spain

Sebastián Ventura
Department of Computer Sciences
University of Córdoba
Córdoba
Spain

Rafael Bello
Center of Information Studies
Central University "Marta Abreu" of Las
  Villas
Santa Clara, Villa Clara
Cuba

Chris Cornelis
Department of Applied Mathematics,
  Computer Science and Statistics
Ghent University
Ghent
Belgium

Amelia Zafra
Department of Computer Science
  and Numerical Analysis
University of Córdoba
Córdoba
Spain

Dánel Sánchez-Tarragó
Central University "Marta Abreu" of Las
  Villas
Santa Clara, Villa Clara
Cuba

Sarah Vluymans
Department of Applied Mathematics,
  Computer Science and Statistics
Ghent University
Ghent
Belgium

ISBN 978-3-319-83815-1   ISBN 978-3-319-47759-6   (eBook)
DOI 10.1007/978-3-319-47759-6

© Springer International Publishing AG 2016
Softcover reprint of the hardcover 1st edition 2016
This work is subject to copyright. All rights are reserved by the Publisher, whether the whole or part
of the material is concerned, specifically the rights of translation, reprinting, reuse of illustrations,
recitation, broadcasting, reproduction on microfilms or in any other physical way, and transmission
or information storage and retrieval, electronic adaptation, computer software, or by similar or dissimilar
methodology now known or hereafter developed.
The use of general descriptive names, registered names, trademarks, service marks, etc. in this
publication does not imply, even in the absence of a specific statement, that such names are exempt from
the relevant protective laws and regulations and therefore free for general use.
The publisher, the authors and the editors are safe to assume that the advice and information in this
book are believed to be true and accurate at the date of publication. Neither the publisher nor the
authors or the editors give a warranty, express or implied, with respect to the material contained herein or
for any errors or omissions that may have been made.

Printed on acid-free paper

This Springer imprint is published by Springer Nature
The registered company is Springer International Publishing AG
The registered company address is: Gewerbestrasse 11, 6330 Cham, Switzerland

Preface

Multiple instance learning (MIL) is a recent learning framework that has become very popular lately. In this framework, objects are represented as sets of feature vectors (or bags, in MIL terminology). This kind of representation is well suited for certain problems, such as the prediction of structure–activity relationships, image classification, document categorization or the prediction of protein binding sites. In fact, MIL provides a much more natural representation than the one used in classical machine learning, where a single feature vector is used per object.

The first papers on MIL appeared in the early nineties. Their main interest is solving classification problems where input data are represented as multiple instances. This field, known as multiple instance classification (MIC), is the most popular subparadigm of MIL, but not the only one. In recent years, papers have also appeared on multiple instance regression (multi-instance learning with a continuous output) and multi-instance clustering. This book aims to present a general and comprehensible overview of the MIL paradigm, providing a formal definition of the framework and covering the subparadigms it comprises, the most relevant algorithms and the most representative applications.

The book is divided into three main parts. The first part (Chaps. 1–3) introduces the most important concepts of the discipline that will be necessary to understand the remainder of the book. Chapter 1 contains some introductory concepts on knowledge discovery in databases, data preprocessing, and data mining, whereas Chap. 2 introduces the multiple instance learning paradigm from a descriptive perspective. The first part finishes with a chapter focused on MIC. Besides including a formal definition of the problem and a taxonomy for MIC algorithms, it also carries out a study of two important issues, namely distance metrics and alternative learning hypotheses.

The second part of the book (Chaps. 4–7) provides an exhaustive review of the different MIL algorithms. Chapters 4 and 5 describe the most important classification algorithms, following the taxonomy introduced in Chap. 3. Chapter 6 introduces multiple instance regression, the other main task in supervised learning. Chapter 7 covers two unsupervised learning tasks in the MIL framework: clustering and association rule mining.

The last part of the book (Chaps. 8–10) deals with other recent areas. Data reduction for MIL is addressed in Chap. 8. Chapter 9 discusses the problem of learning with imbalanced multi-instance data. Finally, Chap. 10 introduces multiple instance multiple label learning, a new learning framework that combines MIL with multi-label learning.

The target audience for this book is anyone interested in a good understanding of this important paradigm of machine learning, as well as a deep description of the current state of the art in the discipline. Practitioners in the industry and enterprise should find new insights and possibilities in the breadth of the topics covered. Researchers and data scientists in universities, research centers, and companies could appreciate this comprehensive review and uncover new ideas for productive research efforts.

Granada, Spain   Francisco Herrera
Córdoba, Spain   Sebastián Ventura
Santa Clara, Cuba   Rafael Bello
Ghent, Belgium   Chris Cornelis
Córdoba, Spain   Amelia Zafra
Santa Clara, Cuba   Dánel Sánchez-Tarragó
Ghent, Belgium   Sarah Vluymans

Contents

Chapter 1
Introduction

Abstract This book reviews the multiple instance learning paradigm. This concept was introduced as a type of supervised learning, dealing with datasets that are more complex than traditionally encountered and presented. Before formally describing multiple instance learning, its methods, developments and applications, this introductory chapter first recalls the general background of the knowledge discovery process in data collections. In Sect. 1.1, we describe the steps involved in this process and the traditional representation of data. Section 1.2 considers one particular knowledge discovery step, namely that of data preprocessing. We continue in Sect. 1.3 with a discussion on data mining methods that are applied on the preprocessed data in order to uncover some novel and useful information. Finally, Sect. 1.4 focuses on classification problems and their evaluation.

1.1 The Knowledge Discovery Process

In everyday life, academics and industry, large amounts of data are collected and stored. Examples include video data obtained from security cameras monitoring public and private areas, interaction data extracted from social networks, transaction data detailing online and in-store purchases, sensor data observing the growth of crops in greenhouses and many more. Since an abundance of information is available and easily collected and storage has become cheap, databases of enormous sizes can be constructed. Small portions of data can still be processed manually, but this task quickly becomes intractable with increasing database size. A supermarket chain, that registers thousands or even millions of transactions on a daily basis, can for instance use this data to model customer behavior and preferences. It requires automated methods to do so.

Knowledge discovery in databases (KDD) involves the extraction of useful knowledge from raw data. The term is commonly credited to [14]. It is the automated procedure that makes sense of data that is too large or complex to be humanly interpreted. The full KDD process involves the understanding of the problem domain and research goals, the collection and formatting of data as well as the modeling of the information contained in it. Several models, going from raw data to understandable information, have been developed both from an academic and industrial perspective [10]. We recall a popular hybrid model, used in industry and academics, that divides this full process into six stages [9]:

1. **Understanding the problem domain**: in the first stage, the problem is defined and background information about the domain in which it is situated is gathered. This can for instance involve familiarizing oneself with the domain jargon. The research objectives are specified.
2. **Data understanding**: the data is collected. It is evaluated whether this data is appropriate and useful for the project aims and tools selected in later steps.
3. **Data preprocessing**: the previous phase collects raw data. In this step, the data is prepared to the correct input format for the next stage. This can involve transformation and reduction procedures. A more detailed discussion of the methods applied in this step is presented in Sect. 1.2.
4. **Data mining**: specific methods are applied to derive the hidden knowledge from the data prepared in the previous step. In Sect. 1.3, we provide more background information on this phase.
5. **Knowledge evaluation**: the results obtained from the data mining method are interpreted and validated. This involves a verification whether the derived information is novel and useful.
6. **Use of the discovered knowledge**: usage of the derived knowledge, either directly in the application that the researcher had in mind when executing this process or in some other domain to evaluate its strength there.

Within this scheme, the data preprocessing step is commonly estimated to take up the most effort (e.g. [10]). The final knowledge extracted from the data may be represented in the form of classification rules, association rules, decision trees, clusters of related samples and many others. A visual overview of the six steps is provided in Fig. 1.1. The figure shows that all stages are linked in the two possible directions, which indicates the iterative nature of the KDD process. Feedback loops are explicitly allowed. Several specific examples are motivated in e.g. [10]:

- From *data understanding* to *understanding the problem domain*: after the data has been collected, it can become evident that more or better domain knowledge is required to understand it.
- From *data preprocessing* to *data understanding*: a clearer interpretation of the data may be needed to set up the preprocessing step, e.g. the choice of algorithm. For example, the proper way to deal with missing values may be derived from characteristics of the data itself.
- From *data mining* to *understanding the problem domain*: when the selected data mining method does not yield adequate results in this phase, the objectives set in the first step may have to be revised. The selection of a different data mining method can also lead the user back to the first step.
- From *data mining* to *data understanding*: the data mining step is not guaranteed to yield good results. This can possibly be caused by an incorrect or incomplete understanding of the data. A common example is the misinterpretation and misuse of a categorical feature as a numeric one.

Fig. 1.1 The six steps in the
knowledge discovery process

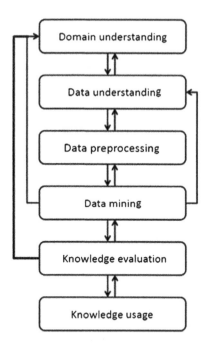

- From *data mining* to *data preprocessing*: when the prepared format in the pre-processing step does not fit all the requirements set by the selected data mining methods, additional preprocessing actions need to be performed.
- From *knowledge evaluation* to *understanding the problem domain*: when the discovered knowledge is validated and a negative result is obtained, e.g. by testing it against knowledge provided by domain experts, the entire KDD process needs to be executed again.
- From *knowledge evaluation* to *data mining*: when the discovered knowledge is correct, but not interesting or new, the data mining step can be repeated with a different method, to possibly obtain more useful results.

The traditional data format lists each observation in a row. An observation (also called sample, element or instance) is described by a number of features or attributes. The values of these features can be ordered in a vector. Possibly, depending on the application, an observation can have an associated outcome. We distinguish two main types of descriptive features. They can be either quantitative (also numeric) or qualitative (also categorical). Both types are further divided into two groups. Quantitative features can be either continuous or discrete. In the former case, the feature takes on real values, in the latter integer values. An example of a continuous feature can be the weight of a woman, while a discrete feature is the number of pregnancies she has had. The division of the qualitative features depends on whether an order can be defined on the feature. If it can, the feature is ordinal. In the other case, it is nominal. Example values for an ordinal feature are categories like 'good', 'neutral'

Table 1.1 A small example dataset

A_1	A_2	A_3	Class
Left	−1.5	1	P
Left	1.5	2	N
Left	1.5	1	N
Center	0.6	2	P
Center	1.1	4	P
Right	−3.9	1	P
Right	0	1	P
Right	−0.9	3	N
Right	−2.2	4	N
Right	0	2	N

and 'bad', which exhibit a clear order between them. For a nominal feature, we can observe categories like 'black', 'yellow' and 'red', on which no order is naturally defined. We note that ordinal qualitative features are sometimes encoded as integers, e.g. by using 0 for 'bad', 1 for 'neutral' and 2 for 'good'. These numbers represent the ordinal relation. This encoding makes ordinal qualitative features somehow related to discrete quantitative features, although the domain of ordinal features is always limited to the predefined categories. For example, there is no interpretation for 4 in this example.

An example dataset is presented in Table 1.1. This is a small artificial dataset, that could correspond to a survey on the voting behavior of citizens with respect to a proposal to increase social benefits. It consists of ten observations, which correspond to voters taking part in the survey. Each observation is described by three features A_1, A_2 and A_3 and has an associated outcome in the form of a class label. There are two possible classes, positive (P) and negative (N), that is, whether the voter would be in favor or not of the proposal. Features A_1 and A_3 are qualitative. The former is nominal and corresponds to the political affiliation of voters, with 'Left', 'Right' and 'Center' as possible categories. The latter is ordinal and is a general evaluation of the respondent of his or her physical condition, which can be 'very poor', 'poor', 'good' or 'very good'. These categories are encoded as integers from 1 to 4. Feature A_2 is quantitative and continuous. It presents the estimated difference in percentage of medical expenses between the previous and current year. This information is collected for all voters completing the survey, together with their disposition towards the social benefit proposal.

This general format is the most common and traditional representation of a dataset. However, this work focuses on multiple instance data, which is a more complex type of data. The datasets in this domain therefore take on a different form than the one presented in Table 1.1. A detailed description will be provided in Sect. 2.1.

1.2 Preprocessing

As explained in the previous section, a crucial step in the KDD process is the transformation of the raw data to a form suitable to be processed by the selected data
mining method. Algorithms performing this step are called preprocessing methods.
The inclusion of the preprocessing step in the general model for KDD is necessary,
since most, if not all, data mining methods require their input data in a specific format.
Furthermore, a certain quality of the data needs to be guaranteed, in order to increase
the probability of obtaining useful results after the data mining step [25]. Procedures
dealing with imperfect data, like noise removal or missing data imputation, may
therefore be necessary.

A recent complete and thorough review on data preprocessing can be found in
[16]. The authors of this work divide these methods into two main groups: *data
preparation algorithms* and *data reduction algorithms*. Data preparation (Sect. 1.2.1)
is the conversion of the raw data to the correct format required by the selected data
mining method. Their application is necessary and enables the application of the
data mining algorithm. Data reduction methods (Sect. 1.2.2) on the other hand are
not used to ensure a correct data format, but rather to actively reduce the size of the
dataset. The reduction step is not always necessary to ensure that the data mining
method can be applied at all, but it can improve its performance and speed up its
computations.

1.2.1 Data Preparation

Data preparation methods provide the correct format for the input data. These algorithms can be divided in three main groups, listed below.

- **Data cleaning**: some corrections are performed on the dataset, e.g., to remove
  bad samples. This category includes two prominent examples. In missing data
  imputation [23], missing values are handled. They are replaced by estimates, for
  example, the mean or most common value for the corresponding feature. The
  second group of popular data cleaning methods are noise identification algorithms
  [28]. They detect noisy observations or feature values in the data. The actual
  removal or replacement of these samples is a data reduction task.
- **Data transformation**: these methods explicitly convert the data to the format
  required by the data mining method, in order to enable its application or improve its
  efficiency. A transformation example is data normalization, which is the process of
  bringing all numeric features to the same scale. This ensures that all these features
  are a priori given the same weight in the data mining step and unexpected results
  are avoided.
- **Data integration**: in some applications, it may be required to merge several data
  sources into a single dataset. An example situation is a clinical study on a specific
  rare disorder, where the data has been collected in a variety of medical centers

that do not store their findings in the same way. Care must be taken, e.g. when the same feature appears under different names in the source datasets.

1.2.2   Data Reduction

Data reduction methods reduce the size of the dataset. This can result in a performance or efficiency gain in the data mining step. We discern five general groups of methods:

- **Feature selection** [21]: the number of features, the dimensionality of the data, is reduced. The aim of these methods is to remove irrelevant and redundant features. Irrelevant features are those that carry little information, or even none at all. An extreme example is a feature that takes on the same value for all observations. Redundant features are those that do not provide any additional useful information on top of that represented by other features present in the dataset. As an example, assume that in a geometry application both the diameter and radius of circles are stored as features. Clearly, providing the diameter of a circle does not yield any new information once its radius is already known. The reduction of the feature set can result in a faster processing in the data mining step and better and easier to interpret results.
- **Instance selection** [22]: this is the orthogonal problem to feature selection. Instead of removing features (columns) from the dataset, observations (rows) are deleted. These methods aim to detect and remove redundant or noisy elements or both. As for features, redundant instances are those that are not very informative. For example, dense areas of highly similar instances, both in terms of their feature values and their outcome, can be reduced. Noisy elements have very similar feature values as instances with a very different outcome. Their initial inclusion in the dataset may have resulted from measurement or data entry errors. The retention of only the informative and non-noisy elements in the dataset can improve the speed and accuracy of the subsequent data mining method.
- **Discretization** [17]: these methods simplify the domain of a quantitative feature by transforming it to a qualitative one. The numeric feature values are divided into ranges that correspond to different categories. For each observation, its corresponding feature value is mapped to the defined category. In this way, the number of possible feature values is reduced. Discretization is used for instance when a data mining method only accepts categorical features as input.
- **Feature extraction** [20]: the feature values of instances are modified and new features are constructed as aggregates of a selection of the existing ones.
- **Instance generation** [30]: new instances are generated. They can be used to replace existing elements in order to gain a better representation of the instance space. Related to instance selection, instance generation can select a subset of the available instances to retain, modify some others and add some new artificial samples.

1.3 Data Mining

As described in Sect. 1.1, the preprocessing stage in the knowledge discovery process is followed by the execution of a data mining method. Data mining is the significant step that extracts information patterns from the preprocessed data. A recent book on data mining methods within the KDD process is [11]. We can also refer the reader to another detailed book [31], that provides an easy-to-understand introduction to the area and describes the most prominent methods accompanied with many illustrative examples.

A data mining method is presented with input data and processes it in such a way to obtain the hidden information contained in this data. As stressed in e.g. [11], it cannot be expected that a single data mining method works well in all possible applications. It may exhibit an excellent performance in some, but yield mediocre or poor results in others. This phenomenon is also referred to as the *no free lunch theorem* [32]. The domain of data mining is divided into three subgroups in [11]:

- **Undirected data mining**: the user has no expectations about the results of the method or their interpretation. This means that the preprocessed data is presented to the method, while the user hopes to find an interesting pattern in the data, although he does not specify what this pattern might be. Any novelty in these results is not guaranteed, the discovered knowledge may simply be an affirmation of previous results.
- **Directed data mining**: the user knows what he is interested in and specifies this as a clear objective. The data is not simply fed to the algorithm, which must make sense of it somehow, but it is rather established what type of information is expected to be retrieved. The example referenced in [11] is the profile characterization of a number of selected supermarket customers.
- **Hypothesis testing and refinement**: in this case, an even clearer objective is provided than in the situation of directed data mining. In his research, the user has formulated a hypothesis and he wishes to corroborate it with the results of the data mining method on the collected data. If he is not satisfied with the conclusions, the hypothesis can be refined and validated anew.

As noted in Sect. 1.1, the samples in the dataset do not necessarily have an associated outcome. The setting where an outcome is provided for all instances is called *supervised learning* (Sect. 1.3.1). When none of the instances are paired with an outcome, we consider *unsupervised learning* (Sect. 1.3.2). In the remaining case, where an outcome is known for some of the instances and not for the others, we deal with *semi-supervised learning* (Sect. 1.3.3). We discuss these three paradigms separately below.

1.3.1 Supervised Learning

In the case of supervised data, an outcome is available for all observations. The learning goal is to construct a prediction model based on a set of observations with known outcomes, in order to predict the outcome of new elements when they are presented to the system. The input data is also referred to as *training or learning data*, while the new observations are called *test data*. The test data can be used to assess the validity of the model, as it was not used in the learning phase.

The constructed prediction model should (i) capture the hidden information present in the training data well and (ii) not be too complex and, ideally, be easy to understand. The latter is an important aspect. The well-known problem of *overfitting* occurs when a learner fits the training data too closely and essentially learns it by heart. Such a complex and detailed model does not generalize well to new, unseen data and leads to poor predictions. In practice, overfitting is often explicitly avoided by the user. This biases the learning process towards simpler models. The twofold aim of a supervised learning method is consequently to understand the structure of the training data as well as to make accurate predictions for the test data.

A first division within this group of methods can be made based on the type of outcomes of the instances. We distinguish between classification and regression problems. In the former, the outcome is categorical and represents a class label. Table 1.1 contains an example classification dataset. In the latter, we deal with numeric outcomes. We list a number of prominent examples of prediction algorithms, that can be used for either classification or regression, below.

- **Neural networks** [7]: methods of this type are inspired by the workings of the human brain, more precisely the processes of neurons. An artificial neuron is modeled as a unit that receives a number of weighted inputs and provides one aggregated outcome. These units are placed together in a network. The network generally consists of several layers: input and output layers as well as a number of hidden layers. As a result, it can model complex data characteristics.
- **Bayesian learning** [6]: these methods are based on Bayes' theorem from probability theory. The Naive Bayes methods assume complete independence between the feature values in the prediction of the outcome. This assumption is rarely satisfied. Nevertheless, the methods still exhibit a strong prediction performance. More complex Bayesian methods do not rely on the independence assumption.
- **Instance-based learning** [3]: these methods are also called lazy learners, a name that refers to the fact that they do not construct a prediction model in the learning phase. Instead, all training observations and their outcomes are kept available in the prediction stage. Aside from the stored observations, a distance measure is provided as well. To predict the outcome of a test element, the nearest stored instances, based on the distance measure, are located. Their outcomes are aggregated into a prediction.
- **Support vector machines** [29]: these methods are originally defined for two-class problems, that is, a classification problem with only two possible class labels. They construct a separating hyperplane between the two classes, such that a maximal

separation is achieved and a minimal amount of errors is made. This hyperplane is not necessarily constructed in the input feature space. Kernel transformations are often applied to obtain linear separability of the classes in a new feature space. When the classes are not linearly separable, errors are unavoidable, that is, some instances will be located on the incorrect side of the constructed hyperplane, amidst instances of the opposite class. In later developments, regression problems and classification problems with more than two classes have been addressed with support vector machine methods as well.

- **Rule induction** [15]: this group of algorithms constructs a set of rules based on the training data to predict the outcome. The rules consist of a number of antecedents, representing conditions on the feature values, and a consequent, the prediction value. The constructed prediction model, that is, the set of rules, has a high interpretability.
- **Decision trees** [26]: this is another group of methods yielding a highly human-interpretable prediction model. The model is structured in the form of a tree, where a path from the root node to a leaf is followed to obtain a prediction for a new element. At each internal node, a division is made based on a feature value. For example, one can imagine a split based on the values of a nominal feature, where the value 'Yes' means that the path is continued to the left child of the node and the value 'No' results in a step to the right child. Each path ends in a leaf node. The outcome associated with this leaf is used as prediction.

We briefly note on a sub-domain within supervised learning called multi-label learning [34]. A multi-label dataset differs from the format presented in Table 1.1, as multiple class labels are associated with each observation. In multi-label applications, observations can naturally belong to several categories, e.g., a movie can belong to both action and comedy categories at the same time. The goal of multi-label classification is to detect as many of the appropriate class labels for each observation as possible.

1.3.2 Unsupervised Learning

In unsupervised learning, as opposed to supervised learning, no outcomes or labels are collected for the observations. The data collection therefore forms an inherently cheaper task than in the case of supervised learning, as the possibly tedious annotation step is avoided. Instead of the construction of a prediction model, the goal of an unsupervised learning method is to extract natural patterns or groups from the training data. As such, the algorithm aims to obtain a thorough and exact data description. Two notable examples of this learning paradigm are described below.

- **Clustering** [2]: these algorithms sort the observations in groups, also called clusters. A good clustering result is one where (i) elements in the same cluster are highly similar and (ii) elements in different clusters are highly dissimilar. The adequacy of these results depends on many components, like the selected cluster similarity measure and the suitability of the selected method to the characteristics of the data. Some methods can for instance be preferred over others when there are regions of very differing densities in the data. Another important question is how many clusters should be constructed. Some methods require this value as a user input, while others determine it automatically.

• **Association rules** [1]: this is another rule induction process, but it differs from the group of supervised rule induction methods listed in Sect. 1.3.1. The supervised methods construct decision rules that are used to predict the outcomes of new instances. Their rule antecedents serve as conditions on the feature values and their consequent is interpreted as the predicted outcome. In unsupervised association rule mining, relations between feature values are determined. Correlations between feature values are encoded into rules, in which both the antecedent and the consequent can refer to several features. An example association rule is 'IF high pollen level AND allergic THEN runny nose AND teary eyes'.

1.3.3 Semi-supervised Learning

On a midpoint between these two paradigms, supervised learning and unsupervised learning, we find semi-supervised learning [8], where part of the training data is annotated with an outcome and the remaining part is not. The number of unlabeled instances is usually the largest, since the annotation step can be costly. Within the domain of semi-supervised learning, we can make a distinction between methods that are either more closely related to the supervised or the unsupervised domains. In semi-supervised classification, for instance, labels are first predicted for the unlabeled part. In a second stage, the now fully labeled training set is used to train a classification model. In semi-supervised clustering, the data is clustered as would be done in unsupervised learning, but the labeled data is used to assist the clustering in the form of conditions that the final grouping should satisfy. These conditions can represent elements that should certainly be grouped in the same clusters or ones that can not be grouped together at all.

1.3.4 Scalability Consideration

One obvious performance measure of data mining methods is the accuracy and suitability of their results. Two additional meaningful standards on which different data mining methods are compared, are the associated runtime costs and their scalability [18]. The efficiency of a method reflects how much time and resources its execution requires. An optimal use of resources (storage, etc.) in a minimum amount of time is aspired. The other important consideration for any data mining method is its scalability to very large databases. This is the question of how well the runtime and resource requirements of the method scale with respect to increasing size and complexity of the data. When it can for instance be theoretically determined that the execution cost of an algorithm is exponential in the number of observations, the method is rendered quite useless. It may perform very well on small datasets, but is not likely to yield a result on larger dataset within a reasonable amount of time. In the development of any new method, the assessment of its theoretical complexity is therefore crucial.

Data mining methods can be specifically designed to deal with large and/or complex data. Examples are algorithms performing parallel and distributed computations [4]. Parallel computing is based on the fact that many methods involve subtasks that can be executed at the same time. In distributed computing, a large dataset is commonly divided in smaller, easier-to-handle chunks. Each chunk is processed separately and these processes can be executed in parallel. Another group of adapted methods are the incremental or online algorithms. They can deal with data that is dynamically presented to the system and process their inputs serially, as they are made available. An example application is the visual tracking of objects, in which the information that needs to be processed by the system clearly changes over time [27].

The research in big data has flourished over the last decade [24]. This term is used to denote applications where the collected data has such a large size and/or presents such a high degree of complexity that traditionally used data mining methods lack the strength to process it. Some relevant big data computing settings are cloud computing and cluster computing. Cloud computing [5] is a form of shared computing. Hardware and software, the cloud, is made accessible by large data centers to its users over the Internet. These resources are shared among all users. It removes the need for individual users (e.g., small companies) to set up the systems themselves. The key aspect of cloud computing is that the services hosted in the data center are made available without geographical concerns, that is, a user may access a cloud in any remote location. In cluster computing [33], a network of connected computers is set up to work together as one system. Together, they form the cluster. As a result, an increase in computer power is obtained. It is ideally suited to run multiple subtasks in parallel. The user must design his project in such a way to optimally take advantage of this architecture. A central component of any cluster system is the scheduler that distributes the tasks over the available nodes and manages these jobs.

1.4   Classification

This is a book on multiple instance learning, a learning paradigm originally developed as an extension of traditional supervised learning. Most advancement in this area has been in classification methods. In classification problems, as stated in Sect. 1.3.1, the goal is to predict a class label. The outcome, which is available for all training instances, is drawn from a finite set of possibilities, the classes. The prediction model represents a relation that maps the feature values to a class decision.

A classification method (also called classifier) aims to discriminate between all possible classes in the training set. The dataset presented in Table 1.1 is an example classification dataset. It represents a two-class problem with positive (P) and negative

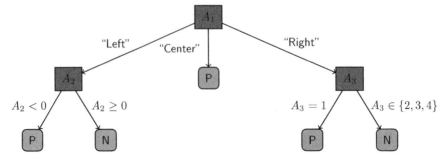

Fig. 1.2 Decision tree learned from the data in Table 1.1

(N) as possible classes. A classifier learned on this data yields a model that is used to decide whether a new element belongs to the positive or negative class. An example model is presented in Fig. 1.2, where a decision tree classifier was learned on the training data in Table 1.1. The constructed classification model is easily interpretable. When a new instance is presented, its value for feature A_1 is first tested. When this feature takes on the value 'Center', the class is immediately predicted as positive. If its value is 'Left', a second test is performed on the A_2 feature. The instance is predicted to belong to the positive class, when the value for A_2 is strictly smaller than zero, and to the negative class otherwise. Finally, when the value for A_1 was 'Right', the second test is performed on the ordinal feature A_3. When its value is 1, the positive class is selected. In all the other cases, the negative class is predicted.

An important question is how to evaluate the prediction performance of a classifier. This involves two separate considerations, namely the selection of the validation scheme on the one hand and the evaluation measure on the other. The former supports the reliability of the conclusions, while the latter measures the classification performance.

1.4.1   Validation Schemes

As described in Sect. 1.3.1, the training data are used to learn a classification model that is afterward applied to make class predictions for unseen elements. The validity of these predictions can only be checked when the real labels of the unseen elements are known. To ensure a faithful evaluation of the prediction strength of a model, a validation scheme is used. In general, the available dataset in split into parts representing the actual training and test sets. A prediction model is learned on the training instances and evaluated on the test instances, for which the class labels are known as well. Several different validation methods can be listed (see e.g. [19]):

- **Holdout**: this is the most straightforward type of validation. The dataset is divided into two parts, one that acts as training set and one that acts as test set. A typical division is to use two thirds of the dataset as training set and the remaining third as test set. The classifier is executed on the training set alone and yields a prediction model. Next, a label is predicted for the elements in the test set, which were not used in the learning phase. The predicted label is compared to their real class, which is known. One of the evaluation measures discussed below can be used to represent the model prediction strength in a single scalar.

- **Repeated holdout**: the holdout method can be repeated several times in order to obtain a more reliable performance estimate. In each repetition, a training and test set is constructed

- **Cross validation**: in k-fold cross validation, the dataset is divided into k roughly equal parts, called partitions or folds. The fold construction can be done by making a random division in the dataset or using a more complex heuristic, like stratified sampling, where the class distribution of the original dataset is reflected in the partitions. A classification experiment is run k times. Every run, a different fold is used as test set. The remaining folds are combined into a training set. After the full process has been completed, the predictions on each of the k test folds are combined into one measure, usually by averaging the values of the evaluation measure computed on the separate folds. Common choices for the number k are 5 and 10. Its selection depends on the characteristics of the dataset, like overall size and class distribution. The extreme case occurs when the number k is set equal to the number of data samples. In this situation, every partition contains a single element, so the test set is reduced to one test element. This setting is referred to as leave-one-out validation.

- **Repeated cross validation**: the fold partitioning process and cross validation is repeated a number of times, in order to decrease the variance of the estimation. The final evaluation value is taken as average over the repetitions.

- **Bootstrapping**: several bootstrap samples of the dataset are created. A bootstrap sample has the same size as the original dataset and is constructed by random sampling with replacement. Duplicate instances can occur. A classifier is learned on each of the bootstrap samples and used to predict the class labels of the full dataset. We note an important difference with the other validation methods. Above, none of the test instances where known at training time. In the bootstrapping procedures, the instances in each training set (bootstrap sample) all occur in the test set (original dataset), possibly multiple times. Due to the sampling with replacement, part of the test instances still remain unknown in the learning phase. This is taken into account when aggregating the prediction values from the different samples, that is, the final prediction strength is not obtained by simply averaging the values corresponding to each bootstrap sample. An example is the .632+ bootstrap estimator from [13].

1.4.2   Evaluation Measures

After deciding which validation scheme will be used, an evaluation metric needs to
be selected. In each schemes above, predicted class labels are compared to the real
labels for the test instances. We list some popular evaluation measures based on these
comparisons for classification data below.

- **Accuracy**: this measure reflects the rate of correctly classified test instances, that
  is, it represents the percentage of test elements for which the real and predicted
  classes coincide. Its value is computed as

$$acc = \frac{corr(Ts)}{|Ts|},$$

  where Ts is the test set and the function $corr(\cdot)$ counts how many elements are
  classified correctly.
- **Error rate**: this value is the complement of the accuracy and computes the rate
  of misclassified test elements. It is given as

$$err = 1 - acc = \frac{|TS| - corr(Ts)}{|Ts|}.$$

- **Gmean**: this measure is computed as the geometric mean of the classwise accuracies, that is,

$$g = \sqrt[c]{\prod_{i=1}^{c} \frac{corr(C_i)}{|C_i|}},$$

  where c is the number of classes in the dataset and C_i is the ith class.
- **Cohen's kappa**: this metric is related to the accuracy, but accounts for random
  hits [12]. It is defined as, using the above notation,

$$\kappa = \frac{|Ts| \sum_{i=1}^{c} corr(C_i) - \sum_{i=1}^{c} |C_i| pred(C_i)}{|Ts|^2 - \sum_{i=1}^{c} |C_i| pred(C_i)},$$

  where $pred(C_i)$ is the number of instances predicted to belong to class C_i. These
  predictions may or may not be correct.

References

1. Adamo, J.M.: Data Mining for Association Rules and Sequential Patterns: Sequential and Parallel Algorithms. Springer Science & Business Media, New York (2012)
2. Aggarwal, C.C., Reddy, C.K.: Data Clustering: Algorithms and Applications. CRC Press, Boca Raton (2013)
3. Aha, D.W., Kibler, D., Albert, M.K.: Instance-based learning algorithms. Mach. Learn. **6**(1), 37–66 (1991)
4. Andrews, G.R.: Foundations of Parallel and Distributed Programming. Addison–Wesley Longman Publishing Co. Inc, Boston (1999)
5. Armbrust, M., Fox, A., Griffith, R., Joseph, A., Katz, R., Konwinski, A., Lee, G., Patterson, D., Rabkin, A., Stoica, I., Zaharia, M.: A view of cloud computing. Commun. ACM. **53**(4), 50–58 (2010)
6. Barber, D.: Bayesian Reasoning and Machine Learning. Cambridge University Press, Cambridge (2012)
7. Bishop, C.M.: Neural Networks for Pattern Recognition. Oxford University Press, Oxford (1995)
8. Chapelle, O., Schölkopf, B., Zien, A.: Semi-supervised Learning. MIT press, Cambridge (2006)
9. Cios, K.J., Kurgan, L.A.: Trends in data mining and knowledge discovery. In: Pal, N., Jain, L. (eds.) Advanced Techniques in Knowledge Discovery and Data Mining, pp. 1–26. Springer, London (2005)
10. Cios, K.J., Pedrycz, W., Swiniarski, R.W., Kurgan, L.A.: Data Mining: A Knowledge Discovery Approach. Springer, New York (2007)
11. Cios, K.J., Pedrycz, W., Swiniarski, R.W.: Data Mining Methods for Knowledge Discovery, vol. 458. Springer Science & Business Media, New York (2012)
12. Cohen, J.: A coefficient of agreement for nominal scales. Edu. Psychol. Meas. **20**(1), 37–46 (1960)
13. Efron, B., Tibshirani, R.: Improvements on cross-validation: the 632+ bootstrap method. J. Am. Stat. Assoc. **92**(438), 548–560 (1997)
14. Frawley, W.J., Piatetsky-Shapiro, G., Matheus, C.J.: Knowledge discovery in databases: An overview. AI Mag. **13**(3), 57 (1992)
15. Fürnkranz, J., Gamberger, D., Lavrač, N.: Foundations of Rule Learning. Springer, Berlin (2012)
16. García, S., Luengo, J., Herrera, F.: Data Preprocessing in Data Mining. Springer, Switzerland (2015)
17. García, S., Luengo, J., Sáez, J.A., López, V., Herrera, F.: A survey of discretization techniques: taxonomy and empirical analysis in supervised learning. IEEE Trans. Knowl. Data Eng. **25**(4), 734–750 (2013)
18. Han, J., Kamber, M., Pei, J.: Data Mining: Concepts and Techniques. Morgan Kaufmann Publishers, Waltham (2011)
19. Kim, J.: Estimating classification error rate: repeated cross-validation, repeated hold-out and bootstrap. Comput. Stat. Data Anal. **53**(11), 3735–3745 (2009)
20. Liu, H., Motoda, H.: Feature Extraction, Construction and Selection: A Data Mining Perspective. Kluwer, Boston (1998)
21. Liu, H., Motoda, H.: Computational Methods of Feature Selection. CRC Press, Boca Raton (2007)
22. Liu, H., Motoda, H.: Instance Selection and Construction for Data Mining, vol. 608. Springer Science & Business Media, Dordrecht (2013)
23. Luengo, J.: García, S., Herrera, F.: On the choice of the best imputation methods for missing values considering three groups of classification methods. Knowl. Inf. Syst. **32**(1), 77–108 (2012)
24. Mayer-Schönberger, V., Cukier, K.: Big Data: A Revolution that Will Transform How We Live, Work, and Think. Houghton Mifflin Harcourt, New York (2013)

25. Pyle, D.: Data Preparation for Data Mining, vol. 1. Morgan Kaufmann Publishers, San Francisco (1999)
26. Rokach, L., Maimon, O.: Data Mining with Decision Trees: Theory and Applications, 2nd edn. World Scientific, Singapore (2014)
27. Ross, D., Lim, J., Lin, R., Yang, M.: Incremental learning for robust visual tracking. Int. J. Comput. Vision. **77**(1–3), 125–141 (2008)
28. Sáez, J.A., Luengo, J., Herrera, F.: Predicting noise filtering efficacy with data complexity measures for nearest neighbor classification. Pattern Recogn. **46**(1), 355–364 (2013)
29. Schölkopf, B., Smola, A.J.: Learning with Kernels: Support Vector Machines, Regularization, Optimization, and Beyond. MIT press, Cambridge (2002)
30. Triguero, I., Derrac, J., García, S., Herrera, F.: A taxonomy and experimental study on prototype generation for nearest neighbor classification. IEEE Trans. Syst. Man. Cybern. Part C **42**(1), 86–100 (2012)
31. Witten, I.H., Frank, E., Hall, M.A.: Data Mining: Practical Machine Learning Tools and Techniques, 3rd edn. Morgan Kaufmann Publishers, Burlington (2011)
32. Wolpert, D.H., Macready, W.G.: No free lunch theorems for optimization. IEEE Trans. Evolut. Comput. **1**(1), 67–82 (1997)
33. Yeo, C., Buyya, R., Pourreza, H., Eskicioglu, R., Graham, P., Sommers, F.: Cluster computing: high-performance, high-availability, and high-throughput processing on a network of computers. In: Zomaya, A. (ed.) Handbook of Nature-inspired and Innovative Computing, pp. 521–551. Springer, New York (2006)
34. Zhang, M., Zhou, Z.: A review on multi-label learning algorithms. IEEE Trans. Knowl. Data Eng. **26**(8), 1819–1837 (2014)

Chapter 2
Multiple Instance Learning

Abstract This chapter provides a general introduction to the main subject matter of this work: multiple instance or multi-instance learning. The two terms are used interchangeably in the literature and they both convey the crucial point of difference with traditional (single-instance) learning. A formal description of multiple instance learning is provided in Sect. 2.1 and we discuss its origins in Sect. 2.2. In Sect. 2.3, we describe different learning tasks within this domain, which may or may not have an equivalent in single-instance learning. Finally, Sect. 2.4 lists a wide variety of applications corresponding to the different multi-instance learning paradigms.

2.1 Formal Description

The traditional data description presented in Chap. 1 corresponds to so-called *single-instance learning*, where each observation or learning object is described by a number of feature values and, possibly, an associated outcome. In our object of study, *multiple-instance learning (MIL)*, the structure of the data is more complex. In this setting, a learning sample or object is called a *bag*. The defining feature of MIL is that a bag is associated with multiple instances or descriptions. Each instance is described by a feature vector, as we saw in single-instance learning, but an associated outcome is never reported. The only information available about an instance, aside from its feature values, is its membership relationship to a bag.

Formally, an instance x corresponds to a point in the instance space $\mathbb{X}$. It is commonly assumed that $\mathbb{X} \subseteq \mathbb{R}^d$, that is, each instance is described by a vector of d real-valued numbers, its feature values. However, as described in Sect. 1.1, datasets often contain mixed types of features. To model these situations, $\mathbb{X}$ can be generalized to $\mathbb{X} \subseteq \mathscr{A}^d = \mathscr{A}_1 \times \cdots \times \mathscr{A}_d$, such that each instance is described by a d-dimensional vector, where each attribute $\mathscr{A}_i$ ($i = 1, \ldots, d$) takes on values from a finite or infinite set $\mathscr{V}_i$. In this way, we can deal with mixed feature sets in which some of the features are categorical and others are numeric.

A bag X is a collection of n instances, where every instance x_i is drawn from the instance space $\mathbb{X}$. Each bag is allowed to have a different size, which means that the value n can vary among the bags in the dataset. Multiple copies of the same instance

© Springer International Publishing AG 2016   17
F. Herrera et al., *Multiple Instance Learning*, DOI 10.1007/978-3-319-47759-6_2

Table 2.1 Structure of a multi-instance dataset with M bags

Bags	Instances	$\mathscr{A}_1$	$\mathscr{A}_2$	...	$\mathscr{A}_d$	Outcome
X_1	$x_{1,1}$	$x_{1,1,1}$	$x_{1,1,2}$	...	$x_{1,1,d}$	y_1
	...	...	...	...	...	
	x_{1,n_1}	$x_{1,n_1,1}$	$x_{1,n_1,2}$	...	$x_{1,n_1,d}$	
...	...	...	...	...	...	...
X_M	$x_{M,1}$	$x_{M,1,1}$	$x_{M,1,2}$	...	$x_{M,1,d}$	y_M
	...	...	...	...	...	
	x_{M,n_M}	$x_{M,n_M,1}$	$x_{M,n_M,2}$	...	$x_{M,n_M,d}$	

can be included in a bag. For this reason, many authors define a bag as $X \in \mathbb{N}^{\mathbb{X}}$, that is, a multi-set containing elements from $\mathbb{X}$ such that duplicates can occur. Different bags are also allowed to overlap and contain copies of the same instance. This forms an indication of the higher level of complexity of MIL compared to single-instance learning. Throughout this work, we use lowercase letters to represent instances (e.g., x, a, b) and uppercase letters to represent bags (e.g., X, A, B).

As an example, Table 2.1 presents the general structure of a multi-instance dataset. The first column represents the bags, sometimes also referred to as exemplars. Each bag contains a number of instances, represented in the second column. Each instance identifier corresponds to a vector description, of which the attribute values are arranged from columns $\mathscr{A}_1$ to $\mathscr{A}_d$. The first instance $x_{1,1}$ in the first bag X_1 is for example represented by the feature vector $\langle x_{1,1,1}, x_{1,1,2}, ..., x_{1,1,d} \rangle$. The last column represents the outcome associated with the bag. It is important to stress that this outcome is only known for a bag as a whole and not for each individual instance. Depending on the learning task (see Sect. 2.3), the outcome may be a class label (classification) or a real value (regression). In clustering applications, there are no outcome values available. We briefly note that the work of [11] showed that the performance of multi-instance learners on datasets with very similar meta-characteristics, like dimensionality and size, can be very different.

2.2 Origin of MIL

The multi-instance learning paradigm was introduced in the seminal work of [16]. It arose in the context of learning tasks where data observations (bags) can have different alternative descriptions (instances). The authors of [16] focused on an application in biochemistry: the drug activity prediction problem. Here, the task is to predict whether or not a given molecule is a good drug molecule, which is measured by its ability to bind to a given target. Each molecule can be represented as a bag, of which the instances correspond to different conformations (molecular structures) of that particular compound. Figure 2.1 depicts this situation for a butane molecule. In

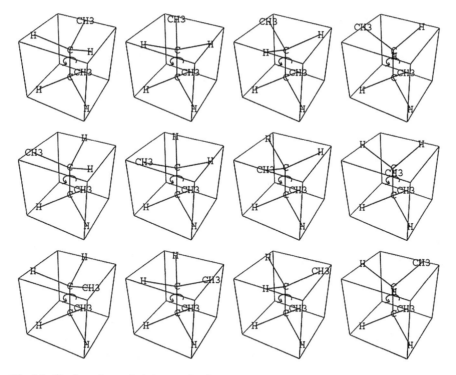

Fig. 2.1 Conformations of a butane molecule

this case, butane would be represented by a bag containing the 12 listed shapes as its instances.

MIL emerged as an extension of supervised learning. bag-instances relationship models the one-to-many relation characteristic of relational databases, since one bag can contain several different instances. More than an extension, MIL can therefore be considered a generalization of single-instance learning and the latter can be understood as a special case of MIL where each bag contains a single instance. Moreover, MIL has proven to be a bridge between two different paradigms: propositional learning on the one hand and relational learning on the other.

2.2.1 Relationship with Propositional Learning

Propositional or attribute-value learning corresponds to the setting described in Sect. 1.1, where the training data is ordered in a single flat table. In single-instance semi-supervised learning (Sect. 1.3.3), only part of the instance outcomes are available and it therefore shows a certain similarity with MIL, where the outcomes are only known for the bags and not their instances. However, there is a fundamental difference between the two: the relationship between instances and bags in MIL does not exist in semi-supervised learning. In the latter, labeled instances are at the same level as unlabeled instances and there is no specific relationship between them. In MIL on the contrary, a secondary structure is present in the dataset, defining the two different levels of bags and instances. All instances in a bag are somehow interrelated, because of their shared membership to the bag.

2.2.2 Relationship with Relational Learning

In relational learning, structured concept definitions are derived from structured training examples [14]. The training data models the different observations as well as the relations between them, for instance by using multiple tables. A clear example is given in [15], where the relational data is represented by two tables, one providing the description of store customers and the other the marital relations between them.

Many learning methods have been developed for propositional learning, but these can only be applied to data organized in a single table and the relations between different observations can not be taken into account. Propositional algorithms can therefore not be directly applied in relational learning problems. Relational data can be transformed into an attribute-value table in a process called propositionalization, but this implies a steep computational cost and its application to real problems is limited as a result of an internal combinatorial explosion [47].

MIL has come to be considered as the missing link between relational and propositional learning, because, as stated above, the bag label models a one-to-many relationship. The contribution of [13] shows that multi-instance problems can also be considered as a special case of inductive logic programming [37]. All inductive logic programming problems (in the form of relational databases) can be transformed by database join operations in a single one-to-many relationship. Such a relation can in turn be naturally represented as a MIL problem [47, 48]. As will be discussed in later chapters, many single-instance learning algorithms have already been adapted to the multi-instance setting. This feature of MIL allows for many relational learning problems to be solved by traditional supervised learning methods.

2.3 MIL Paradigms

As in traditional single-instance learning, discussed in Sect. 1.3, we can distinguish between a number of learning tasks within MIL. In Sect. 2.3.1 we discuss the two supervised learning settings, classification and regression. Section 2.3.2 describes multi-instance clustering. Several other traditional learning tasks, like semi-supervised or multi-label learning, can find a corresponding MIL equivalent (e.g., [44, 82]). However, we must warn the reader that this general similarity between single-instance and multi-instance learning tasks can not be transferred to their solution methods. Due to the relational nature, MIL solution methods are inherently more complex. This also implies that some MIL tasks have no related single-instance setting. The most prominent example is presented in Sect. 2.3.3.

2.3.1 Multi-instance Classification and Regression

In a *multi-instance classification problem*, the goal is to determine the class label of new bags, based on the class labels in the training set or, more specifically, using a prediction model built on the labeled training bags. The outcome associated with the training bags is categorical.

More formally, in a classification problem, we deal with a training set $D = (\mathbf{X}, \mathbf{L})$, where $\mathbf{X} = \langle X_1, \ldots, X_m \rangle$ is a set of bags and $\mathbf{L} = \langle \ell_1, \ldots, \ell_m \rangle$ a set of class labels, with $\ell_i \in \mathbb{L}$ ($i = 1, \ldots, m$) and $\mathbb{L}$ the finite set of all possible class labels. The bag X_i is assigned the class label ℓ_i. Recall that only the class labels of the bags are known and not those of the instances inside them. Later on in this work, we provide a detailed discussion on the contribution of the individual instances to the bag label. Traditionally, MIL has focused on two-class classification problems, dealing with one positive and one negative class. However, in general the number of classes can be larger, that is, $|\mathbb{L}| \geq 2$. The classification objective is to find a function $\mathcal{H} : \mathbb{N}^{\mathbb{X}} \to \mathbb{L}$ based on the training set D. This function is the classification model and is used to predict the class labels of new bags as accurately as possible. More details on multi-instance classification will be provided in Chap. 3.

When the outcomes are known for all training bags, but they correspond to real values rather than class labels, we are dealing with a *multi-instance regression problem*. The data description is highly similar to the one for classification data. The main difference is that the bag class labels are replaced by numerical values, that is, $\mathbb{L}$ corresponds to a range of values in $\mathbb{R}$ rather than to a finite set. Multi-instance regression was proposed in [2, 46], independently at the same conference. This task is discussed further in Chap. 6.

2.3.2 Multi-instance Clustering

As discussed in Sect. 1.3.2, clustering is situated in the unsupervised learning domain. The set of outcomes $\mathbf{L}$ associated to the training bags $\mathbf{X}$ in D is not known or not available. The goal is to group these unlabeled bags based on a given similarity measure. A multi-instance clustering method determines a set of groups $\mathcal{G} = \{G_1, \ldots G_k\}$ and a function $\mathcal{H} : \mathbb{N}^{\mathbb{X}} \to \mathcal{G}$ which assigns bags to groups such that it minimizes the similarity differences between bags of the same group and maximizes the similarity differences between bags of different groups. The choice of an appropriate similarity measure is crucial in multi-instance clustering. As noted in [74], not all instances within a bag contribute equally to the bag prediction, which implies that the bags should ideally not be considered as collections of independent instances in the definition of the similarity metric. Multi-instance clustering is discussed in more detail in Chap. 7.

2.3.3 Instance Annotation

An important task in some MIL applications, which has no counterpart in single-instance learning, is the instance-level classification. In this setting, apart from predicting a class label for a new bag, the assignment of class labels to its instances is a key objective as well. Depending on the application, there are two possible cases.

In the first situation, given the training set $D = (\mathbf{X}, \mathbf{L})$, the objective is to locate the instance or instances that are key to determining the class of the bag. In general, key instances are considered those that are more likely to have the same (hidden) label as their bag. A function $h : \mathbb{X} \rightarrow \mathbb{L}$ is constructed, such that the corresponding aggregation function $H\left(h\left(x_1\right), \ldots, h\left(x_n\right)\right) \rightarrow \mathbb{L}$ can predict class labels of a new bag $X = \{x_1, \ldots, x_n\}$ with maximum possible accuracy. This learning strategy is employed by a large group of multi-instance classification algorithms, described in Chap. 4. Some applications require the identification of key instances not only to classify bags, but also because these instances are themselves relevant to the application (e.g., [30]). An example application where the identification of true positive instances is very informative, is that of the stock selection problem [33]. In that setting, true positive instances correspond to stocks that fundamentally perform well, which is an important subgroup to discern from the other stocks.

In the second case, the training set is represented as $D = (\mathbf{X}, \mathbf{L})$, where $\mathbf{X} = \langle X_1, \ldots, X_m \rangle$ are bags and $\mathbf{L} = \langle \mathscr{L}_1, \ldots, \mathscr{L}_m \rangle$ are sets of instance labels associated to the bags. In this situation, the set $\mathscr{L}_i = \left\{\lambda_1, \ldots, \lambda_{k_i}\right\}$ of explicit instance labels is assigned to the bag X_i. These labels are drawn from a set $\Lambda = \{\lambda_1, \ldots, \lambda_s\}$, which can be different from $\mathbb{L}$. Unlike the traditional MIL approach, some instance labels are known for each bag. The objective is to find a function that, given a new bag, allows us to find instance labels that best describe it. This setting is very popular in applications such as image annotation (e.g., [7]), where the annotation of image segments (instances) can result in a global label for the complete image (bag). Since one observation (bag) is associated with a set of (instance) labels, this approach shows some similarity with multi-label classification (Sect. 1.3.1). However, multi-label and multi-instance learning remain different paradigms. The former represents each observation by multiple instances and a single global class label, while in the latter an observation corresponds to one instance associated with several labels.

2.4 Applications of MIL

In MIL, a more complex structure of data observations can be represented. The multi-instance setting is required to model several real-world applications that we list in this section. There is an inherent level of representation ambiguity in this type of problems and we can distinguish between several sources. MIL data naturally arises in the following situations:

- **Alternative representations**: different views, appearances or descriptions of the same object are available. A classical example in this case is that of drug activity prediction, the application for which MIL was originally developed in [16] (see also Sect. 2.2).
- **Compound objects**: a compound object consists of several parts. In the example of image recognition, an image corresponds to a bag and each image segment forms an instance. An example is found in Fig. 2.2. The image segments can correspond to different breakfast components like the slice of toast, the sausage, the beans, and so on. Together, they form a full English breakfast.
- **Evolving objects**: in these applications, an evolving object is sampled at different time intervals. This is also referred to as a time-series problem. The bag represents the object, while the time point samples are its instances. An example is the study around the use of MIL in bankruptcy prediction presented in [27].

Fig. 2.2 A full English breakfast

The main research focus within the MIL community has been on multi-instance classification problems. A variety of application domains are listed in Sects. 2.4.1–2.4.6. In Sect. 2.4.7, we consider applications of multi-instance regression, while multi-instance clustering applications are discussed in Sect. 2.4.8.

2.4.1 Bioinformatics

We have already discussed the application of *drug activity prediction* in Sect. 2.2. Each bag corresponds to a molecule and its instances are the different molecular shapes, as shown in Fig. 2.1. The objective in the original MIL proposal [16] is the prediction of musky and non-musky molecules. Other drug activity problems concern the mutagenicity prediction of compound molecules [52] and activity prediction of molecules as anticancer agents [6]. Studies like [21, 33, 72, 80] address the drug activity prediction problem with their proposed multi-instance classifiers as well.

Another bioinformatics application of MIL is the *protein identification* task, like the recognition of Thioredoxin-fold proteins, as explored in, e.g., [45, 55, 59]. Binding proteins of the Calmodulin protein are identified in a multi-instance classification process in [36], while the application in [40] is the prediction of binding peptides for the highly polymorphic MHC class II molecules. In [29], multi-instance multi-label classification is used to automate the annotation of gene expression patterns. This method was evaluated on Drosophila melanogaster (fruit fly).

2.4.2 Image Classification and Retrieval

Another widely studied MIL application area is that of *image classification*, where the goal is to, given an image, decide on what it represents or to which of a given set of categories it belongs. As an example, consider the early work of [34] that revolves around the classification of natural scene images, e.g., images of waterfalls. In the data representation, an image corresponds to a bag. The instances within this bag are subimages, encoded as templates describing color and spatial characteristics of that specific region. The subimages can be obtained by a partitioning process or, possibly more appropriately, an image segmentation procedure. In a perfect segmentation, the resulting regions correspond to individual objects. The classification objective is to predict what the complete image represents. If we consider Fig. 2.2, a multi-instance classifier should derive that it is processing an image of a full English breakfast based on the different objects on the plate. This type of region-based image categorization was also evaluated in [3, 9, 10, 24, 42], although not all of these referenced works developed multi-instance classification methods specific for image data. They often consider more general algorithms and evaluate them on a variety of applications. Multi-instance image datasets have indeed become popular benchmarks to evaluate new proposals on. One specific type of image classification, facial recognition, where a bag of instances can represent images taken of the same person from different angles, was studied in, e.g., [8, 19].

More complex models for the mapping of images to multi-instance data were studied in later works. The method of [43] models the interrelations of instances (regions) in a bag (image) to improve the categorization process, while [25] considers image annotation by means of a joint multi-instance mapping and feature selection process. The recent proposal of [20] develops a multi-instance semi-supervised classification method based on sparse representation and evaluates it on image data.

A task related to image categorization is that of *image retrieval*. The aim in this case is to obtain images from a dataset that are semantically relevant to the user, based on his specified query or presented examples of images of interest. Multi-instance approaches to this challenge represent, as above, an image as a bag, containing many of its subimages as instances. Examples can be found in, e.g., [7, 66, 71, 75–77].

2.4.3 Web Mining and Text Classification

Another application domain of MIL lies in web mining. The web index recommendation problem was introduced as a multi-instance problem in [81]. In this application, a bag corresponds to a web index page and its instances refer to other websites to which the page links. The recommendation task is to suggest relevant web pages to users based on their browser history. Such knowledge is useful for the construction of intelligent web browsers. This problem domain was also the central focus of [67, 69], in which genetic programming algorithms were developed to solve it. In [51], a multi-instance classifier based on the Rocchio classifier [49] was developed for this application.

A related task is that of document classification. In [3], the proposed multi-instance classification method is evaluated on a document categorization problem. In this case, a bag corresponds to a document and the instances are particular passages within that document. In the experiments of [45], the dataset obtained in the biomedical study of [5] is used. A bag corresponds to a biomedical article about a particular protein and the instances are the paragraphs of the text. A positive bag is one that can be labeled with a Gene Ontology code, while a negative bag cannot. The classification goal is to discern between positive and negative bags.

2.4.4 Object Detection and Tracking

This domain requires methods that discern an object of interest in image or video data. Examples are the application of the proposed multi-instance boosting method to horse detection and pedestrian detection in [1]. In [32], the detection of landmines based on radar images is studied in a multi-instance classification context. The study of [61] considers the related aspect of saliency detection, which is the detection of the object in the image that draws the visual attention, as humans focus more on some parts of pictures than on others. It is not known in advance what the object is, only that it draws the attention of the observer.

In an object tracking application, a specific object is followed during the course of a video sequence. Online methods have been proposed in, e.g., [4, 73]. In the recent contributions of [31, 83], online multi-instance boosting algorithms for visual object tracking problems are developed.

2.4.5 *Medical Diagnosis and Imaging*

Several studies on multi-instance data focus on applications within the medical domain. In [22], a multi-instance classification framework is developed for computer-aided medical diagnosis, like the detection of tumors. It is shown that the use of this framework significantly improves the diagnostic accuracy in the evaluated applications. The study of [53] concerns the automatic detection of myocardial infarction based on electrocardiography (ECG) recordings. For each patient, a 24-h ECG is taken, which traces his or her heart activity for a full day. Such a recording is too large to be interpreted by a cardiologist. Automated prediction tools are required to detect any heart abnormalities in the data. In the input data for the multi-instance classifier, a bag corresponds to a full ECG, while each instance represents a recorded heartbeat.

The proposal of [41] studies the early detection of illnesses, like frailty and dementia, in senior citizens. This is done in a noninterfering way, namely by using sensor data, collected from a number of sensors monitoring elderly people in nursing homes. A bag consists of 24 hourly sensors measurements (instances) taken in one day for a single patient. The label of a bag is determined based on the report made by a nurse for the patient on that particular day. It indicates whether the patient exhibited health problems (positive) or not (negative).

A fourth study [60] develops a multi-instance classification algorithm for the detection of colonic polyps, abnormal growths in the colon. It revolves around video classification. When a possible polyp is present in the colon, images of it are collected from several viewpoints and combined into a video. Each candidate polyp consequently corresponds to a bag. The different viewpoints or video frames are the instances. The prediction aim is to decide whether the videoed candidate is an actual polyp or not.

2.4.6 *Other Classification Applications*

In this final section on applications of multi-instance classification, we collect a number of miscellaneous applications that do not fall within any of the categories listed in the previous sections.

Multi-instance classification has been applied to *prediction of student perfor-mance* [68]. This problem allows interesting relationships to be obtained that can suggest activities and resources to students and educators that favor and improve both learning and the effective learning process. From the MIL perspective, each student is regarded as a bag which represents the work carried out and is composed of one or several instances where each instance represents the different types of work that the student has done. This representation has shown better results than traditional single-instance representation [68]. The work of [70] proposes a genetic programming model to solve this problem more efficiently.

The study of [35] proposes a method for automatic *subgoal discovery* in reinforce-ment learning [54]. The trajectory of an agent in a reinforcement learning process is encoded as a bag. The observations made along this trajectory are the instances. The bag label states whether the trajectory is successful or not, where the definition of success depends on the problem description.

Multi-instance classification has been applied to several *computer-related tasks* as well, for instance in the work of [50] that focused on computer security applications. Impending failure of computer hard drives is predicted in [38]. A bag corresponds to a single drive and its instances are observations of this drive taken at different time points. In [26], the quality of object-oriented software is estimated. A class hierarchy is transformed into a bag, containing the constituent classes as instances.

The proposed classification method of [33] was evaluated on a *stock selection problem*. In this work, each bag represents a month of trading. A positive bag contains the 100 stocks (instances) with the highest returns in that month, while a negative bag consists of the five stocks with the lowest returns.

The final classification application that we list, is graph mining, the process of extracting knowledge from graph structured data. *Multi-graph learning* is a fur-ther generalization of MIL, where every bag consists of several graphs. In MIL, all instances in the bags are drawn from the same feature space, but this is no longer the case in multi-graph learning. This area was the focus of the recent works [64, 65].

2.4.7 Regression Applications

Although to a lesser extent than for classification problems, we also encounter real-world applications of multi-instance regression. We collect these examples in this section.

The application referenced in one of the original proposals of multi-instance regression [46] is related to the *drug activity prediction problem*. Instead of treating this as a yes-or-no question, as done in the classification scenario, real-valued activity levels are estimated for the molecules. The second initial proposal on multi-instance regression [2] also interpreted drug activity prediction as a regression problem, where the binding strength of a molecule is the prediction objective. The theoretical study on multi-instance regression in [17] refers to the real-valued drug activity prediction problem as an important application as well. In [12], the authors develop a method to predict the binding affinity of molecules based on their three-dimensional structure. They evaluate their method on thermolysin inhibitors, dopamine agonists, and thrombin inhibitors. In later work, [56] considers the prediction of protein-ligand affinities and [18] the prediction of the binding affinity of MHC class II molecules.

The study of [23] uses a real-valued outcome in the interval [0, 1] to express the satisfaction degree of a bag to the concept. One of the evaluated applications is *landmark recognition* for robot vision. In a navigation assignment, robots are required to recognize whether or not they find themselves near one of a given set of landmarks.

Multi-instance regression has also been used in *remote sensing applications*. The contribution of [57] focuses on an agricultural process, namely the modeling of crop yield based on remote sensing data. A bag corresponds to one county in the United States. The instances in the bag are image pixels covering different parts of that county. The same application was evaluated in [58], where the authors developed a multi-instance regression method for structured data. In [62], a climate research application related to aerosols is considered. The prediction value is the so-called aerosol optical depth, which is a number related to the induced attenuation of radiation. This value characterizes aerosols and is central in the construction of climate models. Aerosols are globally monitored by satellites that provide data in the form of multi-spectral images. In this application, a bag corresponds to a set of neighboring pixels (instances) in such an image. The bag is labeled with an aerosol optical depth value. The two remote sensing applications, aerosol optical depth prediction and crop yield modeling, were also studied in [63].

Finally, we also list the multi-instance regression study of [39]. The authors develop a robust system for *age estimation* of a person based on an image of his or her face.

2.4.8 Clustering Applications

In this section, we review the applications for multi-instance clustering that have been presented in the literature. Recall that the goal of this learning paradigm is to arrange the bags in a number of well-separated groups of similar observations.

The proposal of [74] references an application in *biochemistry*. The execution of experiments to determine the functionality of specific molecules can be costly. Multi-instance clustering can be used in the often necessary step to derive the functionality of a molecule by identifying similar molecules with known characteristics. The method of [28] was evaluated on two types of clustering problems. The first one consists of enzyme data, where a bag corresponds to an enzyme and its instances to amino acid sequences. The second problem is the clustering of the molecules in the drug activity prediction datasets taken from [16].

In [78, 79] a multi-instance clustering method based on the maximum margin principle was proposed. It was evaluated on two separate applications. In *image clustering*, the method is used to detect common hidden concepts or patterns in images. As was done in the image classification applications listed in Sect. 2.4.2, the images correspond to bags and the instances are image segments. The second application is *text clustering*. In this case, a bag represents a document and is made up from (possibly overlapping) passages taken from this document.

References

1. Ali, K., Saenko, K.: Confidence-rated multiple instance boosting for object detection. In: Proceedings of the 2014 IEEE Conference on Computer Vision and Pattern Recognition (CVPR 2014), pp. 2433–2440. IEEE, Los Alamitos (2014)
2. Amar, R.A., Dooly, D.R., Goldman, S.A., Zhang, Q.: Multiple-instance learning of real-valued data. In: Brodley, C.E., Danyluk, A. (eds.) Proceedings of the 18th International Conference on Machine Learning (ICML 2001), pp. 3–10. Morgan Kaufmann Publishers, San Francisco (2001)
3. Andrews, S., Tsochantaridis, I., Hofmann, T.: Support vector machines for multiple-instance learning. In: Becker, S., Thrun, S., Obermayer, K. (eds.) Advances in Neural Information, vol. 15, pp. 561–568. MIT press, Cambridge (2002)
4. Babenko, B., Yang, M.H., Belongie, S.: Robust object tracking with online multiple instance learning. IEEE Trans. Pattern Anal. **33**(8), 1619–1632 (2011)
5. Blaschke, C., Leon, E., Krallinger, M., Valencia, A.: Evaluation of BioCreAtIvE assessment of task 2. BMC Bioinform. **6**(1), 1 (2005)
6. Braddock, P., Hu, D., Fan, T., Stratford, I., Harris, A., Bicknell, R.: A structure-activity analysis of antagonism of the growth factor and angiogenic activity of basic fibroblast growth factor by suramin and related polyanions. Br. J. Cancer **69**(5), 890 (1994)
7. Carneiro, G., Chan, A.B., Moreno, P.J., Vasconcelos, N.: Supervised learning of semantic classes for image annotation and retrieval. IEEE Trans. Pattern Anal. **29**(3), 394–410 (2007)
8. Chang, K., Bowyer, K., Flynn, P.: An evaluation of multimodal 2d+3d face biometrics. IEEE Trans. Pattern Anal. **27**(4), 619–624 (2005)
9. Chen, Y., Wang, J.: Image categorization by learning and reasoning with regions. J. Mach. Learn. Res. **5**, 913–939 (2004)
10. Chen, Y., Bi, J., Wang, J.Z.: MILES: Multiple-instance learning via embedded instance selection. IEEE Trans. Pattern Anal. **28**(12), 1931–1947 (2006)
11. Cheplygina, V., Tax, D.: Characterizing multiple instance datasets. In: Feragen, A., Pelilo, M., Loog, M. (eds.) Similarity-Based Pattern Recognition, pp. 15–27. Springer, Switzerland (2015)
12. Davis, J., Costa, V.S., Ray, S., Page, D.: An integrated approach to feature invention and model construction for drug activity prediction. In: Ghahramani, Z. (ed.) Proceedings of the 24th international conference on Machine learning (ICML 2007), pp. 217–224. ACM, New York (2007)
13. De Raedt, L.: Attribute-value learning versus inductive logic programming: the missing links. In: Page, D. (ed.) Inductive Logic Programming. Lecture Notes in Computer Science, vol. 1446, pp. 1–8. Springer, Berlin (1998)
14. De Raedt, L.: Logical and Relational Learning. Springer Science & Business Media, Berlin (2008)
15. Deroski, S.: Relational data mining. In: Maimon, O., Rokach, L. (eds.) Data Mining and Knowledge Discovery Handbook, pp. 887–911. Springer, New York (2009)
16. Dietterich, T.G., Lathrop, R.H., Lozano-Perez, T.: Solving the multiple instance problem with axis-parallel rectangles. Artif. Intell. **89**(1–2), 31–71 (1997)
17. Dooly, D.R., Goldman, S.A., Kwek, S.S.: Real-valued multiple-instance learning with queries. J. Comput. Syst. Sci. **72**(1), 1–15 (2006)
18. El-Manzalawy, Y., Dobbs, D., Honavar, V.: Predicting MHC-II binding affinity using multiple instance regression. IEEE ACM Trans. Comput. Biol. **8**(4), 1067–1079 (2011)

19. Faltemier, T., Bowyer, K., Flynn, P.: Using a multi-instance enrollment representation to improve 3D face recognition. Comput. Vis. Image Underst. **112**(2), 114–125 (2008)
20. Feng, S., Xiong, W., Li, B., Lang, C., Huang, X.: Hierarchical sparse representation based multi-instance semi-supervised learning with application to image categorization. Signal Process. **94**, 595–607 (2014)
21. Fu, G., Nan, X., Liu, H., Patel, R.Y., Daga, P.R., Chen, Y., Wilkins, D.E., Doerksen, R.J.: Implementation of multiple-instance learning in drug activity prediction. BMC Bioinform. **13**(15), 1 (2012)
22. Fung, G., Dundar, M., Krishnapuram, B., Rao, R.B.: Multiple instance learning for computer aided diagnosis. Adv. Neural Inf. **19**, 425 (2007)
23. Goldman, S.A., Scott, S.D.: Multiple-instance learning of real-valued geometric patterns. Ann. Math. Artif. Intel. **39**(3), 259–290 (2003)
24. Han, Y., Qi, X.: A complementary svms-based image annotation system. In: Proceedings of the 2005 IEEE International Conference on Image Processing (ICIP 2005), vol. 1, pp. 1185–1188. IEEE, Los Alamitos (2005)
25. Hong, R., Wang, M., Gao, Y., Tao, D., Li, X., Wu, X.: Image annotation by multiple-instance learning with discriminative feature mapping and selection. IEEE Trans. Cybern. **44**(5), 669–680 (2014)
26. Huang, P., Zhu, J.: Multi-instance learning for software quality estimation in object-oriented systems: a case study. J. Zhejiang Univ.-Sci. C **11**(2), 130–138 (2010)
27. Kotsiantis, S., Kanellopoulos, D., Tampakas, V.: Financial application of multi-instance learning: two greek case studies. J. Converg. Inf. Technol. **5**(8), 42–53 (2010)
28. Kriegel, H.P., Pryakhin, A., Schubert, M.: An EM-approach for clustering multi-instance objects. In: Ng, W., Kitsuregawa, M., Li, J., Chang, K. (eds.) Lecture Notes in Artificial Intelligence, pp. 139–148. Springer, Berlin (2006)
29. Li, Y.X., Ji, S., Kumar, S., Ye, J., Zhou, Z.H.: Drosophila gene expression pattern annotation through multi-instance multi-label learning. IEEE ACM Trans. Comput. Biol. **9**(1), 98–112 (2012)
30. Liu, G., Wu, J., Zhou, Z.: Key instance detection in multi-instance learning. In: Hoi, S., Buntine, W. (eds.) JMLR: Workshop and Conference Proceedings: Asian Conference on Machine Learning, pp. 253–268 (2012)
31. Liu, J., Lu, Y., Zhou, T.: Instance significance guided multiple instance boosting for robust visual tracking (2015). arXiv preprint. arXiv:1501.04378
32. Manandhar, A., Morton, K.D., Collins, L.M., Torrione, P.A.: Multiple instance learning for landmine detection using ground penetrating radar. In: Harmon, R., Holloway, J., Broach, J. (eds.) Proceedings of SPIE, Detection and Sensing of Mines, Explosive Objects and Obscured Targets, pp. 721–835. SPIE, Bellingham (2012)
33. Maron, O., Lozano-Pérez, T.: A framework for multiple-instance learning. In: Jordan, M., Kearns, M., Solla, S. (eds.) Advances in Neural Information, vol. 10, pp. 570–576. MIT press, Cambridge (1998)
34. Maron, O., Ratan, A.L.: Multiple-instance learning for natural scene classification. In: Shavlik, J. (ed.) Proceedings of the 15th International Conference on Machine Learning (ICML 1998), vol. 98, pp. 341–349. Morgan Kaufmann Publishers, San Francisco (1998)
35. McGovern, A., Barto, A.G.: Automatic discovery of subgoals in reinforcement learning using diverse density. In: Brodley, C., Danyluk, A. (eds.) Proceedings of the 18th International Conference on Machine Learning (ICML 2001), pp. 361–368. Morgan Kaufmann Publishers, San Francisco (2001)
36. Minhas, A., ul Amir, F., Ben-Hur, A.: Multiple instance learning of calmodulin binding sites. Bioinformatics **28**(18), i416–i422 (2012)
37. Muggleton, S., De Raedt, L.: Inductive logic programming: theory and methods. J. Logic Program. **19**, 629–679 (1994)
38. Murray, J., Hughes, G., Kreutz, K.: Machine learning methods for predicting failures in hard drives: a multiple-instance application. J. Mach. Learn. Res. **6**, 783–816 (2005)

39. Ni, B., Song, Z., Yan, S.: Web image mining towards universal age estimator. In: Proceedings of the 17th ACM international conference on Multimedia, pp. 85–94. ACM, New York (2009)

40. Pfeifer, N., Kohlbacher, O.: Multiple instance learning allows MHC class II epitope predictions across alleles. In: Crandall, K., Lagergren, J. (eds.) Algorithms in Bioinformatics, pp. 210–221. Springer, Berlin (2008)

41. Popescu, M., Mahnot, A.: Early illness recognition using in-home monitoring sensors and multiple instance learning. Method. Inform. Med. **51**(4), 359 (2012)

42. Qi, X., Han, Y.: Incorporating multiple svms for automatic image annotation. Pattern Recogn. **40**(2), 728–741 (2007)

43. Qi, G.J., Hua, X.S., Rui, Y., Mei, T., Tang, J., Zhang, H.J.: Concurrent multiple instance learning for image categorization. In: Proceedings of the 2007 IEEE Conference on Computer Vision and Pattern Recognition (CVPR 2007), pp. 1–8. IEEE, Los Alamitos (2007)

44. Rahmani, R., Goldman, S.A.: MISSL: Multiple-instance semi-supervised learning. In: Cohen, W., Moore, A. (eds.) Proceedings of the 23rd International Conference on Machine Learning (ICML 2006), pp. 705–712. ACM, New York (2006)

45. Ray, S., Craven, M.: Supervised versus multiple instance learning: an empirical comparison. In: De Raedt, L., Wrobel, S. (eds.) Proceedings of the 22nd International Conference on Machine Learning (ICML 2005), pp. 697–704. ACM, New York (2005)

46. Ray, S., Page, D.: Multiple instance regression. In: Brodley, C., Danyluk, A. (eds.) Proceedings of the 18th International Conference on Machine Learning (ICML 2001), pp. 425–432. Morgan Kaufmann Publishers, San Francisco (2001)

47. Reutemann, P.: Development of a propositionalization toolbox. Master's thesis, Albert Ludwigs University of Freiburg, Germany (2004)

48. Reutemann, P., Pfahringer, B., Frank, E.: A toolbox for learning from relational data with propositional and multi-instance learners. In: Webb, G., Yu, X. (eds.) Lecture Notes in Artificial Intelligence, pp. 421–434. Springer, Berlin (2005)

49. Rocchio, J.J.: Relevance feedback in information retrieval. In: Salton, G. (ed.) The SMART Retrieval System: Experiments in Automatic Document Processing, pp. 313–323. Prentice-Hall, Englewood Cliffs (1971)

50. Ruffo, G.: Learning single and multiple instance decision trees for computer security applications. Ph.D. thesis, Department of Computer Science, University of Turin, Turin, Italy (2000)

51. Sánchez Tarragó, D., Cornelis, C., Bello, R., Herrera, F.: A multi-instance learning wrapper based on the Rocchio classifier for web index recommendation. Knowl.-Based Syst. **59**, 173–181 (2014)

52. Srinivasan, A., Muggleton, S., King, R.D., Sternberg, M.J.: Mutagenesis: ILP experiments in a non-determinate biological domain. In: Wrobel, S. (ed.) Proceedings of the 4th international workshop on inductive logic programming, vol. 237, pp. 217–232. Gesellschaft fr Mathematik und Datenverarbeitung MBH, Bonn (1994)

53. Sun, L., Lu, Y., Yang, K., Li, S.: ECG analysis using multiple instance learning for myocardial infarction detection. IEEE Trans. Bio-Med. Eng. **59**(12), 3348–3356 (2012)

54. Sutton, R.S., Barto, A.G.: Reinforcement Learning: An Introduction. MIT press, Cambridge (1998)

55. Tao, Q., Scott, S., Vinodchandran, N., Osugi, T.T.: Svm-based generalized multiple-instance learning via approximate box counting. In: Greiner, R., Schuurmans, D. (eds.) Proceedings of the 21st International Conference on Machine Learning (ICML 2004), p. 101. ACM, New York (2004)

56. Teramoto, R., Kashima, H.: Prediction of protein-ligand binding affinities using multiple instance learning. J Mol. Graph. Model. **29**(3), 492–497 (2010)

57. Wagstaff, K.L., Lane, T.: Salience assignment for multiple-instance regression. In: Proceedings of the ICML 2007 Workshop on Constrained Optimization and Structured Output Spaces. Citeseer (2007)

58. Wagstaff, K.L., Lane, T., Roper, A.: Multiple-instance regression with structured data. In: Bonchi, F., Berendt, B., Giannotti, F., Gunopulos, D., Turini, F., Zaniolo, C., Ramakrishnan, N., Wu, X. (eds.) Proceedings of the 2008 IEEE International Conference on Data Mining Workshops (ICDMW 08), pp. 291–300. IEEE, Los Alamitos (2008)

59. Wang, C., Scott, S., Zhang, J., Tao, Q., Fomenko, D.E., Gladyshev, V.N.: A study in modeling low-conservation protein superfamilies. CSE Technical reports, p. 35 (2004)
60. Wang, S., McKenna, M.T., Nguyen, T.B., Burns, J.E., Petrick, N., Sahiner, B., Summers, R.M.: Seeing is believing: video classification for computed tomographic colonography using multiple-instance learning. IEEE Trans. Med. Imaging 31(5), 1141–1153 (2012)
61. Wang, Q., Yuan, Y., Yan, P., Li, X.: Saliency detection by multiple-instance learning. IEEE Trans. Cybern. 43(2), 660–672 (2013)
62. Wang, Z., Radosavljevic, V., Han, B., Obradovic, Z., Vucetic, S.: Aerosol optical depth prediction from satellite observations by multiple instance regression. In: Apte, C., Park, H., Wang, K., Zaki, M. (eds.) Proceedings of the 2008 SIAM International Conference on Data Mining, pp. 165–176. SIAM, Philadelphia (2008)
63. Wang, Z., Lan, L., Vucetic, S.: Mixture model for multiple instance regression and applications in remote sensing. IEEE Trans. Geosci. Remote 50(6), 2226–2237 (2012)
64. Wu, J., Zhu, X., Zhang, C., Yu, P.S.: Bag constrained structure pattern mining for multi-graph classification. IEEE Trans. Knowl. Data. Eng. 26(10), 2382–2396 (2014)
65. Wu, J., Pan, S., Zhu, X., Cai, Z.: Boosting for multi-graph classification. IEEE Trans. Cybern. 45(3), 416–429 (2015)
66. Yang, C., Lozano-Pérez, T.: Image database retrieval with multiple-instance learning techniques. In: Proceedings of the 16th International Conference on Data Engineering, pp. 233–243. IEEE, Los Alamitos (2000)
67. Zafra, A., Romero, C., Ventura, S., Herrera-Viedma, E.: Multi-instance genetic programming for web index recommendation. Expert Syst. Appl. 36(9), 11470–11479 (2009)
68. Zafra, A., Romero, C., Ventura, S.: Multiple instance learning for classifying students in learning management systems. Expert Syst. Appl. 38(12), 15020–15031 (2011)
69. Zafra, A., Gibaja, E.L., Ventura, S.: Multiple instance learning with multiple objective genetic programming for web mining. Appl. Soft Comput. 11(1), 93–102 (2011)
70. Zafra, A., Ventura, S.: Multi-instance genetic programming for predicting student performance in web based educational environments. Appl. Soft Comput. 12(8), 2693–2706 (2012)
71. Zhang, C., Chen, X.: Region-based image clustering and retrieval using multiple instance learning. In: Leow, W., Lew, M., Chua, T., Ma, W., Chaisom, L., Bakker, E. (eds.) Lecture Notes in Computer Science, pp. 194–204. Springer, Berlin (2005)
72. Zhang, Q., Goldman, S.A.: EM-DD: an improved multiple-instance learning technique. In: Dietterich, T., Becker, S., Ghahramani, Z (eds.) Advances in Neural Information, pp. 1073–1080. MIT press, Cambridge (2001)
73. Zhang, K., Song, H.: Real-time visual tracking via online weighted multiple instance learning. Pattern Recogn. 46(1), 397–411 (2013)
74. Zhang, M.L., Zhou, Z.H.: Multi-instance clustering with applications to multi-instance prediction. Appl. Intell. 31(1), 47–68 (2009)
75. Zhang, Q., Goldman, S.A., Yu, W., Fritts, J.E.: Content-based image retrieval using multiple-instance learning. In: Sammut, C., Hoffman, A. (eds.) Proceedings of the 19th International Conference on Machine Learning (ICML 2002), pp. 682–689. Morgan Kaufmann Publishers, San Francisco (2002)
76. Zhang, C., Chen, S.C., Shyu, M.L.: Multiple object retrieval for image databases using multiple instance learning and relevance feedback. In: Proceedings of the 2004 IEEE International Conference on Multimedia and Expo (ICME 2004), vol. 2, pp. 775–778. IEEE, Los Alamitos (2004)
77. Zhang, C., Chen, X., Chen, M., Chen, S.C., Shyu, M.L.: A multiple instance learning approach for content based image retrieval using one-class support vector machine. In: Proceedings of the 2005 IEEE International Conference on Multimedia and Expo (ICME 2005), pp. 1142–1145. IEEE, Los Alamitos (2005)
78. Zhang, D., Wang, F., Si, L., Li, T.: M3IC: maximum margin multiple instance clustering. In: Proceedings of the 21st International Joint Conference on Artificial Intelligence (IJCAI 2009), vol. 9, pp. 1339–1344 (2009)

79. Zhang, D., Wang, F., Si, L., Li, T.: Maximum margin multiple instance clustering with applications to image and text clustering. IEEE Trans. Neural Netw. **22**(5), 739–751 (2011)
80. Zhao, Z., Fu, G., Liu, S., Elokely, K.M., Doerksen, R.J., Chen, Y., Wilkins, D.E.: Drug activity prediction using multiple-instance learning via joint instance and feature selection. BMC Bioinform. **14**(Suppl 14), S16 (2013)
81. Zhou, Z., Jiang, K., Li, M.: Multi-instance learning based web mining. Appl. Intell. **22**(2), 135–147 (2005)
82. Zhou, Z.H., Zhang, M.L., Huang, S.J., Li, Y.F.: Multi-instance multi-label learning. Artif. Intell. **176**(1), 2291–2320 (2012)
83. Zhou, T., Lu, Y., Qiu, M.: Online visual tracking using multiple instance learning with instance significance estimation. Comput. Res. Repos. (2015)

Chapter 3
Multi-instance Classification

Abstract In the machine-learning community, the most widely used MIL paradigm is Multi-Instance Classification (MIC). Most contributions in MIL are related to this predictive task and a considerable number of problems have been solved successfully. In Sects. 3.1 and 3.2, we introduce the MIC problem, give a formal definition, and describe the evaluation metrics. Section 3.3 recalls a general taxonomy, describing the main categories established within MIC. An in-depth study of the different methods in each category is made in later chapters. In Sects. 3.4 and 3.5, we discuss two specific design aspects related to MIC algorithms. In the former, we present the different assumptions that can be used to relate class labels of instances within a bag to the class label of the bag itself. The latter section describes the main distance metrics that allow to determine similarity between bags. We conclude this chapter by listing common MIC case studies found in the literature in Sect. 3.6 as well as the relevant MIC software tools in Sect. 3.7.

3.1 Introduction

The classification task in MIL consists of predicting the class label of new bags, based on a training set of bags with known labels. The general procedure is shown in Fig. 3.1. The MIC algorithm uses the training data to learn a classifier, which is subsequently used to predict the class label of new observations. The objective of MIC is the same as that of traditional single-instance classification (Sect. 1.3.1). The main difference between both paradigms lies with the representation of training objects. As specified in Sect. 1.3.1, single-instance classification represents each learning pattern with one instance in the form of a feature vector. For example, in an image classification problem that tries to classify an image of the category *lion*, the image would be represented by one instance as a feature vector (Fig. 3.2a). Each observation has an associated class label (label *lion* or label *no lion*). In the multi-instance representation (Sect. 2.1), each observation, denoted as a bag in MIL terminology, is represented with several instances or feature vectors. Figure 3.2b shows the same image, interpreted as a bag of instances that each represents a patch of the original image. The bag as a whole has an associated label (label *lion* or label *no lion*), but

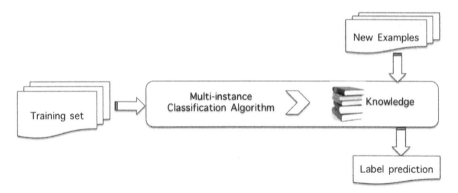

Fig. 3.1 Procedure of classification problem

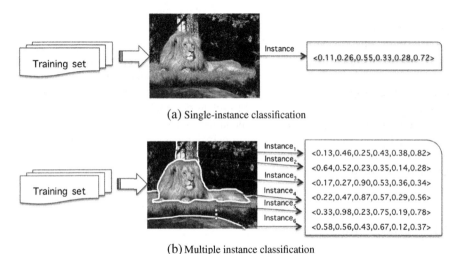

(a) Single-instance classification

(b) Multiple instance classification

Fig. 3.2 Training data set for classification task

class labels of instances inside it are not known. In this example, we know that if the bag label is *lion*, at least one instance (image patch) contains a lion. However, it is not known which instance contains the learning object nor whether there is more than one instance containing it.

Although the multi-instance representation gives us a very natural and flexible way to represent complex learning objects, solving MIC problems is complicated, since the relationship between instances and bags can be different depending on the nature of the problem at hand. In the image classification example in Fig. 3.2b, the representative information of an object is contained in only one instance (the lion). The remaining instances are not relevant and can even confuse the learning process, e.g., when they represent other animals.

(a) Beach   (b) Desert   (c) Ocean

Fig. 3.3 Identifying the concept beach

(a) Desert1   (b) Desert2   (c) Forest

Fig. 3.4 Identifying the concept forest

In other problems, a different relation between instance class labels and the bag class label can exist. For example, in an image classification problem with learning target *beach*, it would be difficult to say which single part of an image is informative. We would need to identify several objects (such as water and sand) to say that the image is a beach scene. If only one instance type is present, the image may be a desert or ocean scene (see Fig. 3.3). This reasoning can be extended to cases where the mere presence of particular objects is not sufficient. For example, we can consider the question of how many trees are required to identify an image as a forest (see Fig. 3.4). In this situation, a certain fraction of instances or a particular number of them is required to represent the learning object and therefore most (or even all) instances can be informative.

Having described the large representation flexibility and the learning complexity of MIC, the following section provides a formal definition of the problem.

3.2 Formal Description

Given a multi-instance dataset with n training bags, we structure the training set as $D = (\mathbf{X}, \mathbf{L})$, where $\mathbf{X} = \langle X_1, \ldots, X_n \rangle$ is a set of bags and $\mathbf{L} = \langle \ell_1, \ldots, \ell_n \rangle$ a set of class labels. The ith training object is represented by $\langle X_i, \ell_i \rangle$, where the bag X_i is associated with the label ℓ_i. As defined in Sect. 2.1, each bag X_i is drawn from $\mathbb{N}^{\mathbb{X}}$, the set of all multi-sets containing elements from $\mathbb{X}$, and $X_i = \langle x_{i1}, \ldots, x_{in_i} \rangle$ is a collection of n_i instances described by d-dimensional vectors, that is, each instance

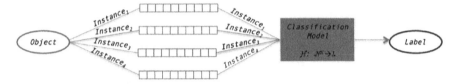

Fig. 3.5 Multiple instance classification

$x_{ij} \subset \mathbb{X}$ is a vector of d dimensions ($\mathbb{X} \subseteq \mathbb{R}^d$). The labels ℓ_i are drawn from $\mathbb{L}$, the finite set of all possible class labels. In MIC, the classes are weakly associated with the bags, since although a bag may be labeled with a class, some (or even most) of its instances may not be truly related to that class.

The MIC objective is to construct, based on the training set D, a function $\mathcal{H}$: $\mathbb{N}^{\mathbb{X}} \rightarrow \mathbb{L}$ that allows to predict class labels of new bags as accurately as possible. The process is shown in Fig. 3.5 where the input is a bag of instances and the output is a single label. The fact that each pattern is represented by several instances complicates the situation. The learning process needs to consider that the bag can have both instances representing the concept to learn and others that do not. This task can be addressed in two possible ways. On the one hand, an instance-level model can be constructed to obtain instance labels, deriving bag labels from instance labels after that. On the other hand, a bag-level model can attempt to obtain bag labels directly from bag discrimination information, working with each bag as an inseparable entity. The following chapters will examine these solution methods further. In the current chapter, the idea is to show that the classification function has to consider the relation between instances and bags in each particular problem. Such relations are not trivial and do not need to be taken into account in single-instance classification. There exist a great number of possibilities to model the relation between the set of instances and its label. This provides a high level of flexibility in representing complex objects, but makes it very difficult to define the most appropriate relationship. The instances inside each bag can have ambiguity, redundancy, interactions, and other properties to explore.

It is interesting to emphasize the case of $|\mathbb{L}| = 2$. This situation deals with two-class classification problems (one positive class and one negative class) and is undoubtedly the most widely addressed problem in the MIC literature. A considerable number of methods described in the following chapters have been specifically designed for $|\mathbb{L}| = 2$. They can only be applied in that context and require modifications when more than two classes are present.

Finally, with respect to the output space, the output of a multi-instance classifier consists of one class label. Therefore, the metrics to evaluate the performance of multi-instance classifiers can be the same as the ones used in single-instance classification. A considerable number of performance metrics have been defined in the literature, such as accuracy, sensitivity, and specificity. In Sect. 1.4, we listed the most commonly used ones.

3.3 Taxonomy

Currently, MIC algorithms cover virtually all categories of machine-learning methods. From decision rules and tree methods to the more sophisticated connectionist and evolutionary methods or support vector machines, all of them have been adapted in various ways to MIC. The growing number of MIC algorithms has created the need to clearly and systematically list their characteristics. For this purpose, various categorization systems have been proposed that try to capture distinctive features of MIC methods. However, as is the case in traditional single-instance learning, it is not possible to create a taxonomy that is both exhaustive and exclusive at the same time, because any nontrivial categorization system will contain classification methods that can be included in two or more categories.

One of the first attempts to order MIC methods was presented by Xu [43]. Two important categories can be found in this taxonomy:

- **Instance-based methods**: these methods first try to determine instance class labels, which are then used to derive class bag labels with an explicit rule.
- **Metadata-based methods**: these methods determine the bag class labels from information extracted directly from the bags.

Later, Foulds [20] proposed a very different categorization, considering three categories widely followed by most works developed from 2009 onward. The categories are set up according to their relationship with traditional single-instance classification algorithms:

- **Purpose-built**: algorithms specifically designed to learn multi-instance concepts.
- **Upgraded**: adaptations of single-instance classification algorithms to MIC.
- **Wrappers**: methods that transform the structure of the multi-instance dataset to a single-instance representation in order to apply existing single-instance classification algorithms without modification.

This categorization has lost support in the last years, because as the number of proposals increased, it could result in confusion. On the one hand, the purpose-built algorithms can also be categorized into one of the well-established learning methods. For example, Xu [43] shows that some methods included in this category, such as APR MIL methods [18] and Diverse Density [31] can be seen as different implementations of the maximum likelihood principle. On the other hand, the category of the upgraded methods is too wide, since it includes both instance-based (upgraded) and bag-based (upgraded) methods.

More recently, Amores [3] presented a MIC algorithm taxonomy of three clear groups of methods. Currently, this taxonomy is the more widely followed. The categories are:

- **Instance space paradigm**: algorithms that seek discriminant functions in the instance space. The bag label is derived using a multi-instance assumption linking labels of instances with that of the bag.

- **Bag space paradigm**: methods that work in the bag space and define similarity or distance measures between bags, allowing them to determine spatial relationships between bags and classes.
- **Embedded space paradigm**: algorithms that work in an embedded space. They transform the original input space into a new (embedded) space, where bags are described by single attribute vectors. Single-instance algorithms can be applied in the induced space.

Another categorization was presented by Foulds and Frank [21]. These authors proposed a hierarchy of MIC algorithms based on the multi-instance assumptions that they implicitly or explicitly embody. Although interesting and very thorough, this categorization was not widely followed by later works. Two facts could explain this. On the one hand, although there is a clear trend toward generalized assumptions and many recent works have implicitly or explicitly dropped the standard assumption, it is not often clearly stated what particular assumptions are used nor is their relation with other assumptions specified. On the other hand, the classification of [21] divides the methods into a higher number of categories and several of them are disconnected from the rest.

Based on these previous studies, this book attempts to specify an adequate taxonomy which covers most algorithms and is easy to follow for the machine-learning community. Concretely, based on the work of Amores [3], the proposed taxonomy is divided into two main categories, instance-based methods and bag-based methods. The latter are in turn divided into two categories that differ in their use of an embedded space or not. We consider this an appropriate taxonomy, on the one hand because it is relatively easy to recognize this categorization in any algorithm in the literature and on the other hand because all previous proposals implicitly or explicitly take into account this feature (with the exception of Fould [20]). However, since this grouping still considers too many methods in each category, a second level of categorizing is necessary. For this second level, we are not in accordance with Amores [3] and consider a more convenient second division based on one of the ideas proposed by Fould [20], where algorithms are divided in classic categories used in traditional single-instance classification. The reason to choose this criterion is that the supervised learning literature provides many single-instance algorithms that are well supported both theoretically and empirically and can provide a solid foundation from which to formulate MIC algorithms. Second, a significant number of publications followed this criterion to group MIC algorithms in their work, because they are very familiar to all members of the machine-learning community and simple to understand and follow.

The proposed taxonomy is shown in Fig. 3.6. We provide a brief description below. An in-depth discussion of each category, together with a review of the corresponding methods and an experimental study, will be presented in later chapters.

1. **Instance-based methods**: these are algorithms whose learning process occurs at the level of the instances. They assume the existence of different classes of instances, i.e., instances have hidden class labels. Their second assumption is that of an explicit relation between the class labels of instances in a bag and the class

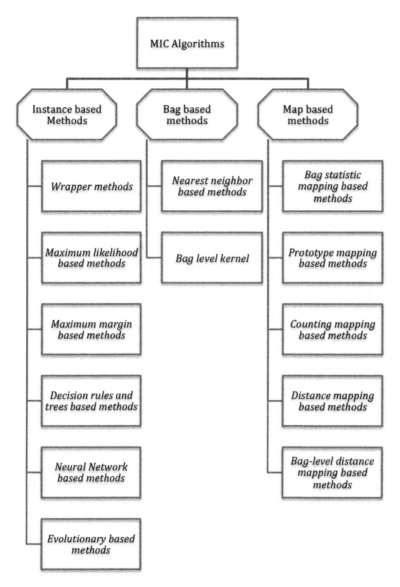

Fig. 3.6 Taxonomy of multiple instance classification algorithms

label of the bag itself. This relation is called the multi-instance (MI) assumption. Instance-based methods construct a learning model to estimate instance class labels in a bag and then, based on the MI assumption, they determine the bag class label. Different assumptions establishing the relation between instance and bag class labels are specified in Sect. 3.4. These methods can be divided into six classic single-instance paradigms, that are described in detail in Chap. 4:

- Wrapper methods
- Maximum likelihood based methods
- Instance-level support vector machine
- Decision rules and trees
- Neural networks
- Evolutionary-based methods

2. **Bag-based methods**: these are algorithms whose learning process occurs at the bag level. They do not attempt to determine sub-concepts or class labels for individual instances, but instead consider the bag as a whole entity. These methods are divided into two subcategories, methods that work in the original bag space and methods that work in a mapped bag space.

    - *Original bag space based methods* include classifiers that define a distance or similarity measure between bags to work directly in the original bag space. These methods rely on a bag comparison function and a method for estimating bag labels. With regard to the former, a distance function can be used (Sect. 3.5), while there are two predominant methods for the latter:
      - Nearest neighbor based methods
      - Bag-level SVM
    - *Mapped bag space based methods* include classifiers that transform each bag to a single-instance representation, such that the learner can train any single-instance classifier to label new bags. Map-based methods differ from each other in the specific way they perform the mapping process, namely:
      - Bag statistics mapping
      - Prototype concatenation mapping
      - Counting-based mapping
      - Distance-based mapping
      - Bag-level distance mapping

    An extensive study of the bag-based methods can be found in Chap. 5.

3.4   MI Assumptions

As specified in Sect. 3.1, a MIC problem represents its learning objects as bags of feature vectors. The bag class labels are available, but the class labels of the individual instances are not defined. This type of representation allows to represent complex objects in a very natural way and many different relations between instances in a bag and bag class labels can be defined. This is where the different MI assumptions, which define these relations, play a relevant role to solve MIC problems.

In initial MI research, a strong assumption was made. It is normally referred to as the *standard MI assumption* and states that each instance has an unknown class label which identifies it as either positive or negative. A bag is considered to be positive if and only if it contains at least one positive instance. This assumption is reasonable in the musk drug activity prediction problem [18], where a molecule is represented by its different conformations and has the desired drug effect if and only if one or more of its conformations binds to the target binding site. It is possible to say that a single positive instance (a specific molecule conformation) is informative enough to determine the bag class label. However, there are other MIC problem domains where this assumption may not be applied. Alternative, more generalized, assumptions are needed. For example, as stated in Sect. 3.1, the classification of concepts as *beach* or *forest* in an image requires a certain fraction of instances (image patches) to represent the concepts. In these cases, most or all instances could be informative.

Different assumptions can be applied depending on the MIC problem and the chosen representation. It is not possible to state that one particular assumption is the most effective heuristic applicable to the whole range of MIC problems. A given assumption can be appropriate for one specific domain, but not advisable in others, because its implied relation does not hold there. Generalized assumptions in a MI scenario deserve special attention for solving the problem appropriately.

It is clear that if the standard MI assumption is relaxed, alternative interactions between instances and bag class labels are possible. However, there are other points that are not so obvious. First, the literature is not in agreement on whether the generalized version of the MI problem belongs within MIL or whether it is a separate problem. There are works that state that alternative MI assumptions are generalized MIL [32, 43], while others state that they are alternative MI assumptions within the multi-instance framework [12, 21] and others compare multi-instance learning with group-based learning [8, 15]. Second, while many recent works have implicitly or explicitly dropped the standard assumption and use different alternative assumptions, they do not state the particular assumptions they use nor how these relate to other assumptions. Therefore, it can be difficult to recognize the many existing MI assumptions in the literature.

This section aims to present the different assumptions and how they are related. Following the categorization used in Sect. 3.3, MIC methods are divided into three categories: instance-based, bag-based, and map-based methods. In this section, we pay attention to the assumptions considered by instance-based classifiers. Our starting point is the work of Foulds and Frank [21]. Bag-based methods are not considered in this study. Although the definition of similarity or dissimilarity creates implicit assumptions about which instances are important, they need fewer assumptions about the relations between instances and bags.

A summary of the different assumptions is shown in Fig. 3.7. Below, we describe them following the formulation given in Sect. 3.2, where $\mathbf{X} = \langle X_1, \ldots, X_m \rangle$ is a set of m bags and each bag is given as $X_i = \langle x_{i1}, \ldots, x_{in_i} \rangle$. The set of bag class labels is $\mathbf{L} = \langle \ell_i, \ldots, \ell_m \rangle$, where $\ell_i \in \mathbb{L}$. A binary classification is assumed ($|\mathbb{L}| = 2$), which is the most widely used in MIC. This makes the specification more understandable (the bags are positive or negative) and it could easily be extended for the case where $|\mathbb{L}| > 2$. A function $h : \mathbb{X} \to \Lambda$ is defined that estimates instance class labels, where Λ is the set of possible instance labels. The MI assumption is a function $H : \mathbb{N}^\Lambda \to \mathbb{L}$ that relates the label of each bag with the labels of its instances.

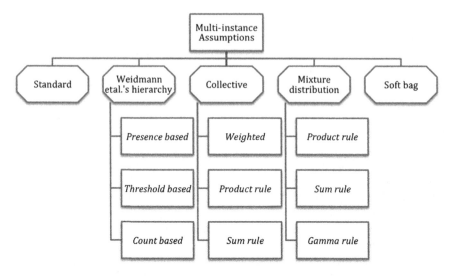

Fig. 3.7 Multiple instance learning assumptions

3.4.1   Standard MI Assumption

The standard MI assumption states that each instance has a hidden class label $\ell_i \in \mathbb{L}$. Under this assumption, a bag is positive if and only if at least one instance is positive. If the positive class is represented with value 1 and the negative class with value 0, the bag class label can be interpreted as the disjunction of instance class labels:

$$H\left(X_i\right) = \bigvee_{x_{ij} \in X_i} \left\{h\left(x_{ij}\right)\right\}. \tag{3.1}$$

Alternatively, if the labels are arithmetically interpreted, then the standard MI assumption can be described as

$$H\left(X_i\right) = \max_{x_{ij} \in X_i} \left\{h\left(x_{ij}\right)\right\}. \tag{3.2}$$

3.4.2   Weidmann et al.'s Hierarchy

Weidmann et al.'s hierarchy [41] is a fundamental reference on this topic, clearly describing and relating different MI assumptions. In this hierarchy, three paradigms are considered in increasing order of generality: the presence-based, the threshold-based, and the count-based paradigms. The positive class is again represented with value 1 and the negative class with value 0 to describe these assumptions.

- **Presence-based MI assumption**: this assumption states that a bag is positive if and only if it contains one or more instances that belong to a set of required instance-level concepts. It coincides with the standard assumption when only one concept is considered. Let $C = \{c_1, c_2, \ldots, c_p\}$ be the set of required instance-level concepts and let $\triangle(X_i, c_j)$ be the number of occurrences of concept c_j in the bag X_i. The bag label is defined as

$$H(X_i) = \begin{cases} 1 & \text{if } (\forall c_j \in C)(\triangle(X_i, c_j) \geq 1) \\ 0 & \text{otherwise.} \end{cases} \qquad (3.3)$$

- **Threshold-based MI assumption**: this assumption states that a bag is positive if and only if there are at least a certain number of instances in the bag that belong to each of the required concepts. Each concept can have a different threshold. The bag label is defined as

$$H(X_i) = \begin{cases} 1 & \text{if } (\forall c_j \in C)(\triangle(X_i, c_j) \geq z_j) \\ 0 & \text{otherwise,} \end{cases} \qquad (3.4)$$

  where $z_j \in \mathbb{N}$ is the lower threshold for concept c_j.
- **Count-based MI assumption**: under this MI assumption, there is a maximum and a minimum number of instances of each concept which each bag has to cover to be considered positive. Each concept can have different thresholds. Using $z_j \in \mathbb{N}$ and $t_j \in \mathbb{N}$ as the lower and upper threshold for concept c_j, the label of bag X_i is given by

$$H(X_i) = \begin{cases} 1 & \text{if } (\forall c_j \in C)(z_j \leq \triangle(X_i, c_j) \leq t_j) \\ 0 & \text{otherwise.} \end{cases} \qquad (3.5)$$

3.4.3 Collective Assumption

This group consists of the heuristic known as the collective assumption [22, 43] and its proposed extensions.

- **Collective assumption**: this is an MI assumption where all instances in a bag contribute equally to its label. It is a probabilistic rule that relates the probability that a bag is assigned to certain class with the likelihood that the instances in the bag are assigned to that class. Although it is not required that instances are divided in the same classes as the bags, it is necessary to determine the contribution of each instance (or its class) to different classes of bags. To do so, $p\left(\ell|x_{ij}\right)$ must be determined to compute for each instance x_{ij} its influence or degree of relationship with each class $\ell \in \mathbb{L}$ of the bag space (ℓ can be either positive $+$ or negative $-$). The values $p\left(\ell|x_{ij}\right)$ can be interpreted as a probability distribution of the instances x_{ij} over the bag classes $\mathbb{L}$, i.e., $(\forall x_{ij} \in X_i)(\sum_{\ell \in \mathbb{L}} p\left(\ell|x_{ij}\right) = 1)$. In the probabilistic understanding of the collective assumption, instances of a bag are a random sample of an underlying instance population of the bag. The class probability function at the bag level is the expected class value of the population, which is estimated by the sample mean:

$$p\left(H\left(X_{i}\right)=\ell\right)=\frac{1}{n_{i}}\sum_{j=1}^{n_{i}}p\left(\ell|x_{ij}\right). \tag{3.6}$$

- **Weighted collective assumption**: this extension of the collective assumption was proposed in [20] and incorporates a weight function over the instance space. It asserts that each instance contributes independently, but not necessarily equally, to the class label of the bag. It assigns weights $\omega_{x_{ij}}$ to all instances $x_{ij} \in X_i$ and computes the bag label as

$$p\left(H\left(X_{i}\right)=\ell\right)=\frac{1}{\sum_{j=1}^{n_{i}}\omega_{x_{ij}}}\sum_{j=1}^{n_{i}}\left[p\left(\ell|x_{ij}\right)*\omega_{x_{ij}}\right]. \tag{3.7}$$

- **Product rule assumption**: Li et al. [29] state that, following the assumption of instance independence, the label of a bag should be computed with the product rule. Given a bag X_i, its instances are assumed to be conditionally statistically independent. This means that, given the label of a bag ℓ_i (either positive or negative), the instances are drawn independently:

$$p(x_{i1}, x_{i2}, \cdots, x_{in_i}|\ell_i) = \prod_{j=1}^{n_i} p(x_{ij}|\ell_i).$$

By writing the probability density function $p(x_{ij}|+)$ that an instance x_{ij} is drawn from a positive bag as $f^+(x_{ij})$ and from a negative bag as $f^-(x_{ij})$, the independence assumption can be rewritten as

$$p(x_{i1}, x_{i2}, \cdots, x_{in_i}|+) = \prod_{j=1}^{n_i} f^+(x_{ij}),$$
$$p(x_{i1}, x_{i2}, \cdots, x_{in_i}|-) = \prod_{j=1}^{n_i} f^-(x_{ij}). \tag{3.8}$$

The product rule can be used to combine the instance classifications into the label of the bag. The product of the posteriors of instances, weighted by the bag prior, is used to decide the bag label. We classify the bag X_i as positive if $p(+|X_i) \geq p(-|X_i)$, where $p(+|X_i)$ or $p(-|X_i)$ respectively denote the posterior probability that the bag X_i is positive or negative, or equivalently if

$$p(+)^{-(n_i-1)} \prod_{j=1}^{n_i} p(+|x_{ij}) \geq p(-)^{-(n_i-1)} \prod_{j=1}^{n_i} p(-|x_{ij}),$$ (3.9)

where $p(+|x_{ij})$ and $p(-|x_{ij})$ reflect the information that the instance x_{ij} contains to predict its bag to be positive or negative respectively and $p(+)$ and $p(-)$ denote the prior probabilities for positive and negative bags.

- **Sum rule assumption**: Li et al. [29] show that the product rule (3.9) is very sensitive to estimation errors of the posteriors. In case of large errors, it is preferable to use the more robust sum rule, which can be derived as an approximation of the product rule

$$(1 - n_i)p(+) + \sum_{j=1}^{n_i} p(+|x_{ij}) \geq (1 - n_i)(p(-)) + \sum_{j=1}^{n_i} p(-|x_{ij}).$$ (3.10)

3.4.4 Mixture Distribution Assumption

The mixture distribution assumption considers a recent group of assumptions (not included in the review of Foulds and Frank [21]), where instances are modeled by a mixture distribution of the concept and the nonconcept, which leads to a convenient way to solve MIC as a classifier combining problem [29].

This assumption states that there exist both a concept C that defines the difference between the positive and negative bags, and a nonconcept $\overline{C}$ that denotes the background region shared by both positive and negative bags. As such, there are two distinct distributions to generate instances from: $f^C(\cdot)$ for the concept C and $f^{\overline{C}}(\cdot)$ for the nonconcept $\overline{C}$. The instances in a negative bag are all drawn from $\overline{C}$, while the instances in a positive bag are from a mixture of both C and $\overline{C}$, with a fraction α of instances sampled from the concept C. Concretely,

$$f^-(x_{ij}) = f^{\overline{C}}(x_{ij}),$$ (3.11)

$$f^+(x_{ij}) = \alpha f^C(x_{ij}) + (1 - \alpha)f^{\overline{C}}(x_{ij}),$$ (3.12)

with $0 < \alpha < 1$. The density of the concept $f^C(x)$ can be written as

$$f^C(x_{ij}) = \frac{f^+(x_{ij}) - (1 - \alpha)f^-(x_{ij})}{\alpha}.$$

We denote the prior probabilities for positive and negative bags as $p(+) = \beta$ and $p(-) = 1 - \beta$, respectively, with $0 < \beta < 1$. The prior probabilities for the concept C and the nonconcept $\overline{C}$ are $p(C) = \alpha\beta$, $p(\overline{C}) = 1 - \alpha\beta$.

- **Product rule assumption**: with the mixture assumption (3.11) and (3.12), the label of a bag X_i can be determined from the classification of its instances x_{ij} into the concept or nonconcept [29]. By using the relation between the probability distribution functions and their posteriors, it can be deduced that

$$p(+|X_i) = p(C|x_{ij}) + \frac{\beta - \alpha\beta}{1 - \alpha\beta} p(\overline{C}|x_{ij}), \tag{3.13}$$

$$p(-|X_i) = \frac{1 - \beta}{1 - \alpha\beta} p(\overline{C}|x_{ij}), \tag{3.14}$$

where $p(C|x_{ij})$ and $p(\overline{C}|x_{ij})$ denote respectively the probability that x_{ij} belongs to the concept C or the nonconcept $\overline{C}$.

Substituting (3.13) and (3.14) into the decision rule (3.9), we find

$$\begin{aligned}
\beta^{-(n_i-1)} &\prod_{j=1}^{n_i} \left(p(C|x_{ij}) + \frac{\beta - \alpha\beta}{1 - \alpha\beta} p(\overline{C}|x_{ij}) \right) \\
&\geq (1 - \beta)^{-(n_i-1)} \prod_{j=1}^{n_i} \frac{1 - \beta}{1 - \alpha\beta} p(\overline{C}|x_{ij}).
\end{aligned} \tag{3.15}$$

If the posteriors $p(C|x_{ij})$ and $p(\overline{C}|x_{ij})$ can be accurately estimated, an optimal solution (in the sense of the Bayes error) for the bag label can be obtained from (3.15).

- **Sum rule assumption**: the product rule above can also be approximated by the more robust sum rule of [29]:

$$\begin{aligned}
(1 - n_i)\beta + &\sum_{j=1}^{n_i} \left(p(C|x_{ij}) + \frac{\beta - \alpha\beta}{1 - \alpha\beta} p(\overline{C}|x_{ij}) \right) \\
&\geq (1 - n_i)(1 - \beta)^{-(n_i-1)} + \sum_{j=1}^{n_i} \frac{1 - \beta}{1 - \alpha\beta} p(\overline{C}|x_{ij}).
\end{aligned} \tag{3.16}$$

- γ-**rule assumption**: if the posterior probabilities cannot be estimated properly and it is only known that an instance is more probable to belong to the concept C or the nonconcept $\overline{C}$, the label of a bag is predicted by counting how many instances are estimated to belong to the concept. The optimal threshold to label a bag as positive is based on the sum rule defined in (3.16). It is preferred over the product rule since there can be large estimation errors in the posteriors.

  Assume that there are n_i instances in bag X_i and a fraction g of them, so $g \cdot n_i$ instances, are estimated to be from the concept, then (3.16) can be rewritten as

$$(1 - n_i)\beta + \sum_{x_{ij} \in C} (\hat{p}(C|x_{ij}) + \frac{\beta - \alpha\beta}{1 - \alpha\beta} \hat{p}(\overline{C}|x_{ij}))$$

$$+ \sum_{x_{ij} \in \overline{C}} (\hat{p}(C|x_{ij}) + \frac{\beta - \alpha\beta}{1 - \alpha\beta} \hat{p}(\overline{C}|x_{ij}))$$

$$\geq (1 - n_i)(1 - \beta)^{-(n_i - 1)} + \sum_{x_{ij} \in C} \frac{1 - \beta}{1 - \alpha\beta} \hat{p}(\overline{C}|x_{ij})$$

$$+ \sum_{x_{ij} \in \overline{C}} \frac{1 - \beta}{1 - \alpha\beta} \hat{p}(\overline{C}|x_{ij}),$$

(3.17)

where $\hat{p}(C|x_{ij})$ and $\hat{p}(\overline{C}|x_{ij})$ denote the estimated posteriors. There are $g \cdot n_i$ instances in the summation $\sum_{x_{ij} \in C}$ and $(1 - g) \cdot n_i$ instances in the summation $\sum_{x_{ij} \in \overline{C}}$. To simplify, the posterior $\hat{p}(C|x_{ij})$ is assumed to equal one if the instance x_{ij} is classified to the concept and zero if it is classified to the nonconcept. Using this, the above equation becomes

$$\gamma = \frac{(1 - \alpha\beta)(1 - 2\beta)}{2(1 - \beta)n_i} + \alpha\beta.$$

A bag is classified to be positive if γ is larger than this threshold. The decision criterion is called the γ-rule.

3.4.5 Soft Bag MI Assumption

The soft bag definition [30] includes a new consideration of multi-instance problems. Previous generalized assumptions assume that all instances of negative bags are negative examples. There is no ambiguity in these objects. The new formulation assumes negative bags can also contain positive instances. As a result, negative bags can also have a noisy instance composition. For example, if we consider the problem of classifying images for the concept *flower*, negative images could include regions of flowers. This labeling noise is common in weakly supervised learning, where human annotators are asked to label data with a few keywords. The absence of the *flower* label does not mean that there are no flowers in the image, just that the annotator did not think of *flower* as one of its predominant concepts. This means that negative bags can frequently contain positive instances.

To address this problem, Li et al. [30] consider a more general definition of MIL, where both positive and negative bags are soft. A soft bag X_i is a set of instances that are sampled independently from two distributions $p_{X_i}^+(x_{ij})$ (positive source) and $p_{X_i}^-(x_{ij})$ (negative source). The positive source is the distribution of the target concept (e.g., image patches of *flower*), the negative source is the distribution of background material (e.g., image patches of everything else).

A soft bag X_i is a set of n_i instances, where $n_i \geq n$ and $n \in \mathbb{N}$ is a lower bound on bag size. The bag label would be determined as follows. Let $0 < \mu \leq N$ be a lower bound on the number of positive examples per positive bag. A soft bag X_i is μ-positive if $n_i^+ \geq \mu$ and μ-negative otherwise. Although a μ-negative soft bag can contain positive instances, their number has to be less than that of a μ-positive soft bag. Conventional supervised learning corresponds to $n_i = \mu = 1$, where a bag contains either a positive or negative instance.

3.5   Distance Metrics

Intuitively, a distance is a numerical measure of how far two places or objects are from each other. It refers to the difference in spatial location. In a broader sense, related to classification, it can refer to the difference between any two objects. In this context, distance metrics are a possible way to evaluate similarity and objects at a closer distance are interpreted as being more similar.

It is very complicated to precisely determine the distance between objects and many contributions deal with this problem in single-instance learning [26]. In MIL, the process becomes more challenging. On the one hand, a multi-instance object is represented as a bag of instances, such that the distance between objects is a set-to-set distance. Compared to single-instance data for which we can use a vector distance (e.g., Euclidean distance), distance estimation in MIL is inherently more difficult. On the other hand, in MIL, labels are assigned to bags but not instances which is known as weak label association. As a result, although a bag belongs to a class, some or most of its instances may not be truly related to that class. The distance metric should consider these particularities for obtaining appropriate results. For example, Fig. 3.8 shows two images categorized as *Fox* and one categorized as *Cat*. Two figures represent a red fox in different backgrounds, one of them in the snow and the other in a forest. The third image represents a cat in a forest. When all image regions are compared, the image background could determine a higher similarity between images that represent different concepts. Appropriately modeling the distance between the image regions could improve the similarity relation between images that really represent the same concept.

(a) Red fox in the snow   (b) Red fox in the forest   (c) Cat in the forest

Fig. 3.8 Differences between animals in different backgrounds

To compute distances between any type of objects, we need a precise definition in the form of a distance function or metric. Formally, given a set of objects X, a metric is a function $D : X \times X \rightarrow \mathbb{R}$ with the following properties for all $A, B, C \in X$:

1. $D(A, B) \geq 0$ (nonnegativity)
2. $D(A, B) = 0$ if and only if $A = B$ (self-identity axiom)
3. $D(A, B) = D(B, A)$ (symmetry)
4. $D(A, B) \leq D(A, C) + D(C, B)$ (triangle inequality)

The spatial structure defined by the distance D and the set of objects X is called a metric space. Several types of metrics can be defined on any set X, each of them capturing different aspects of the objects under comparison or properties of the spatial structure [17, 26].

In some applications, the use of a similarity function can be more appropriate than a distance function. Given a set of objects X, a function $S : X \times X \rightarrow \mathbb{R}$ is a similarity function if it is nonnegative, symmetric and if $S(A, B) \leq S(A, A)$ holds for all $A, B \in X$, with equality if and only if $A = B$. Distance and similarity are inversely related notions. A distance function D can be obtained from a similarity function S by using an appropriate transformation [17]. For example, often used transformations are $D = 1 - S$, $D = \frac{1-S}{S}$, $D = -\ln S$ and $D = \arccos(S)$.

Kernel functions, often used in SVMs, are basically similarity functions. Many kernel functions have been developed for unconventional data structures such as strings, trees, or graphs [23, 25]. They can also be transformed into distance functions. The most popular transformation is

$$D(A, B) = \sqrt{K(A, A) - 2K(A, B) + K(B, B)},$$

where $K(A, B)$ denotes a kernel function defined over bags A and B. Other transformation methods may be used as appropriate [25].

Below, we describe some distance functions widely used in MIL. We define them considering the distance between any two bags A and B with n_a and n_b instances, respectively. Following the work of Cheplygina et al. [14], we distinguish between two different approaches to classify the distance metrics. The first considers each bag as a point set, defining the distance as an aggregation of a set of distances between two point sets. The second approach considers each bag as a distribution of points and defines the distance by comparing the distributions represented by each point set.

3.5.1 Bags as Point Sets

In this approach, the metric considers each bag as a point set or a subset of a high-dimensional space. Typically, a distance between two bags is defined as an aggregation of distances between particular instances of each bag. The Euclidean distance is typically used to measure the distance between instances, although other metrics can be applied as well, such as the Manhattan or Chebyshev distance [11].

Hausdorff Distance

One possible metric is based on the Hausdorff distance. Several variants have been proposed in the literature.

- **Minimal Hausdorff distance** [37]: this measure is defined as the minimum distance between all instances of bags A and B. For each instance, the closest instance in the other bag is located. The minimum among these closest distances defines the bag distance. Concretely,

$$\mathsf{D}_{Hausdorff-min}(A, B) = \min_{a \in A} \min_{b \in B} d(a, b), \tag{3.18}$$

  where $d(a, b)$ represents a distance function between instances. This measure is symmetric, but it does not satisfy the identity property, since a zero distance does not imply $A = B$ when an instance in A coincides with an instance in B. The triangle inequality is not always satisfied either. This measure is therefore not a metric.
- **Maximal Hausdorff distance** [37]: this distance is defined as the maximal distance between an instance in A and its closest instance in B and vice versa. For each instance, the closest instance in the other bag is located and the maximum of these distances is used as the bag distance, given as

$$\mathsf{D}_{Hausdorff-max}(A, B) = \max\{\mathsf{h}(A, B), \mathsf{h}(A, B)\}, \tag{3.19}$$

  where

$$\mathsf{h}(A, B) = \max_{a \in A} \min_{b \in B} d(a, b). \tag{3.20}$$

  Since $h(A, B) \neq h(B, A)$, the measure h is not symmetric. The additional step (3.19) is necessary for the symmetry criterion. This ensures that this distance is a metric, because it satisfies the identity, symmetry, and triangle inequality properties. However, it could be too sensitive to outliers.
- **Average Hausdorff distance** [49]: this metric is the average distance between an instance in A and its closest instance in B and vice versa. The bag distance is given by

$$\mathsf{D}_{Hausdorff-avg}(A, B) = \frac{\sum_{a \in A} \min_{b \in B} d(a, b) + \sum_{b \in B} \min_{a \in A} d(a, b)}{|A| + |B|}. \tag{3.21}$$

  This measure satisfies the identity, symmetry, and triangle inequality properties.
- **Adapted Hausdorff distance** [46]: this distance combines the previous ones. Since the information contained in instances depends on the class that their bag belongs to, the metric is different when it evaluates the distance between two posi-

tive or negative bags or between one positive and one negative bag. The following distinction is made based on the standard MI assumption:

- If both bags are negative, we can be sure that there is no instance in the pattern that represents the positive concept. Therefore, an average distance is used to measure the distance between these bags, because all instances are guaranteed to be negative: $D_{Hausdorff-adap}(A, B) = D_{Hausdorff-avg}(A, B)$.
- If both bags are positive, we know that at least one instance in each of them represents the positive concept, but there is no information about which particular instance or instances. The minimal distance is used to measure the distance between the bags, because the positive instances have a higher probability of being close to each other: $D_{Hausdorff-adap}(A, B) = D_{Hausdorff-min}(A, B)$.
- Finally, if we evaluate the distance between bags where one of them is a positive bag and the other is a negative one, the maximal Hausdorff distance is used to calculate the distance between the two bags: $D_{Hausdorff-adap}(A, B) = D_{Hausdorff-max}(A, B)$.

- **k-th ranked Hausdorff distance** [37]: this distance tries to improve the robustness of the maximum Hausdorff distance against outliers, to which the max and min operators are sensitive. Concretely, the maximum Hausdorff distance (3.20) is redefined as

$$h(A, B) = k^{th} \min_{\substack{a \in A \ b \in B}} d(a, b), \tag{3.22}$$

where k^{th} represents the k-th largest value. When $k = |A|$, the k-th ranked Hausdorff distance reduces to (3.20).

OWA Operator-Based Distances

Ordered weighted averaging operators (OWA) [44] can replace the classical max and min operators to improve the performance of the Hausdorff distances. The OWA aggregation of a sequence V of m scalar values is computed by first sorting the values of V in decreasing order and assigning the weight $w_i \in [0, 1]$ to the value at the ith position, such that $\sum_{i=1}^{m} w_i = 1$. The weighted average is computed as

$$OWA_W(V) = \sum_{i=1}^{m} w_i c_i,$$

where c_i represents the ith largest value in V and $W = \langle w_1, \ldots, w_m \rangle$ is the weight vector.

The OWA operator can be seen as a generalization of any aggregation operation that can be made over a set of values. For example, the classical maximum operator over a set of values V can be modeled with the weight vector $\langle 1, 0, \ldots, 0 \rangle$. If the value at the first position is an outlier, the aggregation result will be inappropriate. A softened version of the maximum operator can be obtained by using a weight vector that distributes the weight among many values, putting more weight in the first positions (the highest values) and putting less and less weight in the following positions.

In the OWA version of the maximal Hausdorff distance, (3.20) is replaced by

$$h^{OWA}(A, B) = OWA_{W_{max}} \underbrace{OWA_{W_{min}} \underbrace{\|a - b\|}_{b \in B}}_{a \in A}. \tag{3.23}$$

The OWA version of the average Hausdorff distance (3.21) is defined as

$$D^{OWA}_{Hausdorff-avg}(A, B) = \frac{\sum_{a \in A} \underbrace{OWA_{W_{min}} \|a - b\|}_{b \in B} + \sum_{b \in B} \underbrace{OWA_{W_{min}} \|a - b\|}_{a \in A}}{|A| + |B|}. \tag{3.24}$$

The weight vectors W_{max} and W_{min} are used to approximate the maximum and minimum operators, respectively. Two weight vector schemes are suggested in [35]. For the maximum operator, the linearly decreasing weight vector is defined as

$$W_{max-L} = \left\langle \frac{2}{m+1}, \frac{2(m-1)}{m(m+1)}, \cdots, \frac{4}{m(m+1)}, \frac{2}{m(m+1)} \right\rangle \tag{3.25}$$

and the inverse additive weight vector as

$$W_{max-IA} = \left\langle \frac{1}{1 \sum_{i=1}^{m} \frac{1}{i}}, \frac{1}{2 \sum_{i=1}^{m} \frac{1}{i}}, \cdots, \frac{1}{(m-1) \sum_{i=1}^{m} \frac{1}{i}}, \frac{1}{m \sum_{i=1}^{m} \frac{1}{i}} \right\rangle, \tag{3.26}$$

where m is the length of the weight vector, i.e., the number of values on which the OWA operator is applied. The weight vector for the minimum operator is the reverse sequence of the maximum weight vector. Vluymans et al. [35, 36] showed that these OWA variants of Hausdorff distances are quite robust against outliers.

3.5.2 Bags as Probability Distributions

In this approach, each bag is considered as a probability distribution in the instance space. Bag differences are characterized in terms of differences between the distribution of their instances. For each bag, a probability density has to be estimated. It is very hard to estimate a high-dimensional probability density function in a high-dimensional feature space and very computationally demanding to estimate the difference, or overlap, between two distributions. The instance distributions are approximated and the distances are computed between the approximated distributions.

Earth Movers Distance

This distance measures the effort that is needed to transform the probability distribution A ('pile of earth') into another probability distribution B ('hole in the ground'). It is assumed that each instance in bag A with n_a instances contains $\frac{1}{n_a}$ of the total probability mass. Therefore, the pile consists of n_a smaller piles and the hole consists of n_b smaller holes. The distribution distance of earth movers distance is defined as

$$D_{EDM}(A, B) = \sum_{a \in A, b \in B} f(a, b) d(a, b), \qquad (3.27)$$

where $d(a, b)$ is the Euclidean distance between points (the ground distance between piles and holes) and $f(a, b)$ is the flow that minimizes the overall distance, subject to constraints that ensure that only available amounts of earth are transported into available holes and that all the earth is indeed transported:

- $f(a, b) \geq 0$,
- $\sum_{a \in A} f(a, b) \leq \frac{1}{n_b}$,
- $\sum_{b \in B} f(a, b) \leq \frac{1}{n_a}$,
- $\sum_{a \in A, b \in B} f(a, b) = 1$

Mahalanobis Distance

This distance approximates the distribution of each bag by a Gaussian with mean μ and covariance matrix $\sum$. The Mahalanobis distance is defined as the difference between two Gaussian distributions

$$D_{Mahalanobis}(A, B) = (\mu_a - \mu_b)^T \left(\frac{1}{2} \sum_a + \frac{1}{2} \sum_b \right)^{-1} (\mu_a - \mu_b). \qquad (3.28)$$

When the number of instances per bag is low and the feature dimensionality is high, it can become hard (or even impossible) to invert the averaged covariance matrix.

Cauchy–Schwarz Divergence

This distance tries to solve the fact that a Gaussian distribution can be too restrictive. It uses a multivariate Gaussian (or a Parzen density with a smaller width parameter) instead. The Cauchy–Schwarz divergence is defined as the divergence between the estimated distributions

$$D_{Cauchy-S}(A, B) = -log \left(\frac{K_{\sigma_a + \sigma_b}(A, B)}{(K_{2\sigma_a}(A, B) K_{2\sigma_b}(A, B))^{1/2}} \right), \qquad (3.29)$$

where

$$K_\sigma(A, B) = \sum_{a \in A, b \in B} \frac{exp(\frac{1}{-2\sigma^2}(a - b)^T(a - b))}{(2\pi \sigma^2)^{d/2}}. \qquad (3.30)$$

According to [9, 14], when the distributions are form the same data source, $\sigma_a = \sigma_b$ holds.

3.6   Real-World Applications

In Chap. 2, the main application fields for MIC were described. Following the grouping established there, the most representative case studies of each application field are listed in this section. The experimental studies conducted in later chapters will use a selection of the data sets described in this section. With the purpose of highlighting the data used in experimental studies, these will be printed in bold.

3.6.1   Bioinformatics

As commented in Sect. 2.4.1, in drug activity prediction, the task is to determine whether a molecule has the desired activity, that is, whether it binds strongly to a target protein. Molecules may adopt a wide range of shapes or conformations which influence their binding properties. Different molecules have different numbers of conformations. It is known that a molecule is active when at least one shape can bind well (although it is not known which one) and it is inactive when none of its conformations can bind well.

- *Musk* [18]: this problem consists of predicting whether a molecule has a musky smell or not. A molecule is described by its different conformations. This problem has become a classic benchmark to evaluate MIL algorithms. Its assumption is based on the standard MI assumption: if at least one of the conformations can cause a molecule to smell musky, the molecule is positive for the musky class. If none of the conformations have this property, the molecule is negative. There are two datasets, Musk1 and Musk2. The Musk1 dataset is smaller, both in having fewer molecules (bags) and fewer instances per molecule. Many molecules are shared between the two data sets, but Musk2 set includes more instances for the shared molecules.
- *Mutagenesis* [33]: this problem consists of predicting the mutagenicity of the molecules, that is, determining whether a molecule is mutagenic or not. A molecule is described by the different conformations. The standard MI assumption can be used: if at least one of the conformations has the mutagenic property, the molecule is positive for the mutagenic class. It is non-mutagenic otherwise. There are three datasets: mutagenesis-atoms, mutagenesis-bonds, and mutagenesis-chains.

The second bioinformatics task in protein identification. These problems compare the sequences of each protein family and try to identify new families by examining the structures. Normally, the similarity between sequences of different families is low, so it is difficult to identify new families by just modeling the primary sequence.

Table 3.1 Description of case studies for the bioinformatics domain

Domain	Application	Dataset (Download)	Attributes	Pos. bags	Neg. bags	Total bags	Instances
Bio-informatics	Molecule activity prediction	Musk1 [5, 16, 47]	166	47	45	92	476
		Musk2 [5, 16, 47]	166	39	63	102	6598
		Mut. Atoms [16, 47]	10	125	63	188	1618
		Mut. Bonds [16, 47]	16	125	63	188	3995
		Mut. Chains [16, 47]	24	125	63	188	5349
	Protein identifica-tion	Thioredoxin-fold [19]	8	25	168	193	26611

The secondary structure, such as the presence of certain patterns (called motifs) in the sequence, is used instead. An example is the *thioredoxin-fold* dataset. The task is to identify thioredoxin-fold proteins, which is a protein superfamily that is important for understanding redox processes in cells. A primary sequence of each protein is described by all the motifs in the sequence. The given proteins are first aligned with respect to a motif that is known to be conserved in members of the family. Each aligned protein is represented by a bag and an instance in the bag corresponds to a position in a fixed length sequence around the conserved motif. Each position is described by properties of the amino acid at that position and smoothed using the same properties from its 16 neighbors.

Datasets of both applications are summarized in Table 3.1 where the most relevant information about each dataset is shown.

3.6.2 Image Classification and Retrieval

As described in Sect. 2.4.2, this problem consists of identifying the intended target object(s) in images. The major difficulty is that images may contain multiple and possibly heterogeneous objects. The global description of a whole image is therefore too coarse and identifying the object of interest is a very challenging open problem in traditional learning frameworks. In the MIL setting, bags are images and the instances are parts of the images, such as pixels, blobs, or segments.

This problem has been tackled with different assumptions which can be more or less appropriate depending on the types of images in question. The standard assumption, where a positive bag has at least one instance contains the target object,

Table 3.2 Description of case studies for the image classification domain

Domain	Application	Dataset	Attributes	Pos. bags	Neg. bags	Total bags	Instances
Image classification	Animals	Elephant [5, 16, 47]	230	100	100	200	1220
		Fox [5, 16, 47]	**230**	**100**	**100**	**200**	**1320**
		Tiger [5, 16, 47]	230	100	100	200	1391
	Corel	African [16]	**9**	**100**	**1900**	**2000**	**7947**
		Horses [16]	**9**	**100**	**1900**	**2000**	**7947**
		Cars [16]	9	100	1900	2000	7947
		Beach [16]	**9**	**100**	**1900**	**2000**	**7947**
		Mountains [16]	9	100	1900	2000	7947
		Waterfalls [16]	9	100	1900	2000	7947
		Historical [16]	9	100	1900	2000	7947
		Food [16]	9	100	1900	2000	7947
		Antique [16]	9	100	1900	2000	7947
		Buses [16]	9	100	1900	2000	7947
		Dogs [16]	9	100	1900	2000	7947
		Battleships [16]	9	100	1900	2000	7947
		Dinosaurs [16]	9	100	1900	2000	7947
		Lizards [16]	9	100	1900	2000	7947
		Skiing [16]	9	100	1900	2000	7947
		Elephants [16]	9	100	1900	2000	7947
		Fashion [16]	9	100	1900	2000	7947
		Desserts [16]	9	100	1900	2000	7947
		Flowers [16]	9	100	1900	2000	7947
		Sunset [16]	9	100	1900	2000	7947

seems applicable when we consider each instances as a patch of image. Nevertheless, other assumptions can be more appropriate in other cases. For example, if instances are pixels, it might not be suitable to define pixels as belonging to the target concept. Perhaps a fraction of positive instances is more suitable. Or, if instances are several patches of an image which represent complex concepts, such as beach concept, it would be difficult to say which part of the image is informative. In this case, it would be necessary to identify several objects (such as water and sand) to say that it is a beach. If only one type of instance is presented, it might be a desert scene or an ocean scene. This reasoning can be extended even further to consider cases where simply the presence of particular objects is not enough, for example, consider how much of an image has to be covered by trees for you to call it a forest. In these cases, a certain fraction of instances or a particular number of them is required for the positive class label, and therefore most, or even all instances can be informative.

This problem has been widely tackled in MIL. Concretely, Tiger, Fox, and Elephant are considered benchmark for evaluating new proposals in MIL. Following, some of most representative case studies are considered and Table 3.2 summarizes these case studies.

- *Tiger*, *Fox*, and *Elephant* datasets [4] are popular benchmarks for evaluating new MIL proposals. For each of them, the task is to identify whether a given image contains the animal. The standard MI assumption is most popular here, where an image is considered as positive when at least one of its segments contains the required animal. Although not very usual, other assumptions have been used [38].
- *Corel* dataset [12]: this problem consists of identifying 20 different categories in images, such as, African, Horses, Cars, and so on. The dataset is commonly divided in 20 different subproblems, using one of the classes as the positive class. The standard assumption can be used [12], although other assumptions have been considered as well [14, 38].

3.6.3 Web Mining and Text Classification

A document, such as an article, email discussion or website can be represented as a collection of its parts, such as paragraphs or individual webpages, which are often described by bag-of-words histograms. The goal is to assign a category to unlabeled document. Different assumptions might be applicable here, which can be more or less appropriate depending on the types of documents and document categories in question. The standard assumption, where a positive bag has at least one positive instance, seems applicable when we consider articles as relevant or not for a particular topic. If at least one paragraph is relevant, then the whole article is considered relevant. When classifying general-purpose documents, such as websites or email discussions, the situation might be different. For example, most social websites could have a page describing the security settings, but it would be wrong to put these websites in the security category.

Similar to image classification, the case studies that cover this application are very difficult to solve, because a text may contain multiple and heterogeneous topics. These are hard problems in traditional learning and the use of a learning framework with more generalized representations, such as MIL, is considered more appropriate. Some case studies in this application field are described following and Table 3.3 summarizes these case studies.

- *Newsgroup* [52]: this problem consists of identifying 20 different news groups. It is very widely used for assessing text classification methods. The bags are news articles and the instances are paragraphs fixed to a specific number of words. For MIC, this dataset is divided in 20 text categorization datasets and the standard assumption is considered. Concretely, 50 positive and 50 negative bags are generated for each of the 20 news categories. Each positive bag contains 3 % posts

Table 3.3 Description of case studies for the web mining and text classification domains

Domain	Application	Dataset	Attributes	Pos. bags	Neg. bags	Total bags	Instances
Textual classification	Newsgroup	comp.graphics [16]	200	100	100	200	5443
		comp.os.ms-windows.mis [16]	200	100	100	200	5443
		comp.sys.ibm.pc. hardware [16]	200	100	100	200	5443
		comp.sys.mac. hardware [16]	200	100	100	200	5443
		comp.windows.x [16]	200	100	100	200	5443
		rec.autos [16]	200	100	100	200	5443
		rec.motorcycles [16]	200	100	100	200	5443
		rec.sport.baseball [16]	200	100	100	200	5443
		rec.sport.hockey [16]	200	100	100	200	5443
		sci.crypt [16]	200	100	100	200	5443
		sci.electronics [16]	200	100	100	200	5443
		sci.med [16]	200	100	100	200	5443
		sci.space [16]	200	100	100	200	5443
		misc.forsale [16]	200	100	100	200	5443
		talk.politics.misc [16]	200	100	100	200	5443
		talk.politics.guns [16]	200	100	100	200	5443
		talk.politics.mideast [16]	200	100	100	200	5443
		talk.religion.misc [16]	200	100	100	200	5443
		alt.atheism [16]	200	100	100	200	5443
		soc.religion.christian [16]	200	100	100	200	5443
	TREC9	TST1 [5]	66552	200	200	400	3224
		TST2 [5]	66153	200	200	400	3341
		TST3 [5]	66144	200	200	400	3246
		TST4 [5]	**67085**	**200**	**200**	**400**	**3391**

(continued)

Table 3.3 (continued)

Domain	Application	Dataset	Attributes	Pos. bags	Neg. bags	Total bags	Instances
		TST7 [5]	66823	200	200	400	3367
		TST9 [5]	66627	200	200	400	3300
		TST10 [5]	66082	200	200	400	3453
	Web index recommendation	User 1 [16]	5999	21	92	113	3423
		User 2 [16]	**5999**	**21**	**92**	**113**	**3423**
		User 3 [16]	5999	21	92	113	3423
		User 4 [16]	5999	89	24	113	3423
		User 5 [16]	**5999**	**89**	**24**	**113**	**3423**
		User 6 [16]	5999	89	24	113	3423
		User 7 [16]	**5999**	**55**	**58**	**113**	**3423**
		User 8 [16]	5999	55	58	113	3423
		User 9 [16]	5999	55	58	113	3423

randomly drawn from the target category and the other instances (and all instances in negative bags) are randomly and uniformly drawn from the other categories [52].

- *TREC9* [4] : this dataset is also known as OHSUMED. The task is to identify different categories on MEDLINE articles. MEDLINE documents are annotated with MeSH terms (Medical Subject Headings), each one defining a binary concept. The total number of MEsH terms in TREC9 was 4903, but the dataset used in Andrews et al. [4] is smaller. It contains the first seven categories of the pretest portion. For MIC, this dataset is divided into passages using overlapping windows of maximal 50 words each and at least 200 positive examples and the rest is randomly selected of the other categories.
- *Web Index Recommendation* [45]: the task is to classify a webpage as interesting or not. In total, nine users rate webpages, such that there are nine different datasets. A webpage is a bag and the links on the webpage are its instances. Webpage links are represented using word frequency. This problem has been addressed using the standard MI assumption, that is, if a user is interested in at least one link, the web page is interesting to him/her.

3.6.4 Medical Diagnosis and Imaging

Many applications in the medical domain could be classified as image classification, because they often work with images. However, as the learning objective is related to

Table 3.4 Description of case studies for the medical diagnosis and imaging domains

Domain	Application	Dataset	Attributes	Pos. bags	Neg. bags	Total bags	Instances
Image clas-sification	Medical diagnosis and imaging	Messidor [16]	687	654	546	1200	12352
		UCBS breast [16]	708	26	32	58	2002

medical diagnosis, these problems are included in the applications on computer-aided medical diagnosis. Table 3.4 summarizes these case studies.

- *Messidor* [28]: the problem consists of predicting whether a medical image is of a patient with diabetes or a healthy patient. A bag is an eye image and an instance is a patch of 135×135 pixels. Patches, which do not have a sufficient amount of foreground, are discarded. Different assumptions can be used [28].
- *UCBS Breast* [27]: the goal is to classify cancer images as malignant or benign. The bags correspond to images and the instances are image equal-sized 7×7 patch. It is assumed that a bag is assigned the positive label if its corresponding image includes a diseased region [27].

3.6.5 Acoustic Classification

In this case study, the task is to classify the species present in an audio recording. A bag corresponds to a spectrogram, a graph of the spectrum of a signal as a function of time, of a recording and each instance is a fragment of that spectrogram. In the *Birds songs* dataset [7], 13 different bird species are responsible for the sound in the recordings. Each bag is a 10 seconds audio recording. This dataset is divided in 13 different problems and the standard assumption is used [7]. Table 3.5 summarizes these case studies.

3.7 Some Comments on Software Tools

To conclude this chapter, the main tools currently used to work with MIC problems are briefly introduced. The features of MIL require specialized software to solve these problems appropriately. The most noteworthy are three open-source tools developed in Java which solve MIC problems.

- **Weka** [24]. It is a collection of machine-learning algorithms for data mining tasks, such as, preprocessing, classification, regression, clustering, association rules, and

Table 3.5 Description of case studies for the acoustic classification domain

Domain	Application	Dataset	Attributes	Pos. bags	Neg. bags	Total bags	Instances
Acoustic classification	Birds songs	Brown creeper [16]	38	197	351	548	10232
		Winter wren [16]	38	109	439	548	10232
		Pacific-slope flycatcher [16]	38	165	383	548	10232
		Red-breasted nuthatch [16]	38	82	466	548	10232
		Dark-eyed junco [16]	38	20	528	548	10232
		Olive-sided flycatcher [16]	38	90	458	548	10232
		Hermit thrush [16]	38	15	533	548	10232
		Chestnut-backed chickadee [16]	38	117	431	548	10232
		Varied thrush [16]	38	89	459	548	10232
		Hermit warbler [16]	38	63	485	548	10232
		Swainsons thrush [16]	38	79	469	548	10232
		Hammonds flycatcher [16]	38	103	445	548	10232
		Western tanager [16]	38	46	502	548	10232

visualization. Weka is very flexible and allows to develop new machine-learning schemes easily. It can be executed from a GUI or via the command line.

Originally, the multiple instance learning module was a separated package, but from Weka version 3.5.3 on it is part of the software. A specific dataset format is required to work in the MIC context, but Weka provides two filters to convert from propositional format to multi-instance format and vice versa. Several MIC algorithms are included: classic methods, such as, diverse density, diverse density with expectation maximization, and other methods based on logistic regression, methods based on support vector machines, methods based on nearest neighbors, a simple wrapper method for applying standard propositional learners to multi-instance data, and so on. This tool is available via http://www.cs.waikato.ac.nz/ml/weka.

- **KEEL** [2]. It can be used for a large number of knowledge data discovery tasks, such as preprocessing techniques, classification, regression, clustering, association rules, and visualization. It also has interesting statistical methodologies module for contrasting experiments. KEEL has been designed for both research and education purposes. It can be executed from a GUI. Multiple instance learning is a specific module within KEEL and requires a specific dataset format. Similar to the Weka tool, it includes different MIC algorithms, such as the classic APR algorithms, methods based on diverse density and diverse density with expectation maximization, methods based on nearest neighbors, and methods based on evolutionary algorithms. This tool is available via http://www.keel.es.

- **JCLEC** [34]. It is a software system for evolutionary computation research. It provides a high-level software framework to execute any kind of evolutionary algorithm, providing support for genetic algorithms (binary, integer, and real encoding), genetic programming (Koza's style, strongly typed and grammar based), and evolutionary programming. It can be executed from the command line.

  Multiple instance learning is a specific module in this tool and requires a specific dataset format. Different evolutionary algorithms in MIC are included. The tool is available via http://jclec.sourceforge.net.

Finally, we also list the page web http://lamda.nju.edu.cn, where the reader can find different datasets and MATLAB implementations of multi-instance algorithms.

References

1. Agrawal, R., Mannila, H., Srikant, R., Toivonen, H., Verkamo, A.I.: Fast Discovery of Association Rules. Lect. Notes Artif. Int. **12**(1), 307–328 (1996)
2. Alcalá, J., Fernández, A., Luengo, J., Derrac, J., García, S., Sánchez, L., Herrera, F.: Keel data-mining software tool: data set repository, integration of algorithms and experimental analysis framework. J. Mult.-Valued Log. Soft Comput. **17**(2–3), 255–287 (2010)
3. Amores, J.: Multiple instance classification: review, taxonomy and comparative study. Artif. Intell. **201**, 81–105 (2013)
4. Andrews, S., Tsochantaridis, I., Hofmann, T.: Support vector machines for multiple-instance learning. In: Hanson, S.J., Cowan, J.D., Giles, C.L. (eds.) Proceedings of 15th Conference on Advances in neural information processing systems (NIPS 2002), pp. 561–568. MIT Press, Cambridge (2002)
5. Andrews, S., Tsochantaridis, I., Hofmann, T.: MIL dataset repository. http://www.cs.columbia.edu/~andrews/mil/datasets.html
6. Banfield, J.D., Raftery, A.E.: Model-based Gaussian and non-Gaussian clustering. Biometrics **49**(3), 803–821 (1993)
7. Briggs, F., Fern, X.Z., Raich, R.: Rank-loss support instance machines for MIML instance annotation. In: Goethals, B. (ed.) Proceedings of the 18th ACM International Conference on Knowledge discovery and data mining (SIGKDD 2012), pp. 534–542. ACM, New York (2012)
8. Brossi, S.D., Bradley, A.P.: A comparison of multiple instance and group based learning. In: Langford, J., Pineau, J. (eds.) Proceedings of the International Conference on Digital Image Computing Techniques and Applications (DICTA 2012), pp. 1–8. IEEE, Los Alamitos (2012)
9. Budka, M., Gabrys, B., Musial, K.: On accuracy of PDF divergence estimators and their applicability to representative data sampling. Entropy **13**(7), 1229–1266 (2011)
10. Cambridge Dictionary of English. Cambridge University Press (2016). http://dictionary.cambridge.org/
11. Cha, S.H.: Comprehensive Survey on Distance/Similarity Measures between Probability Density Functions. Math. Mod. Meth. Appl. Sci. **4**(1), 300–307 (2007)
12. Chen, Y., Bi, J., Wang, J.Z.: MILES: Multiple-instance learning via embedded instance selection. IEEE Trans. Pattern Anal. Mach. Intell. **28**(12), 1931–1947 (2006)

13. Chen, Y., Wu, O.: Contextual Hausdorff dissimilarity for multi-instance clustering. In: Liu, Y. (ed.) Proceedings of the 9th International Conference on Fuzzy Systems and Knowledge Discovery (FSKD 2012), pp. 870–873. IEEE, Los Alamitos (2012)
14. Cheplygina, V., Tax, D.M., Loog, M.: Multiple instance learning with bag dissimilarities. Pattern Recogn. **48**(1), 264–275 (2015)
15. Cheplygina, V., Tax, D.M., Loog, M.: On classification with bags, groups and sets. Pattern Recogn. Lett. **59**, 11–17 (2015)
16. Cheplygina, V., Tax, D.M.J.: MIL dataset repository (matlab format). http://www.miproblems. org/datasets
17. Deza, M.M., Deza, E.: Dictionary of Distances. Elsevier, Amsterdam (2006)
18. Dietterich, T.G., Lathrop, R.H., Lozano-Pérez, T.: Solving the multiple instance problem with axis-parallel rectangles. Artif. Intell. **89**(1), 31–71 (1997)
19. Doran, G.B.: TRX protein sequence classification dataset (C4.5 format). http://engr.case.edu/ doran_gary/code.html
20. Foulds, J.R.: Learning instance weights in multi-instance learning. Master thesis, The University of Waikato, New Zealand (2008)
21. Foulds, J., Frank, E.: A review of multi-instance learning assumptions. Knowl. Eng. Rev. **25**(1), 1–25 (2010)
22. Frank, E., Xu, X.: Applying propositional learning algorithms to multi-instance data. Master thesis, The University of Waikato, New Zealand (2003)
23. Gärtner, T., Flach, P.A., Kowalczyk, A., Smola, A.: Multi-Instance Kernels. In: Sammut, C., Hoffmann, A. (eds.) Proceedings of the 19th International Conference on Machine Learning (ICML 2002), pp. 179–186. Morgan Kaufmann Publishers, San Francisco (2002)
24. Hall, M., Frank, E., Holmes, G., Pfahringer, B., Reutemann, P., Witten, I.H.: The WEKA data mining software: an update. In: Fayyad, U. (ed.) Proceedings of the 15th ACM International Conference on Knowledge discovery and data mining (SIGKDD 2009), Explorations Newsletter, pp. 10–18. ACM, New York (2009)
25. Haussler, D.: Convolution kernels on discrete structures. Technical report, Department of Computer Science, University of California, Santa Cruz, United States of America (1999)
26. Jousselme, A.L., Maupin, P.: Distances in evidence theory: Comprehensive survey and generalizations. Int. J. Approx. Reason. **53**(2), 118–145 (2012)
27. Kandemir, M., Zhang, C., Hamprecht, F. A.: Empowering multiple instance histopathology cancer diagnosis by cell graphs. In: Golland, P., Hata, N., Barillot, C., Hornegger, J., Howe, R. (eds.) Proceedings of the 17th International Conference on Medical Image Computing and Computer-Assisted Intervention (MICCAI 2014), Lecture Notes Computer Science, vol. 8674, no. 2, pp. 228–235 (2014)
28. Kandemir, M., Hamprecht, F.A.: Computer-aided diagnosis from weak supervision: a benchmarking study. Comput. Med. Imag. Grap. **42**, 44–50 (2015)
29. Li, Y., Tax, D.M., Duin, R.P., Loog, M.: Multiple-instance learning as a classifier combining problem. Pattern Recogn. **46**(3), 865–874 (2013)
30. Li, W., Vasconcelos, N.: Multiple instance learning for soft bags via top instances. In: Durand, F., Freeman W.T. (eds.) Proceedings of the IEEE Conference on Computer Vision and Pattern Recognition (CVPR 2015), pp. 4277–4285. IEEE, Los Alamitos (2015)
31. Maron, O., Lozano-Pérez, T.: A framework for multiple-instance learning. In: Jordan, M., Kearns, M., Solla, S. (eds.) Advances in Neural Information Processing Systems, no. 10. pp. 570–576. MIT press, Cambridge (1998)
32. Scott, S., Zhang, J., Brown, J.: On generalized multiple-instance learning. Int. J. Comput. Int. Sys. **5**(1), 21–35 (2005)
33. Srinivasan, A., Muggleton, S., King, R.D.: Comparing the use of background knowledge by inductive logic programming systems. In: Lavrac, N., Dzeroski, S. (eds.) Proceedings of the 5th International Workshop on Inductive Logic Programming (ICLP 1995), pp. 199–230. Springer, London (1995)
34. Ventura, S., Romero, C., Zafra, A., Delgado, J.A., Hervás, C.: JCLEC: a Java framework for evolutionary computation. Soft Comput. **12**(4), 381–392 (2008)

35. Vluymans, S., Sánchez Tarragó, D.S., Saeys, Y., Cornelis, C., Herrera, F.: Fuzzy multi-instance classifiers. IEEE Trans. Fuzzy Syst. (2016) (in press)
36. Vluymans, S., Sánchez Tarragó, D.S., Saeys, Y., Cornelis, C., Herrera, F.: Fuzzy rough classifiers for class imbalanced multi-instance data. Pattern Recogn. **53**, 36–45 (2016)
37. Wang, J., Zucker, J.D.: Solving multiple-instance problem: A lazy learning approach. In: Langley, P. (ed.) Proceedings of the 17th International Conference on Machine Learning (ICML 2000), pp. 1119–1126. Morgan Kaufmann Publishers, San Francisco (2000)
38. Wang, H.Y., Yang, Q., Zha, H.: Adaptive p-posterior mixture-model kernels for multiple instance learning. In: Getoor, L., Scheffer, T. (eds.) Proceedings of the 26th International Conference on Machine Learning (ICML 2008), pp. 1136–1143. Omnipress, Lille Grand Palais (2008)
39. Wang, H., Huang, H., Kamangar, F., Nie, F., Ding, C.H.: (2011). Maximum margin multiinstance learning. In: Shawe-Taylor, J., Zemel, R.S., Bartlett, P.L., Pereira, F., Weinberger, K.Q. (eds.) Proceedings of 24th Conference on Advances in neural information processing systems (NIPS 2011), pp. 1–9. MIT Press, Cambridge (2011)
40. Wang, H., Nie, F., Huang, H.: Learning Instance Specific Distance for Multi-Instance Classification. In: Wolfram, B., Dan, Roth., Program, C. (eds.) Proceedings of 25th Conference on Artificial Intelligence (AAAI 2011), **2**, pp. 6–15. AAAI Press, Vancouver (2011)
41. Weidmann, N., Frank, E., Pfahringer, B.: A two-level learning method for generalized multiinstance problems. In: Lavrac, N., Gamberger, D., Blockeel, H., Todorovski, L. (eds.) Proceedings of 14th European Conference on Machine Learning (ECML 2003), pp. 468–479. Springer, Berlin (2003)
42. Xu, L., Neufeld, J., Larson, B., Schuurmans, D.: Maximum margin clustering. In: Saul, L.K., Weiss, Y., Bottou, L. (eds.) Proceedings of 17th Conference on Advances in neural information processing systems (NIPS 2004), pp. 1537–1544. MIT Press, Cambridge (2004)
43. Xu, X.: Statistical learning in multiple instance problems. Master thesis, The University of Waikato, New Zealand (2003)
44. Yager, R.R., Kacprzyk, J.: The Ordered Weighted Averaging Operators: Theory and Applications. Springer Science Business Media, New York (2012)
45. Zafra, A., Romero, C., Ventura, S., Herrera-Viedma, E.: Multi-instance genetic programming for web index recommendation. Expert Syst. Appl. **36**(9), 11470–11479 (2009)
46. Zafra, A., Pechenizkiy, M., Ventura, S.: ReliefF-MI: An extension of ReliefF to multiple instance learning. Neurocomputing **75**(1), 210–218 (2012)
47. Zafra, A., Ventura, S.: MIL dataset repository (weka format). http://www.uco.es/grupos/kdis/momil
48. Zhang, D., Wang, F., Si, L., Li, T.: Maximum margin multiple instance clustering with applications to image and text clustering. IEEE Trans. Neural Netw. **22**(5), 739–751 (2011)
49. Zhang, M.L., Zhou, Z.H.: Multi-instance clustering with applications to multi-instance prediction. Appl. Intell. **31**(1), 47–68 (2009)
50. Zhang, T., Liu, S., Xu, C., Lu, H.: M4L: maximum margin multi-instance multi-cluster learning for scene modeling. Pattern Recogn. **46**(10), 2711–2723 (2013)
51. Zhou, Z.H., Jiang, K., Li, M.: Multi-instance learning based web mining. Appl. Intell. **22**(2), 135–147 (2005)
52. Zhou, Z.H., Sun, Y.Y., Li, Y.F.: Multi-instance learning by treating instances as non-iid samples. In: Bottou, L., Littman, M. (eds.) Proceedings of the 26th International Conference on Machine Learning (ICML 2009), pp. 1249–1256. Omnipress, Lille Grand Palais (2009)

Chapter 4
Instance-Based Classification Methods

Abstract Instance-based classification algorithms perform their main learning process at the instance level. They try to approximate a function that assigns class labels to instances. The instance classifier is combined with an underlying MI assumption, which links the class label of instances inside a bag with the bag class label. Many strategies have been devised to construct the instance classifier. We discuss the most prominent of them: wrapper methods (Sect. 4.2), maximum likelihood methods (Sect. 4.3), decision trees and rules methods (Sect. 4.4), maximum margin methods (Sect. 4.5), connectionist methods (Sect. 4.6), and evolutionary methods (Sect. 4.7). An experimental analysis on the performance of representative instance-based classifiers is presented in Sect. 4.8. Summarizing remarks are given in Sect. 4.9.

4.1 Introduction

Instance-based classification algorithms rely on two assumptions: (1) a process h exists to determine the class label of instances and (2) the bag label can be obtained by applying a rule H to the class labels of their instances. Rule H is the MI assumption discussed in Sect. 3.4 which is a fixed choice in the algorithm. The crucial step is to determine the process h to obtain class labels for instances. These methods construct an instance classifier which is the best approximation of that process. Bag labels are determined by direct application of the MI assumption H. The main learning process occurs at instance level, which is why this category of algorithms is called instance-based classification algorithms. Figure 4.1 shows the general architecture of an instance-based algorithm. A bag $X \in \mathbb{N}^{\mathbb{X}}$ containing n instances $x_1, \ldots, x_n \in \mathbb{X}$ is represented. Four choices are involved:

1. **Set $\mathbb{L}$ of bag labels**: the size of $\mathbb{L}$ is the number of classes (infinite, if the task would be regression). Two-class classification problems have been studied most and many classification methods are specifically designed to address this setting. Some methods are also able to handle multi-class classification and a few have been developed to solve multi-instance regression problems.

© Springer International Publishing AG 2016

F. Herrera et al., *Multiple Instance Learning*, DOI 10.1007/978-3-319-47759-6_4

Fig. 4.1 General
architecture of
instance-based algorithms

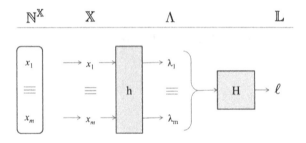

2. **Set Λ of instance labels**: instance labels may correspond to bag subclasses or
   instance-level concepts. Depending on what instances represent in relation to the
   problem, Λ could be the same as $\mathbb{L}$ or could be some different set of classes.
3. **The MI assumption H**: this involves the explicit definition of a mapping from
   the set of instance labels to the set of bag labels. As described in Sect. 3.4, it is
   a function $H : \mathbb{N}^\Lambda \to \mathbb{L}$ that relates the class label of instances inside a bag
   with the bag class label. This function expresses a relationship between the bag
   and the many descriptions that its instances represent. The particular form of this
   function depends on the characteristics of the problem, the semantics of bags and
   instances and their interrelations.
4. **A strategy to find the instance classifier $h : \mathbb{X} \to \Lambda$**: this is the classifier used
   to label instances inside each bag. We do not need the explicit construction of h,
   but do require some method for estimating instance labels or their probabilities
   from the training examples. Depending on the adopted MI assumption, it may
   be sufficient to label certain key instances within each bag. For example, if the
   standard MI assumption is used, identifying a positive instance inside a test bag
   is enough to assign the bag to the positive class. A large variety of methods has
   been used to approximate h and to determine instance labels. In the remainder
   of this chapter, we describe some of the most important methods among which
   are those based on decision rules, decision trees, maximum likelihood, maximum
   margin, connectionist, and evolutionary methods.

4.2 Wrapper Methods to Single-Instance Learning
   Algorithms

Single-instance learners cannot be applied directly to multi-instance data, because
they require a class label for every individual instance. A simple and natural way
of addressing this problem is to assume that each instance in a bag has the same
label as the bag itself. Next, a single-instance classifier can be constructed from the
training data and used to label instances of a new bag. However, what is actually
required, is a classifier for bags. A MI assumption is applied over instance labels
to get the bag label. In Fig. 4.2, we present a learner as a wrapper for a single-

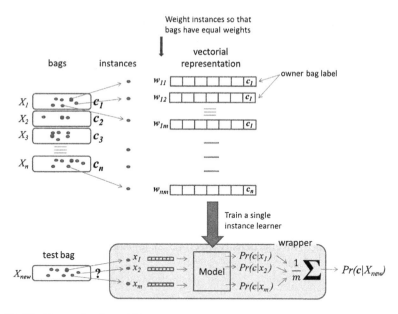

Fig. 4.2 Working mode of a multi-instance wrapper

instance algorithm. The wrapper is an interface between the instance and bag levels. At training time, instances are extracted from the bags by assigning them the label of their parent bag. The wrapper supplies them to the single-instance learner. Instances are properly weighted so that all training bags have equal importance regardless of any differences in their sizes. A single-instance learning model is obtained. Given a new bag to classify, its instances are extracted and classified by the single-instance model. For each instance x, the model can return a class label or, even better, it can return the posterior probability of each class $Pr(c|x)$. The bag label is finally obtained by the wrapper based on the bag's instance labels (or its probabilities) and relying on a given MI assumption.

One of the most influential MI assumptions is the standard MI assumption (Sect. 3.4). Its rationality has been shown in cases like the drug activity prediction problem. A wrapper that uses the standard MI assumption assigns the positive label to a bag if any of its instance is predicted to be positive by the single-instance classifier. However, in Sect. 4.8 we will show that such a MI wrapper can have a low accuracy. The explanation behind this result is clear. We are assigning positive labels to *all* instance in a positive bag, even when we know that many of then can actually be negative, inducing too much noise in the positive class.

The collective assumption (Sect. 3.4) does not suffer from this problem, since it is symmetric. This assumption states that all instances contribute equally and independently to the bag label. In the classification stage, for each instance in the bag to be classified, a class probability estimate for each of the possible classes is provided by the single-instance classifier. These estimates are then averaged to form the prediction for the bag as a whole, yielding the expected class probability under the given assumptions. Although this heuristic leads to biased probability estimates, it works surprisingly well for many datasets, as will be indicated in Sect. 4.8.

4.3   Maximum Likelihood-Based Methods

In traditional machine learning there is an important group of learning methods based on the maximum likelihood principle. Many instance-based MIL methods have been developed on the basis of this statistical approach. In Sect. 4.3.1 we briefly describe the maximum likelihood principle in the single-instance learning setting and present a general strategy for adapting maximum likelihood-based learning algorithms to the MIL setting. Specific MIL algorithms designed under the maximum likelihood principle are described: diverse density (Sect. 4.3.2), logistic regression (Sect. 4.3.3), and boosting (Sect. 4.3.4).

4.3.1   Maximum Likelihood Principle

In single-instance statistical learning, each instance x is regarded as a value of a random variable $\mathscr{X}$ in the attribute space $\mathbb{X}$. Its class label $\ell \in \mathbb{L}$ is a value of the random variable $\mathscr{L}$. The joint probability distribution $p(\mathscr{X}, \mathscr{L})$ describes the relation between $\mathscr{X}$ and $\mathscr{L}$. It allows us to predict the class label ℓ given a new value of x. Although it can be inferred from the training data, it is typically a very difficult problem. By using the product rule of probability, we can state that $p(\mathscr{X}, \mathscr{L}) = p(\mathscr{L}|\mathscr{X}) \, p(\mathscr{X})$. The prior probability $p(\mathscr{X})$ represents the probability of observing x in the data. The posterior class probability $p(\mathscr{L}|\mathscr{X})$ informs us of the probability of a class label, given that the exemplar x is observed. Given $p(\mathscr{L}|\mathscr{X})$ and based on decision theory [5], a classifier h will assign each new instance x to the class ℓ for which $p(\ell|x)$ is larger. In the construction of h, $p(\mathscr{L}|\mathscr{X})$ is inferred from the training data. The parameters Θ of h are trained to maximize the likelihood of $p(\mathscr{L}|\mathscr{X})$. Maximizing the likelihood of $p(\mathscr{L}|\mathscr{X})$ is equivalent to minimizing the expected loss function $E_{\mathscr{X}} E_{\mathscr{L}|\mathscr{X}} [Loss(\mathscr{X}, h)]$ over $\mathscr{X}$ and $\mathscr{L}$. The loss function takes a prediction model as input and produces a single number that indicates how well that prediction model performs. It depends on the true class. This value is unknown for new instances, which is why we use the expectation of the loss function. The expectation $E_p[f]$ of some function $f(x)$ under a probability distribution $p(x)$ is defined as the average value of $f(x)$ weighted by the relative probabilities of the different values of x. By minimizing the expected loss function, a learning algorithm h can obtain the optimal parameters $\hat{\Theta}$ which maximize the likelihood of $p(\mathscr{L}|\mathscr{X})$.

In the MIL setting, another random variable $\mathscr{B}$ is introduced, denoting the bags, and it is $p(\mathscr{L}|\mathscr{B})$ that needs to be determined. A general strategy for adapting a single-instance statistical learning algorithm to MIL requires the definition of three elements [71]:

1. a function f that models $p\left(\mathscr{L}|\mathscr{X}\right)$. Particularly, in a classification problem of two classes ($\mathbb{L} = \{0, 1\}$), f represents the probability $p_{ij} \equiv p\left(\ell_{ij} = 1|x_{ij}\right)$ that the jth instance of the ith bag is classified as positive, given the parameters Θ of a hypothetical instance classifier h.
2. a function g relating the probability $p_i \equiv p\left(\ell_i = 1|X_i\right)$ that the ith bag is positive with the probabilities p_{ij} that its instances are positive, given h. This function implements the MI assumption (whatever it is).
3. a loss function $Loss\left(\mathscr{B}, h\right)$ that takes the expectation of h over all the bags rather than over the instances. The aim is to minimize the expected loss function $E_{\mathscr{B}}E_{\mathscr{L}|\mathscr{B}}\left[Loss\left(\mathscr{B}, h\right)\right]$. Note that h is the instance-level classification model with parameters Θ that determines $p\left(\mathscr{L}|\mathscr{X}\right)$.

In the training stage, an optimization algorithm is executed to minimize the value of the loss function to obtain h and hence an estimation of $p\left(\mathscr{L}|\mathscr{X}\right)$. When classifying a new bag X_{test}, we first calculate $p\left(\mathscr{L}|x_{test}\right)$ and then $p\left(\mathscr{L}|X_{test}\right) = g\left(p\left(\mathscr{L}|x_{test}\right)\right)$, based on the same assumptions used in item 2. We classify X_{test} based on whether $p\left(\mathscr{L}|X_{test}\right)$ is above 0.5.

4.3.2 Diverse Density

Among instance-based MIL methods that rely on statistical learning, the most influential has been Diverse Density (DD) [46]. The classifier $h = \langle w \rangle$ consists of a vector $w \in \mathbb{X}$ representing a positive instance prototype. DD uses a radial shape or Gaussian-like to model $p\left(\mathscr{L}|\mathscr{X}\right)$. The probability that an instance x_{ij} is classified positive for h is defined by a Gaussian centered at the point w:

$$p_{ij} = \exp\left(-\left\|x_{ij} - w\right\|^2\right). \tag{4.1}$$

In [45], two ways are proposed to relate class probabilities of bags with that of their instances. One is the noisy-or (NOR) model described as

$$p_i = 1 - \prod_j \left(1 - p_{ij}\right). \tag{4.2}$$

This model takes into account the influence of all instances of the bag to apply a probabilistic version of the logical OR. The second proposal of [45] is the most-likely-cause model defined as

$$p_i = \max_j \left\{p_{ij}\right\}, \tag{4.3}$$

which considers only the most probably positive instance in the bag, which is the instance closest to the prototype w. However, note that the max operator is not differentiable. In order to apply an optimization algorithm based on gradient descent, it is necessary to use an approximation of the max operator.

Both models of [45] are compatible with the standard MI assumption. A variant of DD that implements the collective assumption has been presented in [22, 71], where

$$p_i = \frac{1}{n_i} \sum_j p_{ij}. \tag{4.4}$$

As bag-level loss function, DD uses the negative binomial log-likelihood defined as

$$\sum_i \left[\ell_i \log (p_i) + (1 - \ell_i) \log (1 - p_i) \right]. \tag{4.5}$$

This function is widely used by single-instance statistical learning algorithms.

In DD, the principle of maximum likelihood is interpreted as the search for the point of instance space where instances from the largest number of positive bags converge and at the same time is farthest from the instances of all negative bags. This point is considered as the prototype of the positive concept and, in this framework, is called the *maximum diverse density point*.

DD is a very popular algorithm and has been widely used as a benchmark for comparison in the development of other MIL classifiers. It has been extended to regression [1] and to learning problems with relational data [48]. It has also been used for scaling attributes [83] and its approach has been widely used in the selection of key instances in the bags [12, 23, 30, 43].

Expectation-Maximization Diverse Density

EM-DD [80] is a variant of DD that uses the expectation-maximization approach (EM) to avoid using approximations of the max operator. It achieves a significant reduction in the computational cost of DD. EM-DD starts with a hypothetical solution w, which is some selected point in a positive bag. The algorithm iterates between expectation and maximization stages. In the expectation step, EM-DD uses the most-likely-cause model to select one instance from each positive bag given the current solution w. In the maximization step, an optimization method based on gradient descent is applied to find a new vector w that maximizes the likelihood of the data formed by all the negative points and the positive points that were selected in the expectation step. Note that, as at this time each instance is assigned a label, the MIL problem has been reduced to a single-instance problem and therefore the use of (4.3) and the problem of its derivative is avoided. A similar method using the NOR model is derived in [52].

4.3.3 Logistic Regression

Logistic regression is a statistical method often used in two-class single-instance classification problems. In this method, the classifier $h = \langle w \rangle$ is a vector w of the instance space $\mathbb{X}$ representing a normal to a hyperplane that separates the two classes. The hyperplane is constructed by applying the logit function to the dependent variable, converting a probability in the log-odds of that probability,

$$\text{logit}\left(E_{\mathscr{L}|\mathscr{X}}\left[\ell_i | x_i \right] \right) = \text{logit}\left(p_i \right) = \ln\left(\frac{p_i}{1 - p_i} \right) = w x_i.$$

The logistic regression method has been adapted to the MIL setting several times. From the logistic function

$$\sigma\left(x \right) = \frac{1}{1 + \exp\left(-x \right)},$$

which is the inverse of the logit function, in MIL, as in the single-instance setting, the probability that an instance x_{ij} is classified positive by h is defined as

$$p_{ij} = \sigma\left(w x_{ij} \right). \tag{4.6}$$

In [72], two ways are proposed to relate class probabilities of bags with that of their instances based on the collective MI assumption. One is by the arithmetic mean of the probabilities of each instance of the bag which is represented by (4.4). This algorithm is called the *arithmetic mean model*. The other way estimates the log-odds function instead of directly estimating the probability function. The log-odds bag-level function is calculated as the average of the log-odds instance-level functions:

$$\ln\left(\frac{p_i}{1 - p_i} \right) = \frac{1}{n_i} \sum_{j=1}^{n_i} \left(\frac{p_{ij}}{1 - p_{ij}} \right). \tag{4.7}$$

It follows that

$$p_i = \frac{\left[\prod_{j=1}^{n_i} p_{ij} \right]^{\frac{1}{n_i}}}{\left[\prod_{j=1}^{n_i} p_{ij} \right]^{\frac{1}{n_i}} + \left[\prod_{j=1}^{n_i} \left(1 - p_{ij} \right) \right]^{\frac{1}{n_i}}}, \tag{4.8}$$

which means that the bag class probability is the normalized geometric mean of the class probabilities of its instances. This algorithm is called the *geometric mean model*. Substituting (4.6) in (4.8), we obtain

$$p_i = \sigma\left(w \bar{x}_i \right),$$

where $\bar{x}_i = \sum_{j=1}^{n_i} x_{ij}$ denotes the average point of the ith bag. Note that this model is equivalent to transforming the multi-instance to single-instance data, representing each bag by the average of its instances and applying the single-instance linear-logistic regression model directly to the transformed data.

The standard MI assumption has also been used to relate class probabilities of bags with that of their instances. Several functions have been used to approximate the non-differentiable maximum operator which characterizes the standard MI assumption. In particular, [22, 59, 71] have used the NOR model (4.2), while in [56] the function $p_i = \text{softmax}(p_{i1}, \ldots, p_{iN})$ is used where softmax is defined as

$$\text{softmax}(x_1, \ldots, x_N) = \sum_{i=1}^{N} \frac{x_i \exp(\alpha x_i)}{\sum_{j=1}^{N} \exp(\alpha x_j)}.$$

Xu [71] showed that it is possible to increase the generalization capacity of multi-instance logistic regression by using simple regularization techniques. The most advanced and efficient regularization methods have been successfully applied to multi-instance logistic regression in [26].

4.3.4 Boosting

Another popular single-instance method which has been adapted to a multi-instance instance-based algorithm is boosting [60], which uses a statistical approach [25]. Like logistic regression, it aims to estimate the log-odds function, but it is based on an additive model. The core idea is to take a (potentially weak) learning algorithm, sequentially train several classifiers $h_t \in \mathcal{H}$ and combine them into an (arbitrarily strong) classifier $\mathbf{h}$. The combination is commonly done by the weighted sum $\mathbf{h} = \sum_{t=1}^{T} \alpha_t h_t(x)$, where α_t are positive weights. Adaptations of boosting to MIL have generally been developed in the gradient boosting framework [25, 47], where each classifier h_t is the best approximation in the space of classifiers $\mathcal{H}$ to the optimal solution of a particular loss function based on a previous approximation. Once h_t is found, the value of α_t is determined by a linear search over the loss function.

Xu and Frank [72] derive a boosting MI algorithm based on the collective assumption. They define the class probability at instance level as

$$p_{ij} = \sigma\left(\mathbf{h}\left(x_{ij}\right)\right) \tag{4.9}$$

and use (4.8) to compute the probabilities of bags, as they relate the log-odds of a bag with that of its instances using the average operator. The optimized loss function is $E_{\mathcal{B}} E_{\mathcal{L}|\mathcal{B}} \left[\exp\left(-\ell \mathbf{H}(X)\right)\right]$, where, following the collective assumption, $\mathbf{H}(X_i) = \frac{1}{n_i} \sum_{j=1}^{n_i} \mathbf{h}\left(x_{ij}\right)$.

Viola et al. [67] propose an adaptation of boosting to MIL based on the standard MI assumption. They also use (4.9) to define the instance probabilities. They relate these values to the bag probability as $p_i = g_j\left(p_{ij}\right)$, where $g\left(\cdot\right)$ is a function that approximates the max operator. The loss function used by Viola et al. is the negative binomial log-likelihood (4.5).

This contribution has had a major impact on the area of visual detection and tracking. Babenko et al. [3] developed an online MIL boosting based on Viola et al.'s Noisy-OR boosting and the works on online boosting of Oza [51] and Grabner et al. [31]. Meanwhile, Zeisl et al. [79] derive a general-purpose semi-supervised online MI boosting method and show that it improves the robustness of the classifier to the problem of the target drift in visual tracking applications. These ideas have inspired many other improvements to the boosting algorithm applied to visual tracking, e.g., [53, 62, 63, 70].

4.4   Decision Rules and Tree-Based Methods

Decision tree learning methods recursively divide the input space into separate regions to build a decision boundary. The regions are created by a greedy optimization process. In each step, the algorithm builds a tree node by selecting the attribute that causes the best separation of classes according to a cost function (e.g., entropy and Gini functions). The cost function measures the impurity of a node, i.e., the heterogeneity of a node regarding the class labels of the training examples in its region. The impurity is maximum when there is an equal number of examples of each class in the node. An important property of ordinary decision trees is that the attribute which achieves maximum reduction of the cost function in a node is also the one who gets the maximum reduction of the cost function in the whole tree. This property allows us to determine the best attribute for a node evaluating the gain of each attribute just locally. Pruning techniques can be applied during or after the tree construction to improve the generalization capability of the model.

Chevalier and Zucker [14] proposed the first instance-based decision tree, ID3-MI, an adaptation of the popular ID3 method [54]. They redefined the entropy and information gain functions based on bag labels rather than instance labels. The entropy of a set S of instances is defined as

$$
\begin{aligned}
Info\left(S\right) = & -\frac{P\left(S\right)}{P\left(S\right)+N\left(S\right)}\log_2\left(\frac{P\left(S\right)}{P\left(S\right)+N\left(S\right)}\right) \\
& -\frac{N\left(S\right)}{P\left(S\right)+N\left(S\right)}\log_2\left(\frac{N\left(S\right)}{P\left(S\right)+N\left(S\right)}\right),
\end{aligned}
$$

where $P\left(S\right)$ and $N\left(S\right)$ denote, respectively, the number of positive and negative bags having instances in S. The information gain of an attribute A partitioning the set S in $\{S_1, \ldots, S_v\}$ is defined as

$$Gain\,(S, A) = Info\,(S) - \sum_{i=1}^{v} \frac{P\,(S_i) + N\,(S_i)}{P\,(S) + N\,(S)} \cdot Info\,(S_i).$$

Note that in instance-based MI trees, instances—not bags—are divided into each node of the tree, which means that instances of the same bag are generally dispersed by different branches of the tree. In the prediction stage, a bag is classified as positive if at least one of its instances reaches a positive leaf node. The instance dispersion tends to produce too complex trees. To keep the tree simple, as soon as an instance of a positive bag is correctly classified, all other instances of the bag are excluded from the induction process [14]. Another problem caused by the dispersion is that the locality property mentioned above is lost. The order in which the nodes are expanded becomes a critical factor.

Blockeel et al. proposed MITI [7], an improved version of ID3-MI with heuristics aimed at correcting the problems caused by the dispersion of the instances. The most important change is that MITI expands nodes in best-first order, prioritizing pure positive nodes covering a larger number of examples. Another heuristic that proved useful was to give more weight to instances of smaller bags.

Both ID3-MI and MITI faithfully adhere to the standard MI assumption. Ruffo [58] proposes a MI decision tree governed by a threshold-based assumption (Sect. 3.4). Ruffo trees learn concepts such as "contains at least three instances with the property P."

Decision rules have also been addressed in MIL. Chevaleyre and Zucker presented RipperMI [14], an extension of the Ripper algorithm [18] to MIL. Ripper is a single-instance rule learning algorithm based on the coverage measure. An observation x is covered by a rule R, denoted $Cover\,(R, x)$, if the attribute values of x satisfy all the conditions of R. Given a set of examples E, the number of these examples covering a rule R is called coverage of R, i.e., $Coverage_E\,(R) = |\{x \in E : Cover\,(R, x)\}|$. The coverage measure is used to decide when to add and remove conditions to the rule during construction. The original definition of coverage is modified in RipperMI, such that it takes into account the number of covered bags instead of the number of instances. Given a set of bags E, Chevaleyre and Zucker [14] redefine the coverage of a rule as

$$Coverage_E\,(R) = |\{X_i \in E : Cover\,(R, X_i)\}|,$$

where

$$Cover\,(R, X) = \bigvee_{x_i \in X} Cover\,(R, x_i).$$

In [15], some deficiencies of RipperMI are discussed and several improvements are proposed, including the growth of partial trees to generate the rules, a global pruning method and a probabilistic coverage measure, which not only informs that a bag is covered by a rule, but also takes into account the number of instances of the bag that have been covered by the rule.

The MITI tree learner is used by Bjerring and Frank [6] to generate decision rules with a system called MIRI. A partial tree is grown until a positive leaf is found. An if-then rule is created based on the path from the root node to the leaf. All bags associated with the leaf are removed from the training set. The partial tree is discarded and built from scratch with the remaining data. Bjerring and Frank show that MIRI accuracy is similar to that of MITI, but MIRI generates much more compact models which favors the interpretability.

The study of decision trees in MIL includes tree ensembles, since it is known that they generally have greater predictive power than individual classifiers. Leistner et al. proposed MIForest [41], which is an ensemble of several MI decision trees, based on the idea of Random Forest [9]. The trees are built over the instance space for which the algorithm must first identify instance labels. Instances are initially assigned the label of their parent bag, after which a preliminary forest is grown. The algorithm tries to predict the true labels of the instances in an iterative manner. Based on the current model, the instance label probability distribution $p\,(\ell|x)$ is sought such that a specific loss function is minimized. The loss function considers the condition that at least one instance in each bag has to be from the target class. Note that it is an extension of the standard MI assumption. Based on $p\,(\ell|x)$, each tree randomly selects new instance labels and updates the model. The cycle is repeated until convergence. The random way in which labels are selected ensures the diversity of the trees, which allows the reduction of generalization error. This approach results in a non-convex optimization problem, which is resolved by a deterministic annealing technique [57].

Another variant of a tree ensemble was developed by Bjerring and Frank [6] using a randomization strategy. A random factor is introduced in the tree construction process allowing to obtain several classifiers from the same dataset to form the ensemble. For each node of the tree, a subset A of the available attributes is selected and the best attribute in A is chosen based on the Gini index or some other criterion. The ensemble output is the mode (or some aggregation) of the tree votes. Bjerring and Frank [6] showed good results with MITI and MIRI ensembles.

4.5 Instance-Level SVM

Support vector machines (SVMs), one of the most widely used classification methods in machine learning, have been recalled in Sect. 1.3.1. Their popularity can be attributed to their robustness and reliability. They require few training examples, and are not affected by the number of dimensions and have a solid theoretical justification. The use of slack variables allows to find an optimal separating hyperplane even when some points are located in the margin or on the wrong side of the hyperplane. Kernel functions, like Gaussian or polynomial functions, are used to solve classification problems with nonlinear decision boundaries. Different kernel types determine different forms of the decision boundary. Many SVM variants have been proposed in the machine learning literature. They primarily differ in the kernel type, the margin optimization formulation and the way in which the latter is solved. Formally, in a two-class problem, let w be the normal vector to the hyperplane separating the two classes and b the hyperplane offset, an SVM is generally defined by the following optimization problem:

$$\min_{w,b,\xi} \frac{1}{2}\|w\|^2 + C\sum_i \xi_i$$
$$s.t. \quad (\forall i)(y_i\,(w \cdot x_i + b) \geq 1 - \xi_i), \qquad (4.10)$$
$$(\forall i)(\xi_i \geq 0),$$

where ξ_i is a slack variable corresponding to x_i and C is a parameter allowing a trade-off between the fit to the training data and the generalization capability (bias–variance trade-off).

The adaptation of SVM to MIL has followed two different lines. The first line works at the instance level, using kernels defined on individual instances. This group of algorithms tries to identify instance labels (either for all instances or for only some key instances) that allow to find an optimal margin between positive and negative bags. These are instance-based methods and are discussed in this section. The second line of multi-instance SVM research works at the bag level. Instead of identifying instance labels, these algorithms use kernels defined over whole bags to optimize the margin between the two classes of bags. This second SVM type will be discussed in Sect. 5.2.2.

The first instance-based SVM methods were presented by Andrews et al. [2] using the standard MI assumption. One of their methods, MI-SVM, tries to identify the key instance of each positive bag, which is the instance that makes the bag positive, assuming that this key instance is the one with the highest positive margin. The remaining instances in positive bags are ignored. Following the standard MI assumption, all instances in negative bags are considered negative. MI-SVM seeks to maximize the margin between instances of negative bags and key instances of positive bags. By incorporating slack variables they arrive at

$$\min_{w,b,\xi} \frac{1}{2}\|w\|^2 + C\sum_{ij} \xi_{ij}$$
$$s.t. \quad (\forall i|y_i = 0)((w \cdot x_{ij} + b) \leq -1 + \xi_{ij}), \qquad (4.11)$$
$$(\forall i|y_i = 1)(\max_j (w \cdot x_{ij} + b) \geq 1 - \xi_{ij}),$$
$$\xi_{ij} \geq 0.$$

This is an optimization program whose second restriction is not convex and is difficult to solve. Andrews et al. choose to transform the problem to a mixed integer program and solve it using an EM-like heuristic method. Unlike MI-SVM, the second method presented by Andrews et al. [2], mi-SVM, does not discard negative instances of positive bags. Both instances from negative bags and negative instances of positive bags are involved in the construction of the negative margin. To this end, mi-SVM tries to identify class labels of each instance in the positive bags. The corresponding optimization program is given by

$$\min_{y_{ij}} \min_{w,b,\xi} \quad \tfrac{1}{2}\|w\|^2 + C\sum_{ij}\xi_{ij}$$

$$
\begin{aligned}
s.t. \quad & (\forall i\,|\,y_i = 0)(y_{ij} = 0), \\
& (\forall i\,|\,y_i = 1)(\textstyle\sum_j y_{ij} \geq 1), \\
& y'_{ij}\,(w \cdot x_{ij} + b) \geq 1 - \xi_{ij} \\
& \xi_{ij} \geq 0,
\end{aligned}
\tag{4.12}
$$

where $y'_{ij} = 2y_{ij} - 1$. This is a mixed integer program, solved by [2] with a heuristic method similar to the one referenced above.

A variant of MI-SVM is presented Bunescu and Mooney [10], aimed at simplifying the optimization program. Consider a positive bag with n instances. Based on the standard MI assumption, there can be up to $n - 1$ negative instances, but at least one of them will be positive. The restriction

$$\sum_j (w \cdot x_{ij} + b) \geq (-1)(n - 1) + 1 = 2 - n$$

is obtained. It may be violated if the margins of negative instances are large, which causes a tendency to narrow margins. To ensure that the margins of all instances in positive bags remain large, the restriction $|w \cdot x_{ij} + b| \geq 1$ is added. Although this program is not convex, the authors show how to solve it with a concave–convex (CCCP) solver [61] and that this algorithm works particularly well in problems with sparse positive bags, where there are few positive instances in each positive bag.

Yang et al. [74] present ASVM, an SVM that introduces an asymmetric loss function under the standard MI assumption. The method is based on the idea that the misclassification costs of positive and negative bags is different. A false negative instance in a positive bag does not necessarily lead to an error on the label of the bag (assuming that there are several positive instances in the bag), while a false positive instance in a negative bag certainly leads to an error in the bag label. ASVM tries to minimize false positives and ensures that all negative instances are on the negative side of the hyperplane. The program is defined as

$$\min_{w,b,\xi} \tfrac{1}{2}\|w\|^2 + C\sum_i \xi_i$$

$$
\begin{aligned}
s.t. \quad & (\forall i)(y_i\,(w \cdot x_i + b) \geq 1 - \tfrac{(y_i+1)}{2}\xi_i), \\
& (\forall i)(\xi_i \geq 0).
\end{aligned}
\tag{4.13}
$$

The authors demonstrated the effectiveness of this algorithm in image annotation applications.

Cheung et al. [13] present an SVM regularization scheme with a loss function, that takes into account both the loss associated with bag labels as well as the loss between the prediction of each bag and the prediction of its instances, based on the standard MI assumption. Instead of using a heuristic method, like in [2], they use a concave–convex optimization which ensures convergence to a local optimum.

Zhou and Xu [84] show that there is a link between MIL and semi-supervised learning (Sect. 1.3.3). According to the standard MI assumption, all instances of negative bags have negative labels, while instances in positive bags can be considered unlabeled with the restriction that at least one instance in each bag is positive. On this basis, they transform the MIL problem into a semi-supervised learning problem and design an SVM which attempts to maximize the margin on both labeled and unlabeled instances, by assigning instances from positive bags to appropriate classes such that the resulting margin is the maximum. A constrained concave–convex procedure [61] is used to solve the optimization problem. Once the instances of a test bag are classified by the SVM, they apply the standard MI assumption to retrieve the bag label.

4.6   Neural Network-Based Methods

Artificial Neural Networks (ANNs) were recalled in Sect. 1.3.1. The operation of an artificial neuron is characterized by its activation function. Given an input signal, the activation function can make the neuron fire, transmitting the signal through its output connections which in turn can activate other neurons. Different types of neurons are characterized by different activation functions. The connections between neurons have numeric weights, which contribute to the calculation of the activation function and can be tuned based on the training data. Several ANNs architectures exist. The most popular ANN model is the feedforward architecture, where connections between the units (neurons) do not form a cycle. Typically, neurons are organized in layers and there are input, hidden, and output layers. The information moves forward, from the input nodes, through the hidden nodes (if any), to the output nodes. This model is known as the multilayer perceptron. In this type of networks, it is common that neurons use a sigmoid function as an activation function and weights are trained using the backpropagation algorithm (BP). ANN models differ from each other in the way in which neurons are connected, the way in which weights are trained and in the activation functions. Many of these models have been adapted to the MIL setting. In this section, we present some of the most representatives adaptations.

4.6.1   Feedforward Neural Networks

Both Ramon et al. [55] and Zhou et al. [85] presented a feedforward neural network derived from the BP algorithm. As they are both based on the classical BP algorithm, their training processes are very similar, but the difference lies in the formal definition of the multi-instance function which measures the error of the neural network. In MIL, this definition has to be changed to consider the discrimination of bags instead of that of instances. Zhou et al. [85] use each instance of a bag as an input to the network, while Ramon et al. [55] provide all the instances of each bag all at once in parallel as input to the network.

On the basis of these first proposals, different extensions have been carried out. Zhang et al. [83] improved BP-MIP by incorporating two different feature selection techniques. The first proposal, BP-MIP-DD, uses feature scaling with Diverse Density [46] and the second one, BP-MIP-PCA, incorporates feature reduction with principal component analysis (PCA) [35]. Zhang et al. [82] extend BP-MIP by means of a new error function to solve multi-instance regression problems. These methods are oriented to solve multi-instance classification problems.

Another extension of the model proposed by Ramon et al. [55] has been developed by Li et al. [43]. Their proposal, called MIBP, selects the most positive instances (points close to instances from positive bags and far from instances in negative bags) for each bag and obtain a descriptor t in the feature space. The classification is carried out by using the descriptor t in combination with differential feature weighting. Recently, Li et al. [44] presented an optimization with respect to the computation time of the previous models, by using parallel computing to speed up the learning process.

One particular type of feedforward neural network is known as a Radial Basis Function Network, as they use radial basis functions as activation functions. Zhang et al. [81] proposed a Radial Basis Function (RBF) for multi-instance problems called RBF-MIP. In this approach, the first layer is composed of clusters of bags formed by merging training bags bottom-up, where the Hausdorff metric [21] is utilized to measure distances between bags and between clusters. Weights of the second layer of the network are optimized by minimizing a sum-of-squares error function and worked out through singular value decomposition. In a later contribution, [8] studied two variants of this architecture. The first applies a RBF network in a classical way, while the second involves a modular neural architecture where each module is an RBF network, called bag unit. This architecture can support a large number of bags. Adding new bags to the system can be done easily without requiring any retraining of the whole neural system, since each bag is modeled as a separate network. This architecture therefore allows incremental learning.

Another particular type of feedforward neural network is the Convolutional Neural Network (CNN), where the connectivity pattern between neurons is inspired by the organization of the animal visual cortex, whose neurons are arranged in such a way that they correspond to overlapping regions of the visual field. CNNs make the explicit assumption that the inputs are images, such that certain properties can be encoded into the architecture. As a result, the forward function is more efficient to implement and the amount of network parameters is vastly reduced. Zhou et al. [33] proposed a framework that integrates MIL with CNNs. Their model is based on an EM method for MIL integrated into a CNN that obtains patch-level predictions for each image. In particular, they assume that there is a hidden variable associated with each image patch, that indicates whether this patch is discriminative, that is, whether the true hidden label of the patch is the same as the true label of the image.

4.6.2   Recurrent Neural Networks

In contrast with a feedforward neural network, a recurrent neural network (RNN) has directed cycles in the connections between its units. This allows the network to create an internal memory and exhibit dynamic temporal behavior. Garcez et al. [27] proposed a recurrent neural network model for MIL. In this approach, first, a prototype vector is learned from the set of instances in a bag. Next, this prototype vector is used in a supervised classification of the bag, given the bag label. In this way, the instance learning can be seen as a kind of preprocessing for subsequent supervised learning at the bag level. Uwents et al. [65] proposed an approach that used different neural networks to represent classes of objects in a kind of unfolding of a recurrent network in time, potentially with the use of different sets of weights. A relational database is used to connect the networks, so that the output of one network can become the input of another.

4.6.3   Decision-Based Neural Networks

A Decision-based Neural Network (DBNN) is an efficient classification neural network with a modular structure. Each subnet is designated to represent one class. Chuang et al. [17] proposed a Generalized Probability Decision Neural Network (GPDNN) to model particular image concepts in the MIL setting. GPDNN uses data distributions instead of data values as network input. These can approximate feature distributions precisely, since image features in the form of distributions can be a better representation than those in numerical form. Xu et al. [73] proposed a Multiple Instance Decision-Based Neural Networks (MI-DBNN) for MIL. MI-DBNN is a probabilistic variant of DBNN. For each concept to be recognized, MI-DBNN devotes one of its subnets to the representation of that particular concept. In order to model all concepts, the discriminant functions in all subnets are designed to capture the MIL nature and are trained by the LUGS two-phase learning: locally unsupervised (LU) learning and the globally supervised (GS) learning.

4.6.4   Network Combinations

Uwents et al. [66] proposed a way to combine different neural networks models by using a cascade correlation method for MIL. They consider the combination of three network architecture models: adapted feedforward networks, recurrent networks, and networks with special aggregation units. The learning process is carried out in a constructive way, adding neurons to the network one by one and looking for a combination that is as simple as possible.

4.7 Evolutionary Based Methods

Evolutionary algorithms are computational modeling tools inspired by biological evolution [32]. Four fundamental paradigms are grouped under this general denomination: genetic algorithms, genetic programming, evolutionary programming, and evolution strategy. All these methods apply the principles of Darwinian theory of evolution [4] to solve problems. They share the following essential features:

- The use of a collaborative learning strategy considering a population of individuals (solutions). In this context, each individual represents a point in the search space of the problem and adds additional information to reach the final solution.
- An evolutionary process to generate new individuals (offspring) by means of genetic operators, such as crossover and mutation.
- The definition of a fitness function to measure the quality of each individual.

Among successful evolutionary algorithm implementations, genetic programming (GP) proposed by John Koza [40] retains a significant position, due to such valuable characteristics as: its great flexibility in representing solutions, the fact that prior knowledge about the statistical distribution of the data is not needed (data distribution free) and it can detect and express unknown relationships that exist among data as a mathematical expression. These characteristics convert these algorithms into a paradigm of growing interest both for obtaining classification rules [42, 64] and for other tasks related to prediction, such as feature selection [19, 50] and the generation of discriminant functions [16, 37]. This shows that GP is a mature field that efficiently achieves low error rates in supervised learning and is still introducing improvements into its methods [36, 39].

An extension of GP is Grammar-Guided Genetic Programming (G3P) [68]. G3P has shown to be an excellent approximation with a high performance in structured problems and is considered one of the most promising areas in GP [49]. This type of algorithms facilitates the efficient automatic discovery of empirical laws and provides a more systematic way of handling typing. More importantly, G3P can constrain the search space so that only grammatically correct individuals are generated. To achieve these goals, G3P employs a context-free grammar, that establishes the syntactical restrictions of the problem to be solved and its possible solutions. Similarly to other evolutionary algorithms, G3P is based on fundamental evolutionary processes, such as selection, reproduction, and replacement [29, 32].

Works on evolutionary algorithms in MIL have focused on G3P algorithms. Concretely, Zafra and Ventura [76] proposed a Grammar-Guided Genetic Programming algorithm for solving MIL problems, called G3P-MI. This method codifies each individual as an IF-THEN rule generated by means of the context-free grammar. The IF part of the rule (antecedent) contains a logical combination of conditions on the feature values and the THEN part (consequent) contains the predicted class for the concepts satisfied by the antecedent of the rule. In the particular case of two-class classification where G3P-MI has been applied, this rule determines if a bag should be considered positive or negative following the standard MI assumption. The individual representation would be

$\Sigma N = \{\langle cond_I\rangle, \langle variable\text{-}cat\rangle, \langle variable\text{-}num\rangle, \langle value\text{-}cat\rangle, \langle value\text{-}num\rangle,$
$\langle cmp\rangle, \langle cmp\text{-}num\rangle, \langle cmp\text{-}int\rangle, \langle cmp\text{-}cat\rangle, \langle op\text{-}cat\rangle, \langle op\text{-}num\rangle, \langle op\text{-}int\rangle\}$
$\Sigma T = \{GE, LT, EQ, NOT\text{-}EQ, IN, OUT, OR, AND\}$

$\langle cond_I\rangle$	$\rightarrow \langle cmp\rangle$
	| **OR** $\langle cmp\rangle\langle cond_I\rangle$
	| **AND** $\langle cond_I\rangle$
$\langle cmp\rangle$	$\rightarrow \langle op\text{-}num\rangle\langle cmp\text{-}num\rangle$
	| $\langle op\text{-}cat\rangle\langle cmp\text{-}cat\rangle$
	| $\langle op\text{-}int\rangle\langle cmp\text{-}int\rangle$
$\langle op\text{-}cat\rangle$	$\rightarrow$ **EQ**
	| **NOT EQ**
$\langle op\text{-}num\rangle$	$\rightarrow$ **GE**
	| **LT**
$\langle op\text{-}int\rangle$	$\rightarrow$ **IN**
	| **OUT**
$\langle cmp\text{-}cat\rangle$	$\rightarrow \langle variable\text{-}cat\rangle\langle value\text{-}cat\rangle$
$\langle cmp\text{-}int\rangle$	$\rightarrow \langle variable\text{-}num\rangle\langle value\text{-}int\rangle\langle value\text{-}int\rangle$
$\langle cmp\text{-}num\rangle$	$\rightarrow \langle variable\text{-}num\rangle\langle value\text{-}num\rangle$
$\langle variable\text{-}cat\rangle$	$\rightarrow$ *Any valid attribute in dataset*
$\langle variable\text{-}num\rangle$	$\rightarrow$ *Any valid attribute in dataset*
$\langle value\text{-}cat\rangle$	$\rightarrow$ *Any valid value*
$\langle value\text{-}num\rangle$	$\rightarrow$ *Any valid value*

Fig. 4.3 Grammar used for representing individuals genotypes in G3P-MI

If $(cond_B(\text{bag}))$ *then*
    bag is an instance of the concept.
Else
    bag is an instance of the concept.
End-If

where $cond_B$ is a condition applied on bags, which can be expressed as

$$cond_B(bag) = \bigvee_{\forall instance \in bag} cond_I(instance), \qquad (4.14)$$

where $\vee$ is the disjunction operator and $cond_I$ is a condition applied on each instance belonging to the bag that is obtained according to the grammar shown in Fig. 4.3. The grammar is defined as the set of non terminals, set of terminals and the set of productions written as Backus-Naur form (BNF) [38]. In this manner, the rule antecedent would be composed by a disjunction (OR) and conjunction (AND) of comparators. The final number of admitted attributes and values would be associated with the attributes and their values defined in the classification problem to solve.

The main steps of G3P-MI are based on a classic generational and elitist evolutionary algorithm (Algorithm 1). Initially, a population of classification rules is generated following a procedure inspired by that defined by Geyer-Shultz [28]. Next, the individuals are evaluated using the product of sensitivity and specificity [76] as fitness function. These measures are, respectively, defined as the proportion of cases correctly identified as meeting a certain condition (true positives) and the proportion of cases correctly identified as not meeting this condition (true negatives). Once the individuals are evaluated with respect to their ability to solve the problem, the main loop of the algorithm is composed of the following operations. The first step represents the parent selection where individuals are selected by means of binary tournaments. The recombination and mutation processes are carried out with a certain probability [76]. Once the offspring is obtained through the previous procedure, these new solutions are evaluated. In the last operation, the population is updated by direct replacement, that is, the resulting offspring replaces the current population. To guarantee that the best individual in the population is not lost during the updating process, the algorithm employs elitism.

Algorithm 1 G3P-MI Algorithm

Input: Multi-instance dataset T, it is used to evaluate individuals. Maximum number of generations $max_{generations}$

Output: The best individual of $P_{max-population}$

1: $P_0 \leftarrow$ initializePopulation() ▷ *generate initial population of rules*
2: $P_0 \leftarrow$ MultiInstanceEvaluator(P_0, T) ▷ *Evaluate individuals (see Algorithm 2)*
3: $t \leftarrow 0$ ▷ *initialize number of generations*
4: **repeat**
5:      ▷ *Select to parents by means of binary tournament*
        $P_{parents} \leftarrow$ tournamentSelector(P_t)
6:      ▷ *Obtain offspring population by means of crossover and mutation*
        $P_{offspring} \leftarrow$ parentReproduction($P_{parents}$)
7:      ▷ *Evaluate individuals of population (see Algorithm 2)*
        $P_{offspring} \leftarrow$ MultiInstanceEvaluator($P_{offspring}, T$)
8:      ▷ *The next individual population is obtained using elitism*
        $P_{t+1} \leftarrow$ updatePopulation($P_{offspring}, P_t$)
9:      ▷ *next generation*
        $t \leftarrow t + 1$
10: **until** (t ≤ max_generations)

Algorithm 2 MultiInstance Evaluator

Input: Multi-instance dataset T. Individual population P

Output: Individual population evaluated $P_{evaluated}$
        ▷ *In MIL the coverage function has to discriminate bags no instances*
1: **for** each individual $\in P$ **do**
2:      $rule \leftarrow$ individual genotype ▷ *Obtain the rule of the individual*
3:      $Coverage_{multi}(rule) \leftarrow \{bag_i | Cover_{multi}(rule, bag_i)\}$
        ▷ *bag_i denotes the $i-th$ bag in the data set*
4:      $Cover_{multi}(rule, bag) \leftarrow \exists$ (instance $\in$ bag) $Cover_{instance}$ (rule, instance)
        ▷ *$Cover_{instance}$ is applied on particular instances*
5: **end for**

Evolutionary algorithms have been applied to different problems in MIL. Using a G3P-based algorithm, Zafra et al. [78] determine if a particular index web page is interesting for a user or not and Zafra and Ventura [75] predict if a student will fail or pass a certain course identifying the most relevant activities to promote learning from the MIL perspective.

Similar to traditional single-instance learning, the classification problem could be considered a multi-objective problem, where there are different contradictory objectives that have to be satisfied simultaneously. An extension of G3P-MI that works over several objectives and obtains well-distributed Pareto solutions in a MIL scenario has been proposed by Zafra and Ventura [77]. The authors proposed a MultiObjective Grammar-Guided Genetic Programming for Multiple Instances (MOG3P-MI). Three different evolutionary approaches were developed following the philosophy of well-known multi-objective algorithms in traditional supervised learning. The first approach (MOG3P-MI$_{v1}$) followed the evolutionary strategy of the Strength Pareto Evolutionary Algorithm (SPEA2) [87], the second one (MOG3P-MI$_{v2}$) is based on the Non-dominated Sorting Genetic Algorithm (NSGA2) [20] and the third one (MOG3P-MI$_{v3}$) is based on Multi-objective genetic local search (MOGLS) [34]. The three versions are compared and a particular proposal called MOG3P-MI is presented as the best option.

4.8   Experimental Analysis

In this section, we empirically compare the performance of some representative instance-based MIC methods. These experiments are only intended for illustration purposes and cannot be taken as a rigorous comparison among classifiers. Datasets coming from various application areas are used. The experimental setup is specified in Sects. 4.8.1 and 4.8.2 presents the results.

4.8.1   Setup

The datasets used in the experimental study are described in Table 4.1, as a selection of the datasets presented in Sect. 3.6. We limit the study to two-class datasets, since this is the kind of problem mostly studied so far. The table shows the total number of bags, as well as the number of bags in each class, the number of instances and the number of features. The datasets comprise different application domains, as described in Sect. 3.6. WIR7 originated from a web mining application [86], but only text rather than multimedia information is used. A strong feature selection process have been applied to the original WIR7 and TREC9-4 datasets, removing both poorly and highly frequent words.

The included algorithms are listed in Table 4.2. They represent different approaches described in this chapter and the two principal MI assumptions used

Table 4.1 Description of the multi-instance datasets used in the comparison

Dataset	#bags	+bags	−bags	#inst	#feat
Musk1	92	47	45	476	166
Musk2	101	39	62	12,179	166
Atoms	188	125	63	1618	10
Bonds	188	125	63	3995	16
Chains	188	125	63	5349	24
WIR7	113	55	58	3423	303
TREC9-4	400	200	200	3391	306
Beach	200	100	100	719	9
Fox	200	100	100	1320	230

Table 4.2 Instance-based classification algorithms to be compared

Algorithm	Approach	MIL assumption
EM-DD	Diverse density	Standard
MILR (Logistic regression)	Traditional statistic	Collective
MIBoost	Ensembles	Collective
MITI	Decision trees	Standard
miSVM	Maximum margin	Standard
MIWrapper	Wrapper	Std/Coll
G3P-MI	Evolutionary	Standard

in the literature. The implementations are taken from the Weka library, except that of G3P-MI which was obtained from the JCLEC library. Both libraries are described in Sect. 3.7. We use the default settings of the algorithms run in Weka. In G3P-MI, we apply the default parameters set in [76]. In MIBoost, we use the classic tree induction Algorithm C4.5 as base classifier and perform 10 boosting iterations. Regarding miSVM, we use an RBF kernel with $C = 1$ and $\gamma = 0.5$. These parameters were selected after a gross grid search over the studied datasets. We use the fivefold cross validation procedure and evaluate the performance of the classifiers by means of their accuracy (Sect. 1.4).

4.8.2 Results and Discussion

For the sake of clarity, we organize the presentation of results in four parts. In Sect. 4.8.2.1, we discuss the results of the wrapper methods of Sect. 4.2, that allow the straightforward use of unmodified single-instance classifiers to multi-instance data. Section 4.8.2.2 presents the results of a representative selection of the most popular and effective instance-based multi-instance learning algorithms. The results of two

MIL boosting methods are provided in Sect. 4.8.2.3. We compare them separately, as they are ensemble methods and it is accepted that they generally outperform single-classifier methods. Finally, Sect. 4.8.2.4 compares the top performing methods taking into account accuracy, model interpretability, and training time.

4.8.2.1   Wrappers for Single-Instance Methods

Section 4.2 discussed wrappers methods that can be used to apply single-instance methods to MIL data. Table 4.3 presents the experimental results for these methods that use the standard (Std) and the collective (Col) MI assumptions. We executed both wrapper types with three single-instance classifiers: C4.5, logistic regression (LR) and a support vector machine (SVM) with RBF kernel and same parameters as described in the setup section. The bottom two rows show the average accuracy and the standard deviation over the nine datasets. The best result in each row is highlighted in bold. We observe the following:

• Different single-instance classifiers are appropriate for different MI problems. SVM dominates in six out of nine datasets, but C4.5 excels in the three mutagenesis datasets and LR works has decent results in text domain datasets. Consequently, we observe that wrappers based on the standard assumption can beat those based on the collective assumption when using C4.5 in mutagenesis datasets or when using SVM in the other datasets. Previous studies have drawn similar conclusions [56].

• Collective assumption-based wrappers learn consistently more accurate models than standard assumption-based wrappers. In almost all cases, the wrapper based on the collective MI assumption has better results than the one based on the standard

Table 4.3 Experimental results for wrapper methods

Method	Std + C4.5	Col + C4.5	Std + LR	Col + LR	Std + SVM	Col + SVM
Musk1	77.17	86.96	77.17	85.87	89.13	**90.22**
Musk2	67.33	81.19	67.33	81.19	83.17	**89.11**
Atoms	68.62	**73.40**	66.49	65.96	66.49	66.49
Bonds	76.06	**77.13**	66.49	67.02	66.49	70.74
Chains	76.60	**85.11**	66.49	71.28	66.49	70.74
WIR	53.98	74.34	60.18	**77.88**	54.87	**77.88**
TREC	74.00	81.25	68.25	80.75	70.50	**82.75**
Beach	63.00	74.00	68.50	79.00	4.50	**80.50**
Fox	55.00	59.00	57.00	55.00	60.00	**62.50**
Average	67.97	**76.93**	66.43	73.77	69.07	76.77
SD	8.50	7.84	**5.29**	9.19	10.15	9.23

MI assumption. The theoretical arguments that were given in Sect. 4.2 are an explanation of these results.

- Taking into account these two points, we can expect that using an appropriate single-instance classifier in conjunction with the collective assumption-based wrapper yields good results in many datasets. The challenge is to find the best single-instance learner.
- On average, the best result is achieved by the collective assumption-based wrapper with the C4.5 single-instance classifier. Even though this method did not reach the highest score in most datasets, its performance was consistently good, as shown by its low standard deviation. For this reason, we include this algorithm in the Sect. 4.8.2.4.

4.8.2.2   Representative Instance-Based Methods

Table 4.4 contains the experimental results of the selected instance-based classifiers. We note the following:

- The evolutionary algorithm G3P-MI dominates. It obtains the highest accuracy in six out of nine datasets and is very close to the best result in the other three. It has the highest average accuracy as well. Additionally, G3P-MI has the lowest standard deviation, which means that it has an important stability in its results. We select G3P-MI for the comparison carried out in Sect. 4.8.2.4.
- The tree induction MI algorithm MITI has a good performance on the three mutagenesis datasets. In Table 4.3, C4.5 yields the best results on the mutagenesis data as well. These observations suggest that the tree induction bias is appropriate to model mutagenesis problems. Conversely, SVMs (both the single-instance version with the wrapper and the multi-instance miSVM) perform poorly in these datasets.

Table 4.4 Experimental results for representative instance-based methods

Method	EM-DD	MILR	MITI	miSVM	G3P-MI
Musk1	84.78	76.09	65.22	**89.13**	88.21
Musk2	**84.16**	75.25	62.38	83.17	83.94
Atoms	75.00	67.55	81.38	66.49	**83.55**
Bonds	73.94	81.91	**82.98**	66.49	82.42
Chains	70.74	78.72	82.45	66.49	**83.81**
WIR	61.06	70.80	61.06	58.41	**72.47**
TREC	52.00	71.00	71.50	69.25	**87.87**
Beach	73.50	78.00	62.50	80.00	**83.54**
Fox	61.00	50.50	56.50	59.00	**67.72**
Average	70.69	72.20	69.55	70.94	**81.50**
SD	10.29	8.76	9.73	10.13	**6.87**

- EM-DD and miSVM obtain good results in some datasets, but not so in others, yielding accuracies that are low on average and highly variable. The results of MILR have less variability, but are considerably lower than those of G3P-MI.

4.8.2.3   Comparing Boosting Methods

In this section, we compare two MIL boosting approaches. The first method is the multi-instance MIBoost algorithm described in Sect. 4.3 using the single-instance C4.5 as base learner. The second is the single-instance AdaBoost method, using the multi-instance MITI method as base learner. Both base learners are tree induction algorithms, but each works in a different learning setting. Boosting methods need base learners that are weak enough so they allow for variability in the learned hypothesis. MITI classifiers readily meet that condition, but in the case of C4.5 we had to increase its pruning level by putting the confidence factor to 0.025 used for pruning in this experiment.

The key difference between these approaches is that in the AdaBoost+MITI scheme, the loss function optimized by the boosting algorithm is used to search a bag-level weak learner H. The error of H is used to compute bag-level weights. In the MIBoost+C4.5 scheme, an instance-level weak learner h is searched and the error of h is used to compute instance-level weights. A second difference is that the AdaBoost+MITI scheme implements the standard MI assumption which is encoded in the base classifier MITI, while the collective assumption is used by the AdaBoost+MITI scheme as part of the loss function optimized by the boosting procedure. Table 4.5 shows experimental results for boosting methods in MIL, from which we can observe the following:

- Compared to Table 4.4, the results of AdaBoost are better than those of the single MITI algorithm in seven out of nine datasets. The best results of AdaBoost are attained in the mutagenesis datasets, precisely where MITI was already the best in its pool.
- MIBoost results are better than those of the C4.5 collective wrapper in eight datasets and worse in one dataset (Chains). Although Adaboost has better results than MIBoost in the mutagenesis datasets, MIBoost has the best performance by a wide margin in the remaining datasets. We select MIBoost for the overall comparison in Sect. 4.8.2.4.

4.8.2.4   Overall Comparison of Instance-Based Methods

We selected the best performing methods from the three previous experiments. These are the evolutionary algorithm G3P-MI, MIWrapper (Col) + C4.5 and MIBoost + C4.5. In this section, we present an overall comparison between them.

Figure 4.4 shows the accuracy of the selected methods in each dataset. Note that the accuracy axis starts at 40 to better distinguish the differences between the methods.

Table 4.5 Experimental results for boosting method

Method	MIBoost + C4.5	AdaBoost + MITI
Musk1	**90.22**	61.96
Musk2	**82.18**	69.31
Atoms	81.91	**84.57**
Bonds	80.85	**84.57**
Chains	82.98	**84.04**
WIR	**83.19**	62.83
TREC	**83.75**	76.75
Beach	**84.00**	71.00
Fox	**60.00**	51.00
Average	**81.01**	71.78
SD	**7.84**	11.14

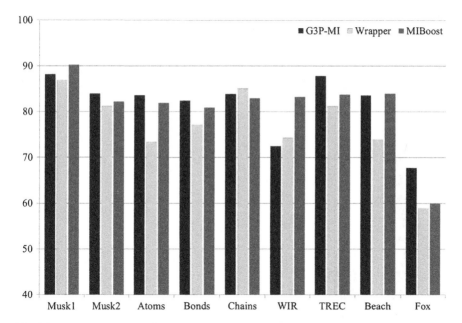

Fig. 4.4 Experimental results for selected methods

Although the differences are only small in some datasets, we count 5 wins for G3P-MI, 3 wins for MIBoost and one for the Wrapper method. The excellent results of G3P-MI show that genetic programming is a powerful tool for learning complex models such as the underlying MIL problems. The behavior of MIBoost suggests that in the multi-instance setting the generalization ability of boosting algorithms is usually better than that of single learners, as also occurs in single-instance learning [69]. In several datasets, Wrapper obtains good results. This is remarkable, since it is a very simple classification method that allows the use of a single-instance classifier such as C4.5. This fact was already observed in previous studies [22, 24].

We must note that while MIBoost and Wrapper achieve these results by using the collective assumption, G3P-MI does so based on the standard assumption. It suggests that the role of the MI assumption in the performance of the classifier might not be as important as other characteristics of the learner.

Aside from accuracy, other important characteristics of a learning algorithm are the training time and the model interpretability. In some applications, the time required to learn the model can be a critical design factor. Figure 4.5 shows the training time for selected classifiers in our experiments. In addition to the three best performing classifiers discussed above, we also include other representative methods in this comparison. G3P-MI has the largest training time. The high-computational cost needed to evolve solutions is a drawback of genetic programming methods. In this context, it is interesting to name the study of Cano et al. [11] that optimizes the execution time of G3P-MI. Methods such as miSVM and EM-DD are time-consuming as well. With respect to EM-DD, it is clear that the intensive computation of the diverse density function and its slow convergence take a long time to be trained. MIBoost, which shows very competitive accuracy, has a moderate training time. It is

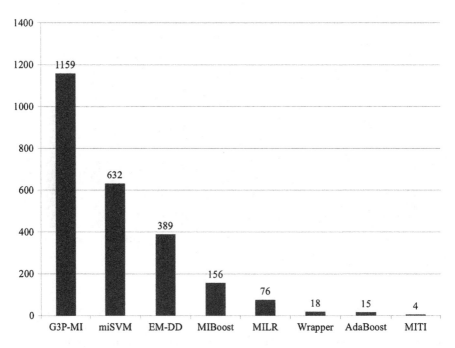

Fig. 4.5 Training time in seconds for the methods in the study

interesting that AdaBoost takes much less time to be trained than MIBoost and even than some single classifiers. One reason of this behavior is that its base classifier is MITI, of which the training time is lower than that of C4.5. The other reason is that the loss function optimized by AdaBoost is less complex than that of MIBoost, as explained in Sect. 4.8.2.3. MILR is not an expensive method and, as was shown in Sect. 4.8.2.2, it can reach acceptable results in some datasets. The Wrapper method is fast and quite accurate. Finally, MITI has the lowest training time. Although it is not among the more accurate methods, MITI has another advantage: since its classification model is a decision tree, it is easy to understand. Two other learning algorithms are also among those that build the most interpretable models. One is the Wrapper method that uses the C4.5 base classifier (which builds a decision tree) and the other is G3P-MI, which represents the model in the form of IF-THEN classification rules, providing a more natural description of the learned knowledge.

4.9 Summarizing Comments

Instance-based classification algorithms are among the most popular MIC methods. In this chapter, we have reviewed a variety of these algorithms such as decision trees, SVMs, and evolutionary algorithms. Most instance-based classification algorithms are adaptations of single-instance classification algorithms to the multi-instance setting. An important exception are the wrapper methods that allow the use of unmodified single-instance classifiers in MIC problems.

In order to find the function that best fits the training data, one general principle is to minimize some loss function relating instance labels provided by a generative model with bag labels of training data through the MI assumption. This optimization process can take the form of a likelihood maximization in many statistical learners, margin maximization in SVMs, information gain maximization in decision tree methods, fitness function maximization in evolutionary algorithms, etc. As an alternative, the adaptation of a single-instance classification algorithm to MIL can rely on any appropriate MI assumption.

In an experimental study, we have compared some representative instance-based classification algorithms, taking into account several quality aspects. The results show that the optimal classifier for a given application depends on both the application domain and priorities such as accuracy, training time, or model interpretability. Instance-based methods that make accurate predictions, have fast training times and construct interpretable models have been identified in this study.

References

1. Amar, R.A., Dooly, D.R., Goldman, S.A., Zhang, Q.: Multiple-instance learning of real-valued data. In: Brodley, C., Danyluk, A. (eds.) Proceedings of the 18th International Conference on Machine Learning (ICML 2001), pp. 3–10. Morgan Kaufmann Publishers, San Francisco (2001)
2. Andrews, S., Tsochantaridis, I., Hofmann, T.: Support vector machines for multiple-instance learning. In: Becker, S., Thrun, S., Obermayer, K. (eds.) Advances in Neural Information Processing Systems, pp. 561–568. MIT Press, Cambridge (2002)
3. Babenko, B., Belongie, S., Yang, M.H.: Visual tracking with online multiple instance learning. In: Flynn, P., Mortensen, E. (eds.) Proceedings of the 2009 IEEE Conference on Computer Vision and Pattern Recognition (CVPR 2009), pp. 983–990. IEEE, Los Alamitos (2009)
4. Bascom, J.: Darwin's theory of the origin of species. Am. Theol. Rev. **3**, 349–379 (1871)
5. Bishop, C.M.: Pattern Recognition and Machine Learning. Springer, New York (2006)
6. Bjerring, L., Frank, E.: Beyond trees: adopting MITI to learn rules and ensemble classifiers for multi-instance data. In: Wang, D., Reynolds, M. (eds.) Lecture Notes in Artificial Intelligence, pp. 41–50. Springer, Berlin (2011)
7. Blockeel, H., Page, D., Srinivasan, A.: Multi-instance tree learning. In: De Raedt, L., Wrobel, S. (eds.) Proceedings of the 22nd International Conference on Machine Learning (ICML 2005), pp. 57–64. ACM, New York (2005)
8. Bouchachia, A.: Multiple instance learning with radial basis function neural networks. In: Pal, N., Kasabov, N., Mudi, R., Pal, S., Parui, S. (eds.) Advances in Neural Information Processing Systems (NIPS Conference), pp. 440–445. Springer, Berlin (2004)
9. Breiman, L.: Random forests. Mach. Learn. **45**(1), 5–32 (2001)
10. Bunescu, R., Mooney, R.: Multiple instance learning for sparse positive bags. In: Proceedings of the 24th International Conference on Machine Learning (ICML 2007), pp. 105–112. ACM, New York (2007)
11. Cano, A., Zafra, A., Ventura, S.: Speeding up multiple instance learning classification rules on GPUs. Knowl. Inf. Syst. **44**(1), 127–145 (2015)
12. Chen, Y., Wang, J.: Image categorization by learning and reasoning with regions. J. Mach. Learn. Res. **5**, 913–939 (2004)
13. Cheung, P., Kwok, J.: A regularization framework for multiple-instance learning. In: Ghahramani, Z. (ed.) Proceedings of the 23rd International Conference on Machine learning, pp. 193–200 (2006)
14. Chevaleyre, Y., Zucker, J.: Solving multiple-instance and multiple-part learning problems with decision trees and rule sets. Application to the mutagenesis problem. In: Stroulia, E., Matwin, S. (eds.) Lecture Notes in Artificial Intelligence, pp. 204–214. Springer, Berlin (2001)
15. Chevaleyre, Y., Bredeche, N., Zucker, J.: Learning rules from multiple instance data: issues and algorithms. In: Proceedings of the 9th International Conference on Information Processing and Management of Uncertainty in Knowledge-Based Systems (IPMU 2002), pp. 455–459. Esia, Annecy (2002)
16. Chien, B.C., Lin, J.Y., Hong, T.P.: Learning discriminant functions with fuzzy attributes for classification using genetic programming. Expert Syst. Appl. **23**(1), 31–37 (2002)
17. Chuang, S.C., Xu, Y.Y., Fu, H.C.: Neural network based image retrieval with multiple instance leaning techniques. In: Khosla, R., Howlett, R., Jain, L. (eds.) Lecture Notes in Artificial Intelligence, pp. 1210–1216. Springer, Berlin (2005)
18. Cohen, W.: Fast effective rule induction. In: Prieditis, A., Russell, S. (eds.) Proceedings of the 12th International Conference on Machine Learning, pp. 115–123. Morgan Kaufmann, San Francisco (1995)
19. Davis, R.A., Charlton, A.J., Oehlschlager, S., Wilson, J.C.: Novel feature selection method for genetic programming using metabolomic 1H NMR data. Chemom. Intell. Lab. **81**(1), 50–59 (2006)
20. Ded, K., Pratap, A., Agarwal, S., Meyarivan, T.: A fast and elitist multi-objective genetic algorithm: NSGA-II. IEEE Trans. Evol. Comput. **6**(2), 149–172 (2002)

21. Deza, M.M., Deza, E.: Dictionary of Distances. Elsevier, Amsterdam (2006)
22. Dong, L.: A comparison of multi-instance learning algorithms. Master thesis, University of Waikato, New Zealand (2006)
23. Feng, S., Xu, D.: Transductive multi-instance multi-label learning algorithm with application to automatic image annotation. Expert Syst. Appl. **37**(1), 661–670 (2010)
24. Frank, E., Xu, X.: Applying propositional learning algorithms to multi-instance data. Technical report 06/03, Department of Computer Science, University of Waikato, Hamilton, New Zealand (2003)
25. Friedman, J., Hastie, T., Tibshirani, R.: Additive logistic regression: a statistical view of boosting (with discussion and a rejoinder by the authors). Ann. Stat. **28**(2), 337–407 (2000)
26. Fu, Z., Robles-Kelly, A.: Fast multiple instance learning via L1,2 logistic regression. In: Proceedings of the 19th International Conference on Pattern Recognition (ICPR 2008), pp. 3815–3818. IEEE, Los Alamitos (2008)
27. Garcez, A., Zaverucha, G.: Multi-instance learning using recurrent neural networks. In: Proceedings of the International Joint Conference on Neural Networks (IJCNN), pp. 1–6. IEEE, Los Alamitos (2012)
28. Geyer-Schulz, A.: Fuzzy Rule-Based Expert Systems and Genetic Machine Learning, vol. 3. Physica Verlag, Heidelberg (1997)
29. Goldberg, D.E.: Zen and the art of genetic algorithms. In: Proceedings of the 3rd International Conference on Genetic Algorithms, pp. 80–85. Morgan Kaufmann Publishers, San Francisco (1989)
30. Gondra, I., Xu, T.: A multiple instance learning based framework for semantic image segmentation. Multimed. Tools Appl. **48**(2), 339–365 (2010)
31. Grabner, H., Grabner, M., Bischof, H.: Real-time tracking via on-line boosting. In: Chantler, M., Trucco, E., Fisher, B. (eds.) Proceedings of the British Machine Vision Conference, pp. 47–56. British Machine Vision Association, Durham (2006)
32. Holland, J.H.: Adaptation in Natural and Artificial Systems: An Introductory Analysis with Applications to Biology, Control and Artificial Intelligence. MIT Press, Cambridge (1992)
33. Hou, L., Samaras, D., Kurc, T.M., Gao, Y., Davis, J.E., Saltz, J.H.: Efficient multiple instance convolutional neural networks for gigapixel resolution image classification (2015). arXiv:1504.07947
34. Jaszkiewicz, A.: Genetic local search for multi-objective combinatorial optimization. Eur. J. Oper. Res. **137**(1), 50–71 (2002)
35. Jolliffe, I.: Principal Component Analysis. Springer, New York (2002)
36. Kattan, A., Agapitos, A., Ong, Y.S., Alghamedi, A., O'Neill, M.: GP made faster with semantic surrogate modelling. Inf. Sci. **355–356**, 169–185 (2016)
37. Kishore, J.K., Patnaik, L.M., Mani, V., Agrawal, V.: Application of genetic programming for multicategory pattern classification. IEEE Trans. Evol. Comput. **4**(3), 242–258 (2000)
38. Knuth, D.E.: Backus normal form vs. Backus Naur form. Commun. ACM **7**(12), 735–736 (1964)
39. Kouchakpour, P., Zaknich, A., Bräunl, T.: Dynamic population variation in genetic programming. Inf. Sci. **179**(8), 1078–1091 (2009)
40. Koza, J.R.: Genetic Programming: On the Programming of Computers by Means of Natural Selection. MIT Press, Cambridge (1992)
41. Leistner, C., Saffari, A., Bischof, H.: MIForests: multiple-instance learning with randomized trees. In: Daniilidis, K., Maragos, P., Paragios, N. (eds.) Computer Vision - ECCV 2010, pp. 29–42. Springer, Berlin (2010)
42. Lensberg, T., Eilifsen, A., McKee, T.E.: Bankruptcy theory development and classification via genetic programming. Eur. J. Oper. Res. **169**(2), 677–697 (2006)
43. Li, C.H., Gondra, I.: A novel neural network-based approach for multiple instance learning. In: Proceedings of the 2010 IEEE 10th International Conference on Computer and Information Technology (CIT), pp. 451–456. IEEE, Los Alamitos (2010)
44. Li, C.H., Gondra, I., Liu, L.: An efficient parallel neural network-based multi-instance learning algorithm. J. Supercomput. **62**(2), 724–740 (2012)

45. Maron, O.: Learning from ambiguity. Ph.D. thesis, Massachusetts Institute of Technology, United States of America (1998)
46. Maron, O., Lozano-Pérez, T.: A framework for multiple-instance learning. In: Jordan, M., Kearns, M., Solla, S. (eds.) Advances in Neural Information Processing Systems, pp. 570–576. MIT Press, Cambridge (1998)
47. Mason, L., Baxter, J., Bartlett, P.L., Frean, M.R.: Boosting algorithms as gradient descent. In: Solla, S., Leen, T., Müller, K. (eds.) Advances in Neural Information Processing Systems, pp. 512–518. MIT Press, Cambridge (2000)
48. McGovern, A., Jensen, D.: Identifying predictive structures in relational data using multiple instance learning. In: Fawcett, T., Mishra, N. (eds.) Proceedings of the 20th International Conference on Machine Learning (ICML 2003), pp. 528–535. The AAAI Press, Menlo Park (2003)
49. Mckay, R.I., Hoai, N.X., Whigham, P.A., Shan, Y., O'Neill, M.: Grammar-based genetic programming: a survey. Genet. Program. Evol. M **11**(3–4), 365–396 (2010)
50. Muharram, M., Smith, G.D.: Evolutionary constructive induction. IEEE Trans. Knowl. Data Eng. **17**(11), 1518–1528 (2005)
51. Oza, N.C.: Online ensemble learning. Ph.D. thesis, University of California, Berkeley, United States of America (2001)
52. Pao, H., Chuang, S., Xu, Y., Fu, H.: An EM based multiple instance learning method for image classification. Expert Syst. Appl. **35**(3), 1468–1472 (2008)
53. Qi, Z., Xu, Y., Wang, L., Song, Y.: Online multiple instance boosting for object detection. Neurocomputing **74**(10), 1769–1775 (2011)
54. Quinlan, J.: Induction of decision trees. Mach. Learn. **1**(1), 81–106 (1986)
55. Ramon, J., De Raedt, L.: Multi instance neural networks. In: Proceedings of the ICML-2000 Workshop on Attribute-Value and Relational Learning, pp. 53–60. Morgan Kaufmann Publishers, San Francisco (2000)
56. Ray, S., Craven, M.: Supervised versus multiple instance learning: an empirical comparison. In: De Raedt, L., Wrobel, S. (eds.) Proceedings of the 22nd International Conference on Machine Learning (ICML 2005), pp. 697–704. ACM, New York (2005)
57. Rose, K., Gurewitz, E., Fox, G.: Deterministic annealing, constrained clustering, and optimization. In: Proceedings of the IEEE International Joint Conference on Neural Networks (IJCNN), pp. 2515–2520. IEEE, Los Alamitos (1991)
58. Ruffo, G.: Learning single and multiple instance decision trees for computer security applications. Ph.D. thesis, University of Turin, Italy (2000)
59. Saul, L.K., Rahim, M.G., Allen, J.B.: A statistical model for robust integration of narrowband cues in speech. Comput. Speech Lang. **15**, 175–194 (2001)
60. Schapire, R.E., Singer, Y.: Improved boosting algorithms using confidence-rated predictions. Mach. Learn. **37**(3), 297–336 (1999)
61. Smola, A.J., Vishwanathan, S., Hofmann, T.: Kernel methods for missing variables. In: Cowell, R., Ghahramani, Z. (eds.) Proceedings of the 10th International Workshop on Artificial Intelligence and Statistics (AISTATS), pp. 325–332. The Society for Artificial Intelligence and Statistics (2005)
62. Song, Y., Li, Q.: Visual tracking based on multiple instance learning particle filter. In: Proceedings of the 2011 IEEE International Conference on Mechatronics and Automation, pp. 1063–1067. IEEE, Los Alamitos (2011)
63. Sternig, S., Roth, P., Bischof, H.: Inverse multiple instance learning for classifier grids. In: Proceedings of the 20th International Conference on Pattern Recognition (ICPR), pp. 770–773. IEEE, Los Alamitos (2010)
64. Tsakonas, A.: A comparison of classification accuracy of four genetic programming-evolved intelligent structures. Inf. Sci. **176**(6), 691–724 (2006)
65. Uwents, W., Blockeel, H.: Classifying relational data with neural networks. In: Kramer, S., Pfahringer, B. (eds.) Lecture Notes in Artificial Intelligence, pp. 384–396. Springer, Berlin (2005)

66. Uwents, W., Blockeel, H.: A comparison between neural network methods for learning aggregate functions. In: Jean-Fran, J., Berthold, M., Horváth, T. (eds.) Lecture Notes in Artificial Intelligence, pp. 88–99. Springer, Berlin (2008)

67. Viola, P., Platt, J., Zhang, C.: Multiple instance boosting for object detection. In: Weiss, Y., Schölkopf, B., Platt, J. (eds.) Advances in Neural Information Processing Systems, pp. 1417–1424. MIT Press, Cambridge (2005)

68. Whigham, P.A.: Grammatically-based genetic programming. In: Rosca, J.P. (ed.) Proceedings of the Workshop on Genetic Programming: From Theory to Real-World Applications, pp. 33–41. University of Rochester, Rochester (1995)

69. Wu, X., Kumar, V., Quinlan, J.R., Ghosh, J., Yang, Q., Motoda, H., McLachlan, G.J., Ng, A., Liu, B., Philip, S.Y., Zhou, Z., Steinbach, M., Hand, D., Steinberg, D.: Top 10 algorithms in data mining. Knowl. Inf. Syst. **14**(1), 1–37 (2008)

70. Xie, Y., Qu, Y., Li, C., Zhang, W.: Online multiple instance gradient feature selection for robust visual tracking. Pattern Recognit. Lett. **33**(9), 1075–1082 (2012)

71. Xu, X.: Statistical learning in multiple instance problems. Master thesis, University of Waikato, New Zealand (2003)

72. Xu, X., Frank, E.: Logistic regression and boosting for labeled bags of instances. In: Dai, H., Srikant, R., Zhang, C. (eds.) Lecture Notes in Artificial Intelligence, pp. 272–281. Springer, Berlin (2004)

73. Xu, Y.Y., Shih, C.H.: Multiple-instance learning via decision-based neural networks. In: Watada, J., Philips-Wren, G., Jain, L., Howlett, R. (eds.) Intelligent Decision Technologies, pp. 885–895. Springer, Berlin (2011)

74. Yang, C.Y.C., Dong, M.D.M., Hua, J.H.J.: Region-based image annotation using asymmetrical support vector machine-based multiple-instance learning. In: Fitzgibbon, A., Taylor, C., LeCun, Y. (eds.) Proceedings of the 2006 IEEE Computer Society Conference on Computer Vision and Pattern Recognition (CVPR 2006), pp. 2057–2063. IEEE, Los Alamitos (2006)

75. Zafra, A., Ventura, S.: Predicting student grades in learning management systems with multiple instance learning genetic programming. In: Barnes, T., Desmarais, M., Romero, C., Ventura, S. (eds.) Proceedings of the 2nd International Conference on Educational Data Mining, pp. 309–318 (2009)

76. Zafra, A., Ventura, S.: G3p-MI: a genetic programming algorithm for multiple instance learning. Inf. Sci. **180**(23), 4496–4513 (2010)

77. Zafra, A., Ventura, S.: Multi-objective approach based on grammar-guided genetic programming for solving multiple instance problems. Soft Comput. **16**(6), 955–977 (2012)

78. Zafra, A., Romero, C., Ventura, S., Herrera-Viedma, E.: Multi-instance genetic programming for web index recommendation. Expert Syst. Appl. **36**(9), 11470–11479 (2009)

79. Zeisl, B., Leistner, C., Saffari, A., Bischof, H.: On-line semi-supervised multiple-instance boosting. In: Boykov, Y., Schmidt, F.R., Kahl, F., Lemptisky, V. (eds.) Proceedings of the 2010 IEEE Conference on Computer Vision and Pattern Recognition (CVPR 2010), pp. 1879–1879. IEEE, Los Alamitos (2010)

80. Zhang, Q., Goldman, S.A.: EM-DD: an improved multiple-instance learning technique. In: Dietterich, T., Becker, S., Ghahramani (eds.) Advances in Neural Information Processing Systems, pp. 1073–1080. MIT Press, Cambridge (2001)

81. Zhang, M., Zhou, Z.: Adapting RBF neural networks to multi-instance learning. Neural Process. Lett. **23**(1), 1–26 (2006)

82. Zhang, M.L., Zhou, Z.H.: A multi-instance regression algorithm based on neural network. J. Softw. **14**(7), 1238–1242 (2003)

83. Zhang, M.L., Zhou, Z.H.: Improve multi-instance neural networks through feature selection. Neural Process. Lett. **10**(1), 1–10 (2004)

84. Zhou, Z., Xu, J.: On the relation between multi-instance learning and semi-supervised learning. In: Ghahramani, Z. (ed.) Proceedings of the 24th International Conference on Machine Learning (ICML 2007), pp. 1167–1174. ACM, New York (2007)

85. Zhou, Z., Zhang, M.: Neural networks for multi-instance learning. Technical report, Department of Computer Science and Technology, Nanjing University, Nanjing, China (2002)

86. Zhou, Z., Jiang, K., Li, M.: Multi-instance learning based web mining. Appl. Intell. **22**(2), 135–147 (2005)
87. Zitzler, E., Laumanns, M., Thiele, L.: SPEA2: improving the strength Pareto evolutionary algorithm. Eurogen **3242**(103), 95–100 (2001)

Chapter 5
Bag-Based Classification Methods

Abstract In bag-based multi-instance methods, the main learning process occurs at the level of bags. In this chapter, we analyze two important subcategories of bag-based MIL classifiers. On the one hand, in Sect. 5.2, we examine classifiers that define a distance or similarity measure between bags to work directly in the original bag space. On the other hand, Sect. 5.3 is devoted to mapping-based classifiers that transform each bag to a single-instance representation such that the learner can train any single-instance classifier to label new bags.

5.1 Introduction

As opposed to instance-based classification methods, the learning process of bag-based methods occurs at bag level. The main feature that distinguishes bag-based from instance-based classifiers is that the former can predict the label of a new bag considering each training bag as a whole entity, without the need to discover any hidden instance labels. Instance-based classification methods need to construct an instance classifier that is as accurate as possible, but this is not a requirement for bag-based methods. Although some types of bag-based classifiers do train an instance-level learning model, it is only used as a rough guide to the main bag-level learning process. Moreover, the MI assumption of bag-based methods need typically not be as precise as is the case for instance-based methods, but can be more flexible and general. We discuss the following two important subcategories of bag-based methods:

- **Bag-based methods that work in the original bag space**: these methods rely on a metric function defined over bags. The metric is used in a distance-based classification algorithm, e.g., a nearest neighbor algorithm. By introducing the bag-wise distance measure, the learner is effectively upgraded to a full-fledged MI classification algorithm. We refer to these methods as *original bag space classification methods* (original-BS methods, for short) and discuss them in more depth in Sect. 5.2.
- **Bag-based methods that work in a mapped space**: these methods transform the multi-instance data into a single-instance representation and train a single-instance

© Springer International Publishing AG 2016
F. Herrera et al., *Multiple Instance Learning*, DOI 10.1007/978-3-319-47759-6_5

classifier on the transformed data. The same transformation is applied to an unseen bag and its class label is predicted by the single-instance classifier learned in the mapped space. We refer to these methods as *mapped bag space classification methods* (mapped-BS methods, for short). They are discussed in Sect. 5.3.

5.2   Original Bag Space Methods

In single-instance learning, each instance is interpreted as a point in a multidimensional space determined by the features of the problem at hand. Many traditional single-instance learning algorithms rely on a distance function between points of this space to determine separating boundaries between classes. In MIL, bags can be understood as regions in the instance space and a bag-wise distance function is required to evaluate similarity relations between them. Using such a bag-wise distance function in a traditional distance-based learning algorithm, it becomes a multi-instance algorithm able to locate bag class boundaries. The two main design options of any bag-distance-based classification method are

- **A distance-based classification method**: we describe two distance-based methods: nearest neighbor methods (Sect. 5.2.1) and kernel methods (Sect. 5.2.2).
- **A bag-wise distance/similarity function**: recall that similarity functions can be used instead of distance functions by inverting the objective function of the learner. Both types of comparison measures are complementary and using one or the other depends on the definition of the bag label prediction method. In Sect. 3.5, we listed several distance and similarity functions that can be used in these algorithms.

5.2.1   Nearest Neighbor Methods

The CitationKNN algorithm was proposed in [20] and extends the traditional single-instance k-nearest neighbors method (KNN) to the level of bags. To classify a new bag X, CitationKNN uses a distance function between bags to determine which training bags are closest to X. Inspired by the concept of citations in the field of information science, this algorithm extends the set of nearest neighbors to consider not only the r bags closest to X (references, Fig. 5.1), but also the bags for which X is among the c closest bags (citers, Fig. 5.2). A voting scheme uses the class labels of both references and citers to determine the class label of X.

Any bag-wise distance function can be used in CitationKNN (see Sect. 3.5). In particular, the study of [20] uses the minimal Hausdorff distance (3.18), maximal Hausdorff distance ((3.19), (3.20)) and k-th ranked Hausdorff distance (3.22).

The distance function employed in CitationKNN has a major impact on its performance [2]. Each application domain can benefit more from a certain distance function than from others and some applications may require the selection of a less

Fig. 5.1 References. The *circle* encompasses the nearest 3-references to X (*filled balls*). The closest references correspond to the (traditional) nearest neighbors

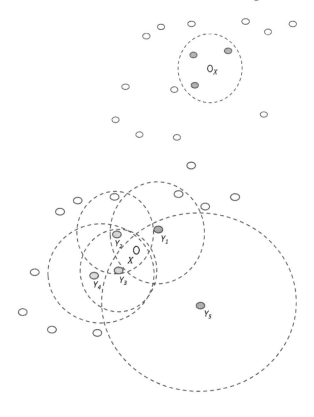

Fig. 5.2 Citers. The 3-citers nearest to X (*filled balls*) are those whose three nearest neighbors include X. Each *circle* contains the three nearest neighbors of the sample located at its *center*. For clarity, we have only represented *circles* including X. These are the 3-nearest citers to X

conventional metric. For example, the work of [27] on a web mining application adapts CitationKNN for text data represented by sets of terms, rather than the traditional attribute-value vector representation suffering from the so-called curse of dimensionality. They represent an instance x by a set of textual terms $\{t_1, t_2, \ldots, t_n\}$, where t_i $(i = 1, \ldots, n)$ is one of the n more frequent terms in the text fragment corresponding to x. They use the minimal Hausdorff distance variant, i.e., $k = 1$ in (3.22), and define a distance function between two instances $a = \{a_1, a_2, \ldots, a_n\}$ and $b = \{b_1, b_2, \ldots, b_n\}$ as

$$\|a - b\| = 1 - \sum_{\substack{i,\, j\, =\, 1 \\ a_i = b_j}}^{n} \frac{1}{n},$$

based on the idea that the fewer common terms two instances share, the greater the distance between them.

CitationKNN has been extended to regression tasks [8], clustering [13] and multi-label classification [24]. It has been used successfully in several application domains, such as textual classification [21] and anomaly detection [23].

5.2.2 Bag-Level SVM

Bag-level kernels are used to measure the similarity between two bags in a transformed representation space. They operate on whole bags and return a single number assessing how close the two bags are. As stated in Sect. 3.5, the similarity is inversely related to the distance. Kernel-based methods, as well as distance-based ones, rely on space metrics to find the separating class boundaries. When a bag-level kernel is used in a standard SVM, the latter becomes able to optimize the margin between bag classes without any modification to the SVM itself. One of the first bag-level kernels was presented by Gärtner et al. [11]. They define the set kernel between two bags A and B as

$$k_{MI}(A, B) = \sum_{a \in A, b \in B} k_I^p(a, b),$$

where k_I is a kernel defined at the instance level. Theoretically, for sufficiently large values of p, this kernel ensures the separability of the training set. Because of the computational cost involved in the MI kernel above, [11] defines a minimax kernel based on the minimum and maximum attribute values of instances in each bag, namely

$$k(A, B) = (\langle s(A), s(B) \rangle + 1)^p,$$

where $s(\cdot)$ defines the attribute transformation

$$s(X) = \left\langle \min_{x \in X} x_1, \ldots, \min_{x \in X} x_m, \max_{x \in X} x_1, \ldots, \max_{x \in X} x_m \right\rangle.$$

In the MI kernels proposed by Gärtner et al. [11], all attributes are treated with equal weight. On the other hand, Blaschko et al. [3] propose conformal kernels which can locally reduce or expand each attribute dimension based on the discriminative importance of each attribute, while preserving the angles between vectors in the transformed space.

Kwok and Cheung [14] present marginalized kernels, that assume that the data are generated by a latent variable model. The observed variable is the bag and the hidden variable is its label. In particular, let $Z_1 = (X_1, \ell_1)$ and $Z_2 = (X_2, \ell_2)$ be two bags with their respective class labels. A joint kernel is defined as

$$k_Z(Z_1, Z_2) = \sum_{i=1}^{n_1} \sum_{j=1}^{n_2} k_\ell(\ell_{1i}, \ell_{1j}) k_x(x_{1i}, x_{2j}),$$

where $k_\ell (\cdot, \cdot)$ is a kernel defined over the instance labels and $k_x (\cdot, \cdot)$ is a kernel defined over the instance space. The marginalized kernel, defined over two observed variables X_1 and X_2, is obtained by taking the expectation of the joint kernel with respect to the hidden variables ℓ_1 and ℓ_2, that is,

$$k (X_1, X_2) = \sum_{\ell_1 \in \mathbb{L}} \sum_{\ell_2 \in \mathbb{L}} P (\ell_1, X_1) P (\ell_2, X_2) k_Z (Z_1, Z_2). \qquad (5.1)$$

It is possible to calculate this marginalized kernel in polynomial time. The posterior distribution of ℓ_1 and ℓ_2 is obtained from a probabilistic model $P (\ell_i | X_i)$ estimated from the data.

Bag-level kernels make an implicit transformation of bags into a single-instance representation such that standard SVMs can be directly applied to multi-instance data. In Sect. 5.3, we show that an explicit transformation of the bags can also be set up to obtain a single-instance dataset on which any single-instance learner can be trained and used to predict bag labels.

5.3   Mapped Bag Space Methods

The multi-instance classification algorithms described in Chap. 4 and Sect. 5.2 are based on single-instance classifiers that have been modified to function in the MIL setting. Although good results have been reported in many applications for these multi-instance algorithms, the high cost of developing new algorithms today limits the applicability of this approach. There is only a small number of multi-instance algorithms compared to the large number of methods and algorithmic variants that have been developed for single-instance learning.

In this section, we examine another approach to solving multi-instance classification problems. Instead of using a modified single-instance classifier, a transformation is applied to the multi-instance data resulting in a single-instance representation of bags. In this new data representation, it is possible to construct a classification model using any traditional single-instance algorithm, effectively solving the multi-instance classification problem. The single-instance representation of multi-instance data not only allows the use of any single-instance classifier, but also the application of data preprocessing techniques, such as editing, cleaning, and dimensionality reduction, which have been well studied in single-instance learning.

In map based methods, the learning process occurs at bag level, but always relies on a mapping process. These methods transform the original multi-instance representation, in which each bag is a set of points (instances) in the attribute space, into another form of representation in which each bag is represented as a single point of the induced space. The multi-instance problem effectively becomes a single-instance problem to which any traditional learning algorithm can be applied.

Map based methods differ among each other in their specific mapping processes. In general, the following procedure is used. The methods are based on a function

$\mathscr{M} : \mathbb{N}^X \to \langle a_1, \ldots, a_d \rangle$ that transforms the multi-instance representation of a bag X into a single vector $\mathscr{M}(X) = \langle a_1, \ldots, a_d \rangle$. The multi-instance training set is transformed in a single-instance training set by applying the function $\mathscr{M}$ to each training bag. Any suitable single-instance classifier is built on the new training set. To classify a new bag, it is first converted to the new space using $\mathscr{M}$ and is then fed to the classifier which predicts a label class. By representing a bag as a point in the new space, some of the inherent ambiguity and imprecision of the multi-instance dataset can be reduced. However, as it is practically impossible to eliminate it completely, some of the original ambiguity remains encoded in the attribute values of each vector. The amount of the ambiguity reduction depends on the design of the mapping function $\mathscr{M}$.

Mapping-based classification algorithms differ primarily in the design of $\mathscr{M}$ and the mapping process. Below, we examine each of these mapping strategies and the classifiers that use them. For a better understanding, we have made a division in four categories, considering the meaning of the attributes in the new representation space

- **Mapping methods based on bag statistics (Sect.** 5.3.1): each attribute of the new mapping space is the value of a statistic that is applied to the set of values of the corresponding attribute in the original representation space.
- **Mapping methods based on representative instance concatenation (Sect.** 5.3.2): each vector of the new mapping space is the concatenation of N instances of the bag, where each instance is a representative of one pattern in the instance space.
- **Mapping methods based on counting (Sect.** 5.3.3): each attribute of the new mapping space indicates presence, amount or frequency of instances of the bag in a specific region of the instance space.
- **Mapping methods based on distance (Sect.** 5.3.4): each attribute of the new mapping space represents the distance (or similarity) of the bag to a specific region of the instance space.

5.3.1 Mapping Methods Based on Bag Statistics

Bag statistics-based methods seek to represent each bag by a single attribute vector that summarizes the statistical information of the bag. Consider a bag $X = \{x_1, \ldots, x_n\}$ in which each instance is described by d attributes, i.e., $x_i = \langle x_i^1, \ldots, x_i^d \rangle$, $\forall i \in [1, \ldots, n]$. The bag can be seen as a set of d random variables with unknown probability distribution, for which we have a sample of size n. Several statistics can be used to characterize the probability distribution of these random variables. In the new attribute space, in which the multi-instance examples are mapped, each attribute of the original space is represented by one or more statistic values, that attempt to capture the shape of the probability distribution of the original variable within the bag. We list some examples of the kind of transformation performed on the bags

- **Average mapping**: $M(X) = \langle m_1, \ldots, m_d \rangle$, where m_j is the mean value of the jth attribute over all the instances of X. This transformation is used by the SimpleMI algorithm described in [7] and included in the experiments of Sect. 5.4.
- **Min-Max mapping**: $M(X) = \langle a_1, \ldots, a_d, b_1, \ldots, b_d \rangle$, where $a_j = \min_i (x_i^j)$ and $b_j = \max_i (x_i^j)$ are the minimum and maximum values of the jth attribute over all the instances in X. This transformation is used by the Min-Max kernel proposed by [11].
- **Moments mapping**: $M(X) = \langle m_1, \ldots, m_d, v_1, \ldots, v_d, s_1, \ldots, s_d, k_1, \ldots, k_d, \rangle$. The values m_j, v_j, s_j and k_j represent the first to fourth statistical moment (i.e., mean, variance, skewness, and kurtosis) of the jth attribute of the instances in X.

The dimension of the new mapped space is the number of dimensions of the original space multiplied by the number of statistics used to describe each variable.

Stratified Bag Statistics

The methods described above are limited to summarize statistical information of *all* instances inside the bag and do not consider that within the same bag different patterns can coexist. In different instance patterns, one or more attributes can have different probability distributions. If all instances of the bag are treated as if they belonged to the same pattern, the statistics will be unable to adequately describe the mixture of distributions. A more sophisticated mapping method can try to discover patterns or classes of instances in the data and represent each bag in the embedded space with the statistics values of each original attribute for each instance pattern separately. We call *stratified bag statistics-based mapping*.

   The most common way to discover instance patterns in the data is to use unsupervised methods, since instance class labels are unknown. Unsupervised methods allow to find groups of instances with shared characteristics. These groups can be considered as different instance classes. We can also use supervised methods, assuming that instances are assigned to the same class labels of their bags. Clearly, this assumption can cause a certain proportion of mislabeled instances, but the goal is to obtain a first approximation of the underlying instance-level patterns. From this first approximation, a learning algorithm can be trained to obtain a more accurate instance-level classifier.

   Learning methods based on stratified bag statistics represent each bag by a single attribute vector with statistical information of the different patterns or instance classes contained in the bag. The new attribute values related to each instance pattern are concatenated in the vector describing the bag. Let $C_1, \ldots, C_k$ be instance patterns found in the data and $\theta : \mathbb{N}^{\mathscr{A}} \to \mathbb{R}$ a statistic (e.g., average, minimum, maximum, or moments) applicable to the d attributes of a set of instances. The stratified bag statistics based mapping is defined as

$$M(X) \mapsto \langle \theta_{11}, \ldots, \theta_{1d}, \theta_{21}, \ldots, \theta_{2d}, \ldots, \theta_{k1}, \ldots, \theta_{kd} \rangle, \tag{5.2}$$

where θ_{ij} represents the statistic value applied to the jth original attribute of the instance subset in the bag belonging to the ith pattern. Equation 5.2 represents the case where each attribute probability distribution is described by a single statistic, but in general several statistics can be used for each attribute. The dimension of the new embedded space is $d \times k \times q$, where d is the number of dimensions of the original space, k is the number of patterns or classes of instances discovered in the data and q is the number of statistics used to describe each original attribute distribution (e.g., in the Min-Max mapping two statistics are used, so $q = 2$).

5.3.2 Mapping Methods Based on Prototype Concatenation

This approach was introduced by Boughorbel et al. [4]. They look for k instance patterns in the data and characterize each pattern C_i through its center p_i. However, instead of using statistics operating on individual attributes, they use a function $\varphi(X, p_i) : \mathbb{N}^{\mathbb{X}} \times \mathbb{X} \to \mathbb{X}$ to select the instance in the bag closest to the center p_i of the ith pattern and use that instance as the pattern representative. The mapping by Boughorbel et al. can be defined as $M(X) \mapsto \langle v_1, v_2, \ldots, v_k \rangle$, where v_i is the instance from X that is closest to the center p_i of the ith pattern. The authors use this transformation to construct an SVM with an ad hoc kernel. However, as with all mapping methods described in this chapter, any other single-instance learning algorithm can be applied to the mapped data as well.

This method can be generalized so that an aggregation of all instances of the bag is used to represent the matching degree between the bag and the instance pattern. Let $S(x, C) \in [0, 1]$ be a function that measures the matching degree between an instance x and a pattern C. A natural way of defining $S(x, C_i)$ is as a similarity measure between instance x and the center of the ith pattern p_i. The vector v_i can be calculated as

$$v_i = \frac{\sum\limits_{x \in X} x \cdot S(x, C_i)}{\sum\limits_{x \in X} S(x, C_i)}, \tag{5.3}$$

which represents the average of the instances weighted by their matching degree with the pattern. This method is related to the stratified statistic mapping method described in Sect. 5.3.1. When the matching function $S(x, C)$ is binary, so that $S(x, C)$ equals 1 if the similarity between x and C is above a given threshold and $S(x, C)$ equals 0 otherwise, we can use (5.2) to compute v_i using the average as the only statistic. In the other case, if the matching function takes on continuous values in the interval [0, 1], we have a generalization of (5.2), where the value of each attribute is weighted with a matching degree.

5.3.3 Mapping Methods Based on Counting

This group of methods represent each bag as a single vector, where each attribute is the number of instances of the bag that are found in a specific region of the instance space. In other words, they describe the relationship between the bag label and instance classes covered by different regions of the instance space.

Multi-instance classifiers using a counting-based mapping are strongly inspired by the MI assumptions hierarchy of Weidmann et al. (Sect. 3.4.2). Some algorithms create binary attributes in the mapping process, where the ith attribute indicates the presence or absence of instances of the bag in the ith region. These algorithms allow to model the presence-based assumption, including the standard MI assumption. Other algorithms create attributes that take on positive numeric values representing absolute or relative frequencies of the instances belonging to the bag and lying inside the corresponding region. These algorithms allow to model the threshold and counting-based MI assumptions.

We can further divide this group into two major categories the acquisition of the MI assumption into account. On the one side are those algorithms for which the designers decide in advance which MI assumption is used. This category is examined in Sect. 5.3.3.1. On the other side we consider the algorithms for which no MI assumption has been specified. They learn the hypothesis from the data during execution. Section 5.3.3.2 is devoted to these methods.

5.3.3.1 Using an a Priori Count-Based MI Assumption

The best known algorithm using a count-based MI assumption is GMIL, which first appeared in [17]. GMIL stands for Generalized Multiple Instance Learning and is indeed a generalization of the standard MI assumption. The presence-based MI assumption of the Weidmann hierarchy is generalized by GMIL as well. However, it cannot represent learning problems obeying the threshold or counting based MI assumption, because the attributes constructed in the mapping are binary.

Like all algorithms using count-based assumptions, GMIL first identifies regions of the instance space that will be used in a second step to map bag attributes. Regions are identified systematically and exhaustively. All possible axis-parallel boxes in the instance space are explicitly enumerated. As an illustration, consider a discrete d-dimensional instance space $\mathbb{X} = \{1, \ldots, v\}^d$ in a two-class classification problem. In a one-dimensional space ($d = 1$), if the attribute has two possible values ($v = 2$), there are three possible axis-parallel boxes as shown in Fig. 5.3. If the space has two dimensions and each dimension can take one of two possible values, there are nine possible axis-parallel boxes as shown in Fig. 5.4. If the space has three dimensions, each with two possible values, there are 27 possible axis-parallel boxes as shown in Fig. 5.5. In general, there are $N = (v(v+1)/2)^d$ possible axis-parallel boxes in a d-dimensional space. The reason why the regions have axis-parallel box shapes is because the infinite norm is used to determine distances in the instance space. This norm defines the length of a d-dimensional vector x as $\|x\|_\infty = \max\{|x_1|, \ldots, |x_d|\}$, the largest absolute value of its components. GMIL creates two Boolean attributes for each box, indicating whether a bag contains an instance within that box. To reduce the number of attributes, boxes containing the same set of points are grouped together and only one representative box for each group is used.

Fig. 5.3 There are three
axis-parallel boxes when
$d = 1$

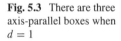

Fig. 5.4 There are nine
axis-parallel boxes when
$d = 2$

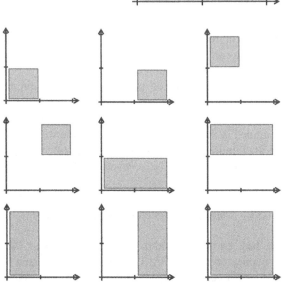

Concretely, GMIL maps a bag X to $M(X) = \langle a_1, \ldots, a_N, \overline{a}_1, \ldots, \overline{a}_N \rangle$. The algorithm sets a_i to 1 if any point of X is contained by the ith box and sets it to 0 otherwise. It sets $\overline{a}_i = 1 - a_i, \forall i \in [1, \ldots, N]$. All information is encoded by the N first attributes. This would be sufficient for many learning algorithms. However, GMIL was originally designed to learn monotone disjunctions using the Winnow classifier [15]. Since Winnow generates formulas generated only containing disjunctions of the input variables, the negations of the first N attributes must also be supplied such that any logical combination of the initial variables can be formed.

Once the bags have been mapped to Boolean attributes, the algorithm tries to learn the target concept using a specific MI assumption based on theoretical results from geometric pattern recognition [12]. In the standard MI assumption, a single positive instance inside a bag determines that the bag belongs to the positive concept. Instance labels are typically determined by the proximity of the instance to a single target point, but GMIL can represent more general concepts. It represents a concept by a set of target points, more specifically, a set of attraction points, which can be seen as instances from an ideal positive bag. GMIL can also include a set of repulsion points, which can be seen as instances from an ideal negative bag. In this setting, a bag is positive if and only if it is sufficiently close to attraction points and sufficiently far from repulsion points.

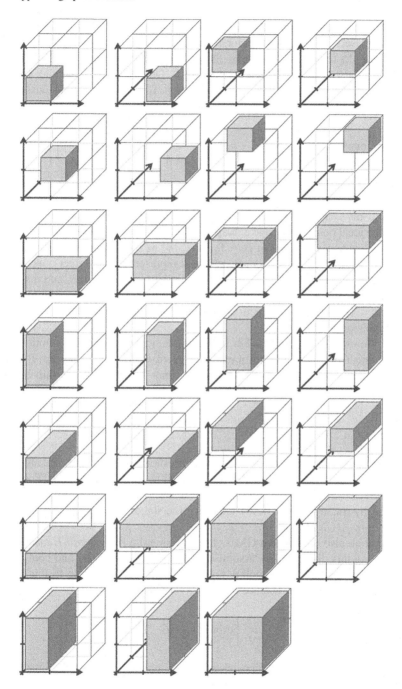

Fig. 5.5 There are 27 axis-parallel boxes when $d = 3$

GMIL's notion of distance between bags is based on the Hausdorff distance. Recall from Sect. 3.5 that the Hausdorff distance between two sets of points P and Q is defined as the largest distance from either a point in P to its nearest neighbor in Q or from a point in Q to its nearest neighbor in P. Due to its use of the max operator, the Hausdorff distance is sensitive to outlier points. To improve the robustness against noise, Scott et al. use the *ranked full-Hausdorff* distance

$$\max\left\{\max_{p\in P}^{s}\left\{\min_{q\in Q}\{\|p-q\|_{\infty}\}\right\}, \max_{q\in Q}^{s}\left\{\min_{p\in P}\{\|p-q\|_{\infty}\}\right\}\right\}, \qquad (5.4)$$

in which instead of using the largest distance, the sth largest distance is used. In (5.4), $\max^{s}$ denotes the sth largest value, P represents the pattern and Q is the model. Positive bags are within a ranked full-Hausdorff distance of some threshold γ from the ideal positive bag and at least a ranked full-Hausdorff distance of γ' away from the ideal negative bag. Let $Q = \{q_1, \ldots, q_k\}$ be the set of attraction points and $\overline{Q} = \{\bar{q}_1, \ldots, \bar{q}_{k'}\}$ the set of repulsion points representing the target concept. The concept can be modeled as a set of k axis-parallel attraction boxes and a set of k' axis-parallel repulsion boxes. A bag is positive if and only if it contains points within at least $r = k - s$ of the k attraction boxes and contains points within at most s of the k' repulsion boxes.

The Winnow algorithm is used in [17] to implement the GMIL assumption. Winnow is a linear-threshold algorithm that learns r-of-k threshold functions. It assigns nonnegative real-valued weights w_a to each attribute a. Weights are iteratively modified to find a hyperplane

$$\sum_{i=1}^{N} a_i w_{a_i} + \bar{a}_i w_{\bar{a}_i} = \theta,$$

which separates both classes, where θ is the threshold determined by the algorithm. The $k + k'$ more weighted attributes are selected at the end of training. The values of the selected attributes correspond to the k attractions plus k' repulsion points identified by the algorithm. In the classification stage, a bag is labeled positive if $a_{i_1} + \cdots + a_{i_k} + \bar{a}_{i_1} + \cdots + \bar{a}_{i_{k'}} \geq r$.

Scott et al. also presented a GMIL variant using the *ranked half-Hausdorff distance*. Using this distance they assume that the model is accurate and compute the distance from the bag to the model, but not vice versa. According to this variant, positive bags are within a distance

$$\max_{q\in Q}^{s}\left\{\min_{p\in P}\{\|p-q\|_{\infty}\}\right\} \qquad (5.5)$$

of some threshold γ to the ideal positive bag and, including repulsion points, beyond a distance

$$\min_{q\in Q}^{s'}\left\{\min_{p\in P}\{\|p-q\|_{\infty}\}\right\} \qquad (5.6)$$

of another threshold γ' to the ideal negative bag. As before, the concept is a set of k axis-parallel attraction boxes and a set of k' axis-parallel repulsion boxes. A bag is positive if and only if it contains points within at least $r = k - s$ of the k attraction boxes and contains points within at most s' of the k' repulsion boxes. Note that, in contrast to the full-Hausdorff distance model, the number of points s which are tolerated to not fall in attraction boxes can be different to the number of points s' which are tolerated to fall in repulsion boxes. Though it was theorized that the half-Hausdorff variant should be more robust against noise and more able to avoid overfitting, empirical results show a higher generalization ability of the full-Hausdorff variant on data from several domains.

GMIL has a theoretically sound foundation. However, it is not a practical learning method, since it has a very high time complexity. In the sequence of Figs. 5.3, 5.4 and 5.5 it can be seen that the number of boxes grows exponentially as d increase. A real application, with a moderate number of attributes, like Musk, is unfeasible to be solved by GMIL. The strategy of using a reduced number of instances to build the learning model [18] fails because, when the dimension is not trivially small, in order to significantly reduce the computational cost, the number of instances must be so small that it becomes insufficient to build an accurate model. A kernel-based reformulation is another strategy used to improve the efficiency of GMIL. The kernel performs the feature mapping implicitly and allows a support vector machine to be applied directly to the data. However, computing the kernel on two bags requires counting the number of boxes that contain at least one instance from each of both bags, which again leads to severe scalability issues and quickly renders the problem intractable as the problem size increases. To address this issue, a fully polynomial randomized approximation scheme (FPRAS) was presented in [19], reducing the time complexity from exponential to polynomial.

5.3.3.2 Learning a Count-Based MI Assumption

In Chap. 4, we showed that instance-based methods make strong assumptions regarding the MI hypothesis. Each instance-based algorithm implements a specific MI assumption: some algorithms are based on the standard MI assumption, others on the collective assumption, and so on. The GMIL algorithm discussed in Sect. 5.3.3.1 has a MI assumption wired in its design as well. In these methods, the MI assumption is not only used in the classification stage to determine the bag label, but also in the training stage to impose restrictions to help determine the class likelihood of instances. If the imposed MI assumption does not conform reasonably well to a given dataset, then the algorithm cannot build an appropriate learning model for it. Each algorithm is only appropriate for those problems which conform to the applied MI assumption.

Unlike instance-based methods and methods like GMIL that have a specific MI assumption embedded in their design, mapping-based algorithms described in this section do not assume a priori the existence of a specific relationship between the labels of each bag and of its instances. This relationship is learned from the data instead, in the form of a count-based MI assumption. Training occurs in two steps

1. The method tries to identify regions in the instance space using either supervised or unsupervised methods. These regions appear as a result of the instance space structure.
2. The underlying MI assumption is learned. This is the relationship between the bag labels and the instance space regions identified in the first step. To this end, a new representation space is built, in which each attribute corresponds to one of the regions. Each bag is mapped into this new space, such that the value of the ith attribute indicates the presence or frequency of instances of the bag in the ith region. Any single-instance learning model can be built on this new single-instance training set.

Methods in this category differ fundamentally in the way they identify instance patterns, i.e., in the first step described above. In the Two-Level Classification (TLC) algorithm [22], a standard decision tree is used for this purpose. The tree is built on all instances of all training bags. Each instance is assigned to its bag's class label. Instances are weighted such that all training bags have equal weight in the construction of the learning model. Each node in the tree represents a region of the instance space. In the second step, each bag is mapped to a new representation in which each attribute contains the number of instances of the bag that have reached the corresponding node in the tree.

Constructive Clustering Ensemble (CCE) [25] uses a clustering algorithm to determine the regions. The k-means algorithm is used to obtain a number of groups whose centers are stored. In the second step, each bag is mapped to a new representation in which each attribute indicates the presence of instances of the bag in the corresponding group. An instance belongs to a group g if its distance to the center of g is less than its distance to the center of the other groups. As it is not possible to determine the optimal number of groups in advance, CCE generates many classifiers, each obtained from a number of different groups, and then combines their predictions in a majority vote.

Since these algorithms do not make a priori assumptions about the nature of the relationship between bags and instances underlying the data, they can learn a wider variety of problems. For example, all algorithms based on the standard MI assumption take for granted that there are two classes of instances (positive and negative). Algorithms learning the MI assumption during training can find an arbitrary number of classes in the instance space and can discover relationships between bags and instances that best fit the training data.

5.3.4 Mapping Methods Based on Distance

In count-based mapping methods, the attribute values of each bag are defined by the location of instances of the bag inside a delimited region of instance space corresponding to that attribute. The notion of an instance membership to a region is strict. It only accepts two extreme possibilities: the point either belongs or does not belong to the region, depending on which side of the border of the region the point is located. The fact that we can only have a vague idea of the borders of the instance regions is ignored. In many applications, perfectly delimited regions boundaries make no sense. For example, if tall people are an important region of the instance space, it is difficult to determine where we should start the region, at 1.70 m, 1.80 m, or 1.85 m? Any such value would be merely conventional. However, we can say that if an instance is near the center of a region we can have a great certainty that it falls within the region. The farther an instance is located from the center, the less likely it belongs to the region. This is the idea behind distance-based mapping methods: each attribute value in the output space is related to the distance from the bag to the center of a region.

These methods try to identify instance regions that are representative of the structure of the instance space. Regions can be obtained through a clustering or classification model constructed from training instances. A prototypical point is recorded at the center of each region. In some cases, prototypes of only one class (usually the positive class) are used. In other cases, they are determined for each class. Each attribute of the induced space corresponds to one of the prototypes found in the original space. The attribute value is a distance measure (or a similarity measure) between the bag and the prototype. Note that the bag contains many points (instances), while the prototype is a single point. Specific distance functions between bags and prototypes have to be used. Distance functions used in these cases are usually aggregations of distances between the instances of the bag and the prototype. Distance-based mapping methods differ in how instance prototypes are determined and in their definition of the distance function.

One of the first algorithms using this type of mapping was DD-SVM [5]. This algorithm selects instance prototypes for both classes based on the values of the diverse density (DD) function. Under the diverse density framework, a prototype for class C is a point of the instance space with a high probability of being found in bags of class C. Prototypes are local extrema of the DD function, where the positive prototypes are maxima and the negative prototypes minima. To locate the prototypes, gradient descent methods are used over the DD function. To find the positive prototypes, optimization processes are started from each instance of the positive bags, while for negative prototypes, searches start from each instance of the negative bags. The located prototypes are used to map each bag to the new representation space. Using T prototypes, a bag X is transformed as

$$\mathcal{M}(X) = \langle S(t_1, X), \ldots S(t_T, X) \rangle, \tag{5.7}$$

where t_i represents the ith prototype and $S(t_i, X)$ is a distance measure between the bag X and t_i. Specifically, in [5] an absolute distance measure $S(t, X) = \min_j \|x_j - t\|$ is used. The authors apply an SVM to the bags represented in the mapped space to obtain a bag classification model. In general, as with all mapping methods, any single-instance learning algorithm can be used to build this model as well.

The MILES algorithm [6] was introduced by the same authors as DD-SVM. Instead of looking for class prototypes in each bag, MILES uses all training instances as reference points to construct the new bag space. In other words, each instance is treated as a prototype. The new representation space has as many attributes as the total number of instances in the training set. More formally, let $\mathbf{X} = \{X_1, \ldots X_m\}$ be the training bag set. We align the instances inside the bags and renumber them to get the set of instances $\{t_k | \exists X_i \in \mathbf{X} : t_k \in X_i\}$, $k = 1, \ldots, T$, where $T = \sum_{i=1}^{m} n_i$. We use (5.7) to map a bag X to the output space. To calculate the value of the ith attribute, MILES uses the Gaussian similarity function given by

$$S(t, X) = \max_{j} \exp\left(-\frac{\|x_j - t\|^2}{\sigma^2}\right), \tag{5.8}$$

where σ is a parameter to scale the attributes.

MILES is more computationally efficient than DD-SVM, because it avoids the expensive optimization procedure over the diverse density function, which DD-SVM must perform for every instance. Chen et al. [6] have shown that MILES is as good as and sometimes superior to DD-SVM in generalization accuracy and it is also more robust with respect to label noise.

The MILES mapping can be seen as a method for determining the weight of each instance. Indeed, the SVM applied to the mapping space calculates a weight for each attribute which is normally used for feature selection. The attributes of the mapped space are precisely the instances of the training bags, which allows to determine the influence of different parts of the instance space. However, MILES does not create a well-defined weight function over the instance space, because the max operator, used in (5.8) that determines the value of each attribute, only takes into account the influence of the nearest instance of the bag to the target point, resulting in a bag-dependent weight function [9]. Foulds et al. [9, 10] proposed the YARDS algorithm, which is similar to MILES in almost everything except in that YARDS can find a true weight function over the instance space. By replacing the max operator with the sum operator, that is, by setting

$$S(t, X) = \sum_{j} \exp\left(-\frac{\|x_j - t\|^2}{\sigma^2}\right),$$

the bag-dependence in the similarity function is removed. In YARDS, each instance of the bag has an influence on the bag-level classification and that influence only depends on the attributes of the instance and not on the rest of the bag.

5.3.5 Bag-Level Distance Mapping Methods

In the mapping methods included in Sects. 5.3.3 and 5.3.4, bags are described by their relationships with instance-level spatial structures. This mapping relates instance space regions with bag classes. Another way to transform a multi-instance problem into a single-instance one is by describing each bag through the spatial relationship it has with the other bags of the training set. In this case, the mapping is done at the bag level, but instance space regions are ultimately related to bag classes, since bags are represented by multiple vectors in the instance space. However, in this mapping each instance maintains the relationship with its bag, making it a more informative mapping than that which only includes instance-level relations.

The idea of bag-level distance mapping methods has been developed by Zhang and Zhou [26] with their BARTMIP algorithm. The work scheme of BARTMIP is shown in Fig. 5.6. A multi-instance clustering model is built on the training bags, dividing them in k groups. Each group is represented by its medoid, i.e., the most central bag. Each bag is mapped to a vector of k attributes, one for each group of bags. The ith attribute value of a bag is the distance from the bag to the ith medoid. All training bags are mapped with this form of representation. It results in a single-instance training set on which a single-instance classification algorithm is trained. In the prediction step, the new bag is mapped in the same way to a vector of k attributes and processed by the single-instance classification model.

The components of this algorithm can be selected from a wide variety of choices. BATRMIP can train any single-instance classification algorithm and use any multi-instance clustering algorithm. Multi-instance clustering algorithms are described in Chap. 7. Specifically, in [26], BARTMIP uses a multi-instance clustering algorithm called BAMIC (Sect. 7.1.4.1), which is an adaptation of the single-instance k-medoids clustering algorithm to the multi-instance setting. Many multi-instance clustering methods depend on a bag-level distance function which in turn uses an instance level distance function. Distance functions at bag and instance levels are other components of the model that should be chosen. The optimal number of groups to be generated in the clustering step can be determined by cross-validation. An alternative is to build several clustering models, each with a different number of groups, and train a classifier model from each grouping. The ensemble prediction is obtained by majority vote.

5.4 Experimental Analysis

In this section, we empirically compare the performance of some representative bag-based MIC methods. We show experimental results for both original-BS methods and mapped-BS methods and compare the two strategies. These experiments are only intended for illustration purposes and cannot be taken as a rigorous comparison

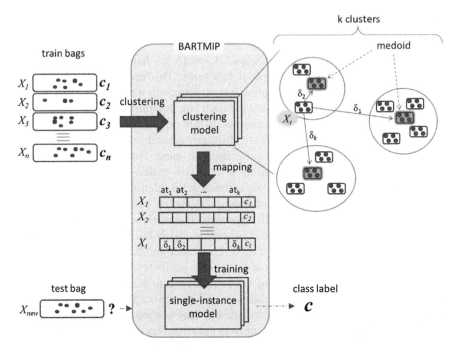

Fig. 5.6 BARTMIP algorithm

among classifiers. The experimental setup is specified in Sect. 5.4.1, while Sect. 5.4.2 presents the results.

5.4.1 Setup

We use the same datasets as in the experimental study of Chap. 4, described in Table 4.1. The algorithms included in the study are named in the first column of Table 5.1. The second column describes the method type. CitationKNN and MISMO are representative algorithms that work on the original bag space. The other algorithms are mapping methods, one of each type described in Sect. 5.3 with the exception of prototype concatenation discussed in Sect. 5.3.2. Prototype concatenation mapping methods have been excluded due to their high memory requirements. They are appropriate to use in small problems, but even for medium-sized datasets (as some are in these experiments) it is difficult to make comparative studies.

Unlike methods that work on the original bag space and construct an specific classifier, a mapping method can train any standard classification algorithm. Their performance depends on both the mapping method and the learner used as base classifier. In order to get a better idea of the mapping method qualities, we try each

Table 5.1 Bag-based classification algorithms to be compared

Algorithm	Category
CitationKNN	Original-BS distance-based methods
MISMO	Bag-level kernel methods
SimpleMI	Bag statistic mapping methods
MILES	Distance-based mapping methods
CCE	Count-based mapping methods
BARTMIP	Bag-level distance mapping methods

alternative with five popular classification algorithms: one nearest neighbor (1NN), C4.5, logistic regression (LR), an SVM and AdaBoost with C4.5 as base classifier (AdaBoost). We use Weka implementations for algorithms in the first four rows of Table 5.1, while the last two were implemented by us. A rough optimization was made for the most important parameters of each method looking for those yielding the best result across all the datasets. We use default parameter settings for each algorithm if not specified otherwise. We use the fivefold cross-validation procedure and evaluate the performance of the classifiers by means of their accuracy (Sect. 1.4).

5.4.2 Results and Discussion

In Sect. 5.4.2.1, we show empirical results of the selected original-BS methods. We compare typical mapped-BS methods with each another using several base classifiers in Sect. 5.4.2.2. Finally, we compare the original-BS and mapped-BS based classifiers in Sect. 5.4.2.3.

5.4.2.1 Original-BS Methods

Table 5.2 presents the experimental results of two original-BS methods, namely CitationKNN and a bag-level SVM. The latter is a standard SVM using the Gärtner et al. MI kernel described in Sect. 5.2.2 with the standard RBF instance-level kernel. The table lists the best results for each algorithm after a simple parameter adjustment was done looking for the best average result over all data. The results shown for CitationKNN were obtained with $C = 2$ and $R = 2$ and those for SVM with $C = 1.0$ and $\gamma = 0.5$. The last two rows of the table show the average accuracy and the standard deviation of each classifier over the nine datasets. The best accuracy is highlighted in bold for each dataset. SVM is the winner in six out of nine cases, while CitationKNN

Table 5.2 Classification accuracy for methods working in the original bag space

Dataset	CitationKNN	SVM
Musk1	**89.13**	88.04
Musk2	**84.16**	83.17
Atoms	70.21	**74.47**
Bonds	74.47	**85.11**
Chains	73.40	**84.57**
WIR	64.60	**69.91**
TREC	47.75	**74.75**
Beach	**82.00**	80.50
Fox	50.00	**61.00**
Average	70.64	**77.95**
SD	14.42	**8.70**

wins in three datasets. The higher average accuracy of SVM supports the idea that it has a significantly better performance than CitationKNN over the studied problem domains. The lower standard deviation of the SVM means that its good performance is more evenly distributed across all datasets than that of the CitationKNN, which instead obtains very good results in a few datasets, but poor results in many of them.

5.4.2.2   Mapped-BS Methods

Table 5.3 presents a summary of the experimental results of the selected mapped-BS methods using five base classifiers. The average accuracy computed over the nine datasets along with the confidence interval with a significance level $\alpha = 0.05$ is shown for each pair of mapping method and classifier. The algorithm parameters were set as follows: $\sigma = 250$ in MILES, 60% of clustering in BARTMIP, five iterations in CCE and 10 iterations in Adaboost. The SVM in all mapping methods uses an RBF kernel with $C = 10.0$ and $\gamma = 0.5$. The most accurate mapped-BS method for each base classifier is highlighted in bold. SimpleMI obtains the best performance for three classifiers: C4.5, SVM, and Boosting. BARTMIP is the best performing mapped-BS method for the 1NN and LogReg classifiers. This suggests that SimpleMI and BARTMIP are two of the most accurate mapped-BS methods overall, since they achieve the highest quality predictions with several base classifiers over a range of datasets from different application domains.

Table 5.4 presents the detailed experimental results of each mapped-BS method executed with its best base classifier following the conclusions of Table 5.3. The highest accuracy for each dataset among the four methods is marked in bold. SimpleMI and BARTMIP are again the most outstanding algorithms, as each one wins in four datasets. With respect to the application domains, it seems that SimpleMI is best suited for molecular activity prediction, while BARTMIP looks like the leader

Table 5.3 Average classification accuracy of mapping methods using different base classifiers

Base classifier	SimpleMI	MILES	BARTMIP	CCE
1NN	74.99 ± 6.32	72.47 ± 5.77	75.24 ± 8.21	70.55 ± 6.79
C4.5	76.73 ± 5.41	68.54 ± 8.04	73.42 ± 6.17	67.19 ± 5.55
LogReg	70.07 ± 5.75	69.81 ± 4.34	78.59 ± 5.75	74.00 ± 5.54
SVM	79.18 ± 6.81	69.09 ± 7.84	78.58 ± 8.47	70.40 ± 6.31
Boosting	76.77 ± 5.19	70.16 ± 8.70	74.81 ± 6.78	69.32 ± 5.19

Table 5.4 Classification accuracy for best performing mapping method schemes

Dataset	SimpleMI	MILES	BARTMIP	CCE
Musk1	91.30	77.17	84.78	80.43
Musk2	91.09	66.34	85.15	74.26
Atoms	73.40	80.85	84.04	78.19
Bonds	84.57	79.79	82.45	79.26
Chains	85.64	79.79	86.17	77.66
WIR	62.83	61.06	63.72	73.45
TREC	75.75	68.25	71.50	68.25
Beach	82.50	80.00	83.00	80.50
Fox	65.50	59.00	66.50	54.00

in the image recognition domain. In the next section, we delve deeper into this topic when we compare all bag-based methods to each other.

5.4.2.3 Overall Comparison

In Sects. 5.4.2.1 and 5.4.2.2, we pointed out the most accurate classifiers of each type. We are now interested to make an overall comparison between original-BS and mapped-BS methods in order to discover their advantages and disadvantages. The best performing model of each type is taken into account in this comparison. Two original-BS methods and four mapped-BS methods are included.

To discover which method is the best option in each case, we first separate the results by application domain. In Fig. 5.7, we depict the accuracy of the methods on the biochemical applications. Note that the accuracy axis values start at 40 to better distinguish the differences between the methods. SimpleMI, BARTMIP, and MISMO dominate in almost all datasets, while CitationKNN and MILES are not stable in their results. It is remarkable that BARTMIP performs quite good in the five datasets.

In Figs. 5.8 and 5.9, we show the accuracy of the methods on datasets from the textual and image domain, respectively. From these charts, we can not identify one algorithm that is superior to the others in any of these domains. The advantage

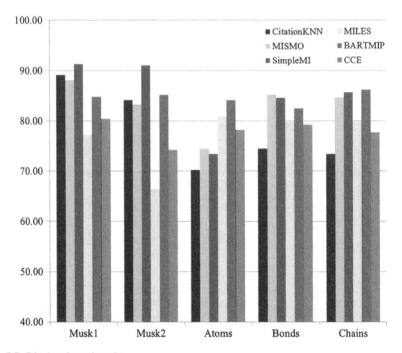

Fig. 5.7 Biochemistry domain

Fig. 5.8 Textual domain

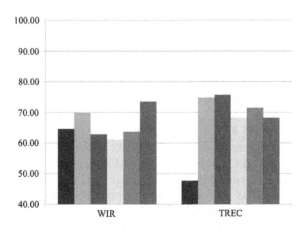

(discussed in the previous section) of BARTMIP over SimpleMI on image datasets
is negligible. We can only point out some general trends. CitationKNN and MILES
have again poorer results compared to the other methods. SimpleMI, BARTMIP and
MISMO excel in most datasets. Figure 5.10 shows the average accuracy of the six
methods over the nine datasets and supports the above statement.

We are also interested in analyzing the training time of the models. Figure 5.11
shows the average training time of the six methods over the nine datasets. Note that

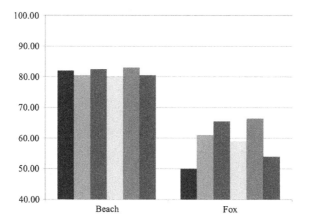

Fig. 5.9 Imaging domain

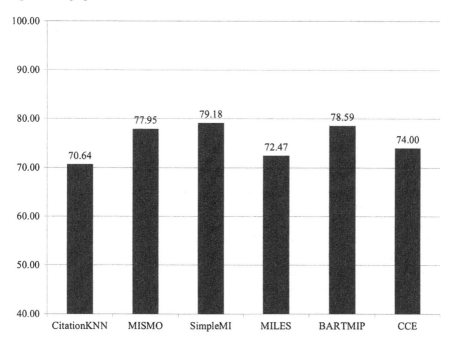

Fig. 5.10 Average accuracy of selected bag-based classification methods over the experimental datasets

a logarithmic scale is used to represent time intervals, such that differences between methods can be correctly perceived. Time values are given in seconds, but we are mostly interested in the relative time proportions of the different models. The training

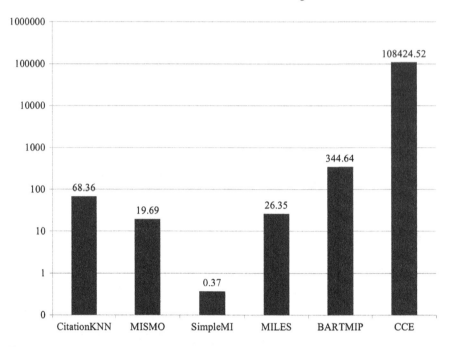

Fig. 5.11 Average training time of selected bag-based classification methods over the experimental datasets

time of CitationKNN is mainly devoted to the calculation of bag-level distances,[1] whereas kernel calculations made by MISMO are three times faster than the work of CitationKNN. The very small training time of SimpleMI is one of the most remarkable things in the figure. The key lies in the simplicity of its mapping method. MILES has a fair training time complexity, which is in line with its moderately simple mapping method. Conversely, BARTMIP training has a considerable time complexity. This method has a much more complex mapping method, that includes bag-level distance calculations and bag-level clustering. Finally, training CCE takes a long time. It includes instance-level distance calculations and instance-level clustering, that are much more time demanding than their bag-level relatives.

5.5 Comparing Instance-Based, Bag-Based, and Traditional Classification Methods

In Chap. 4 and this chapter, we discussed two classifier families that work very differently: one of them learns at the instance level, the other at the bag-level. In both

---

[1]The implementation used for CitationKNN calculates the neighbor list of each bag in the training step.

cases, we have presented comparative experiments on the performance of several representative members of each family. An obvious question is how these two families compare. This does not have an easy answer and has been the subject of study of some recent work [1, 2]. There is another more basic question that some researchers have put forward [1, 16], namely whether multi-instance classifiers outperform single-instance classifiers in all multi-instance datasets.

Ray and Craven [16] found that single-instance classification algorithms can perform well for several MIL problems, outperforming MI classifiers in some cases. This strongly impacts the MIL community, as occasional reports have shown that MI classifiers with good success records were beaten by simple single-instance models in some datasets.

Alpaydin et al. [1] designed artificial datasets with increasing complexity levels, corresponding to more and more complex dependencies between instances in a bag. They compare instance-based, bag-based, and single-instance classifiers on artificial datasets of different sizes and levels. Their conclusion was that, in general, single-instance classifiers can only handle the simplest MIL problems corresponding to the lowest complexity level, instance-based classifiers are good to solve problems from the first and second complexity levels and bag-based classifiers can solve problems from the first three levels. Datasets from the fourth complexity level require even more advanced classification methods. Alpaydin et al. also found that datasets where single-instance classifiers outperform multi-instance methods are those with the lowest complexity level and with a small number of bags, because there is not enough data to train the bag-level classifiers.

This explanation clarifies the general relation that appears between algorithms and data complexity. Nevertheless, we should keep in mind that no classifier exists that can handle all different application domains. Faced with a new MIL problem, the best algorithm might be an instance-based, a bag-based or a traditional classifier.

5.6 Summarizing Comments

Bag-based classification algorithms are an important group of MIC methods. They predict the bag class mainly using information at the bag level. They do not strive to predict instance class labels and have more flexible and generals MI assumptions. Several bag-based methods have appeared in the literature. According to their main features, we organize them in a category system depicted in Fig. 5.12. There are two principal categories of bag-based classifiers: (i) methods that operate on the original bag space by relying on a distance, similarity or kernel function and (ii) methods that use a mapping function to transform the data to a single-instance representation, such that single-instance classifiers can be trained and used to predict bag labels. Several types of transformations have been developed. Some mapping functions are based on simple bag statistics. Others represent the new space by concatenating prototypes extracted from the training bags. Other mapping methods count the number

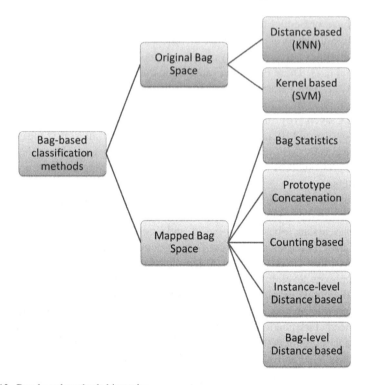

Fig. 5.12   Bag-based methods hierarchy

of instance of the bag falling in specific regions of the instance space and yet others compute the distance from the bag to the centers of these regions.

The experimental study shows that each of the discussed methods can attain high accuracy in some application domains. Nevertheless, we do not recommend CCE because of its large training time and uncertain performance. We advise the use of SimpleMI, because it often attains a very good accuracy and is very fast to train. BARTMIP is also a good option, because of its stable performance over several domains.

References

1. Alpaydin, E., Cheplygina, V., Loog, M., Tax, D.M.: Single-versus multiple-instance classification. Pattern Recognit. **48**, 2831–2838 (2015)
2. Amores, J.: Multiple instance classification: review, taxonomy and comparative study. Artif. Intell. **201**, 81–105 (2013)
3. Blaschko, M., Hofmann, T.: Conformal multi-instance kernels. In: Schölkopf, B., Platt, J.C., Hoffman. T. (eds.) Proceedings of the 19th Conference on Advances in Neural Information Processing Systems (NIPS 2006), pp. 1–6. MIT Press, Cambridge (2006)

4. Boughorbel, S., Tarel, J.P., Boujemaa, N.: The intermediate matching kernel for image local features. In: Proceedings of the International Joint Conference on Neural Networks (IJCNN 2005), pp. 889–894. IEEE, Los Alamitos (2005)
5. Chen, Y., Wang, J.: Image categorization by learning and reasoning with regions. J. Mach. Learn. Res. **5**, 913–939 (2004)
6. Chen, Y., Bi, J., Wang, J.: MILES: multiple-instance learning via embedded instance selection. IEEE Trans. Pattern Anal. **28**, 1931–1947 (2006)
7. Dong, L.: A Comparison of Multi-instance Learning Algorithms. Master thesis, The University of Waikato, New Zealand (2006)
8. Dooly, D.R., Zhang, Q., Goldman, S.A., Amar, R.A.: Multiple-instance learning of real-valued data. J. Mach. Learn. Res. **3**, 651–678 (2002)
9. Foulds, J.: Learning instance weights in multi-instance learning. Master thesis, The University of Waikato, New Zealand (2008)
10. Foulds, J., Frank, E.: A review of multi-instance learning assumptions. Knowl. Eng. Rev. **25**(1), 1–25 (2010)
11. Gärtner, T., Flach, P.A., Kowalczyk, A., Smola, A.: Multi-instance kernels. In: Sammut, C., Hoffmann, A. (eds.) Proceedings of the 19th International Conference on Machine Learning (ICML 2002), pp. 179–186. Morgan Kaufmann Publishers, San Francisco (2002)
12. Goldman, S.A., Kwek, S.S., Scott, S.D.: Agnostic learning of geometric patterns. J. Comput. Syst. Sci. **62**(1), 123–151 (2001)
13. Henegar, C., Clément, K., Zucker, J.D.: Unsupervised multiple-instance learning for functional profiling of genomic data. In: Fürnkranz, J., Scheffer, T., Spiliopoulou, M. (eds.) Proceedings of the 16th European Conference on Machine Learning (ECML 2006), pp. 186–197. Springer, Berlin (2006)
14. Kwok, J., Cheung, P.: Marginalized multi-instance kernels. In: López, R., Veloso, M.M. (eds.) Proceedings of the 20th International Joint Conference on Artificial Intelligence (IJACI 2007), pp. 901–906. IJCAI/AAAI Press, Hyderabad (2007)
15. Littlestone, N.: Learning quickly when irrelevant attributes abound: A new linear-threshold algorithm. Mach. Learn. **2**(4), 285–318 (1988)
16. Ray, S., Craven, M.: Supervised versus multiple instance learning: an empirical comparison. In: De Raedt, L., Wrobel, S. (eds.) Proceedings of the 22nd International Conference on Machine Learning (ICML 2005), pp. 697–704. ACM, New York (2005)
17. Scott, S., Zhang, J., Brown, J.: On generalized multiple-instance learning. Int. J. Comput. Int. Sys. **5**(1), 21–35 (2005)
18. Tao, Q., Scott, S.: A faster algorithm for generalized multiple-instance learning. In: Valerie, B., Zdravko, M. (eds.) Proceedings of the 17th International Florida Artificial Intelligence Research Society Conference (FLAIRS 2004), pp. 550–555. AAAI Press, Menlo Park (2004)
19. Tao, Q., Scott, S.D., Vinodchandran, N.V., Osugi, T.T., Mueller, B.: Kernels for generalized multiple-instance learning. IEEE T Pattern Anal. **30**(12), 2084–2098 (2008)
20. Wang, J., Zucker, J.: Solving the multiple-instance problem: a lazy learning approach. In: Langley, P. (ed.) Proceedings of the 17th International Conference on Machine Learning (ICML 2000), pp. 1119–1126. Morgan Kaufmann Publishers, San Francisco (2000)
21. Wei, H., Yu, W.: Text representation and classification based on multi-instance learning. In: Lan, H., Yang, Y.-H. (eds.) Proceedings of the 10th International Conference on Management Science and Engineering Management (ICMSE 2009), pp. 34–39. IEEE, Los Alamitos (2009)
22. Weidmann, N., Frank, E., Pfahringer, B.: A two-level learning method for generalized multi-instance problems. In: Lavrac, N., Gamberger, D., Blockeel, H., Todorovski, L. (eds.) Proceedings of the 14th European Conference on Machine Learning (ECML 2003), pp. 468–479. Springer, Heidelberg (2006)
23. Yang, W., Gao, Y., Cao, L.: TRASMIL: a local anomaly detection framework based on trajectory segmentation and multi-instance learning. Comput. Vis. Image Underst. **117**(10), 1273–1286 (2013)
24. Zhang, M.: A K-nearest neighbor based multi-instance multi-label learning algorithm. In: Grégoire, E. (ed.) Proceedings of the 22nd International Conference on Tools with Artificial Intelligence (ICTAI 2010), pp. 207–212. IEEE, Los Alamitos (2010)

25. Zhou, Z., Zhang, M.: Solving multi-instance problems with classifier ensemble based on con-
    structive clustering. Knowl. Inf. Syst. **11**(2), 155–170 (2007)
26. Zhang, M., Zhou, Z.: Multi-instance clustering with applications to multi-instance prediction.
    Appl. Intell. **31**(1), 47–68 (2009)
27. Zhou, Z., Jiang, K., Li, M.: Multi-instance learning based web mining. Appl. Intell. **22**, 135–147
    (2005)

Chapter 6
Multi-instance Regression

Abstract Regression is a popular machine learning task that aims to predict a numerical outcome. In multi-instance regression (MIR), each observation can be described by several instances. After a brief introduction to this topic in Sect. 6.1, we present a formal definition of MIR and its appropriate evaluation measures in Sect. 6.2. We organize the MIR methods in two main categories. Algorithms that focus on individual instances of each bag in their construction of a regression model are examined in Sect. 6.3, while Sect. 6.4 discusses methods that treat bags as single entities to create a regression model operating at the bag level. Section 6.5 lists some summarizing remarks.

6.1 Introduction

The multi-instance regression task (MIR) is the natural extension of traditional (single-instance) regression to the multi-instance setting. MIR models the data in the same way as MIC, with the important difference that each bag is associated with a real-valued outcome and not a class. The MIR objective is to approximate, based on the training bags, a function that can predict the outcome of future bags as accurately as possible. In Sect. 6.2, we present a more formal description of MIR. Compared to the traditional regression task, the ambiguity introduced by the multiple descriptions for every bag as well as the lack of information on how these descriptions relate to the bag label make MIR intrinsically more challenging.

MIR has been studied much less than the multi-instance classification task. Nevertheless, it is of great importance for two main reasons. On the one hand, regression provides a theoretical basis to understand many classification methods and can generate useful ideas to the design of more effective classifiers. On the other hand, an important motivation for the development of new algorithms is that many real-life applications can be successfully modeled as MIR problems. These include drug activity prediction, landmark recognition, remote sensing systems, age estimation, and sentiment analysis (see Sect. 2.4.7).

We have already shown that MIC methods can be grouped into two major categories, namely instance-based and bag-based methods. MIR methods can be divided

© Springer International Publishing AG 2016
F. Herrera et al., *Multiple Instance Learning*, DOI 10.1007/978-3-319-47759-6_6

into these two categories as well. Instance-based MIR methods try to determine a regression function for one prime instance, a subgroup of instances or all instances inside the bag. The bag label is a function of the prime instance label or an aggregation of several instance labels. This group of methods is discussed in Sect. 6.3. Bag-based MIR methods treat each bag as a whole entity. These methods can rely on bag-wise distance or kernel functions or can be based on mapping functions that represent bags as single vectors on which single-instance regression models can be learned. Section 6.4 is devoted to bag-based MIR methods.

6.2   MIR Formulation

We begin our discussion on MIR methods with a brief description of the setting and objective of this learning task. Evaluation measures to assess the quality of MIR models are presented as well.

6.2.1   Problem Description

In a MIR problem, the training set $D = (\mathbf{X}, \mathbf{Y})$ consists of m bags $\mathbf{X} = \langle X_1, \ldots X_m \rangle$ and their corresponding real-valued labels $\mathbf{Y} = \langle y_1, \ldots y_m \rangle$ with $(\forall i = 1 \ldots m)(y_i \in \mathbb{R})$. Each bag X_i has n_i instances $\{x_{i1}, \ldots, x_{in_i}\}$ and each instance x_{ij} is described by d features. In the simplest case all features take on real values, but in general real-valued features can be mixed with categorical ones. Instance labels are not available. The goal of MIR is to determine a function f over the bag space $\mathbb{N}^{\mathbb{X}}$ which can make predictions $\hat{y}_i = f(X_i)$ of the label y_i of new bags X_i as accurately as possible.

A geometrical view of MIR is presented in Fig. 6.1. If we project the bag space in a Cartesian plane, each bag can be viewed as a region in that plane. For simplicity, the bag space in Fig. 6.1 has only two features $\mathscr{X}_1$ and $\mathscr{X}_2$. Bag labels are represented as scores on the $\mathscr{Y}$ axis, orthogonal to the $\mathscr{X}_1$–$\mathscr{X}_2$ plane. When there is an infinite number of bags covering the whole bag space, their label ordinates form a surface over the plane. MIR aims to find a function f that is the best possible approximation to that surface. As a consequence, f is sometimes referred to as the regression surface.

6.2.2   Evaluation Measures

Evaluation measures are needed to assess how well the regression function f approximates the real process. Any validation scheme (Sect. 1.4.1) can be used as appropriate to the problem at hand. Despite the difference in data representation, MIR is similar to traditional regression in the type of variable to be predicted. The same evaluation metrics can therefore be used. The most common evaluation measures used for

Fig. 6.1 Geometrical view
of MIR

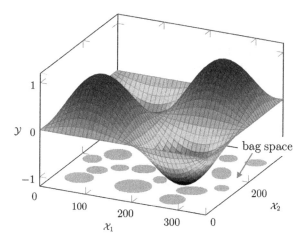

regression are the mean absolute deviation (MAD) computed as

$$MAD = \frac{1}{n} \sum_{i=1}^{n} |y_i - f(X_i)|$$

and the mean squared error (MSE) given by

$$MSE = \frac{1}{n} \sum_{i=1}^{n} (y_i - f(X_i))^2 .$$

In both cases, the actual label y_i is compared with the predicted outcome $f(X_i)$ and their differences are averaged over n test bags. In MSE, these differences are squared, such that larger errors are penalized more.

6.3 Instance-Based Regression Methods

Chapter 4 showed that instance-based classifiers perform their main learning process at instance level. The same goes for instance-based regression methods. Attention is payed to the individual instances within the bags. In general, one representative instance is selected or generated for each bag and a regression model is constructed over these instances. Any traditional single-instance regression learner can be used, since it is fitted with just one instance from each bag. The most important design option of instance-based regression methods is the way to model the relation of instances with the bag label. Two assumptions dominate the MIR literature

- **The prime instance assumption (Sect.** 6.3.1): there is a single instance in every bag which is responsible for the bag label. Algorithms based on the prime instance assumption strive to select this "correct" instance in the bag.
- **The collective assumption (Sect.** 6.3.2): each instance in the bag makes a (possibly different) contribution to the bag label. Methods based on this assumption try to determine the weight that each instance has in the prediction of the bag label.

A second source of differences between instance-based methods lies with the selection of the regression model and solution procedure to be used. Commonly, one assumes a class of regression functions f on X depending on a set of parameters Θ, i.e., $f \equiv f(X, \Theta)$. As an example, consider the class of linear regression functions consisting of a hyperplane determined by a normal vector W. To guarantee that the obtained regression model $f(X, \Theta)$ is the best possible approximation according to the training data, an optimization approach

$$\Theta^* = \arg\min_{\Theta} \sum_{i=1}^{m} L(y_i, f(X_i, \Theta)) + \lambda R(\Theta) \qquad (6.1)$$

must be adopted. In expression (6.1), L is a loss function that indicates how well the prediction model performs and $R(\Theta)$ is a regularization term favoring simple models and thereby avoiding data overfitting. The parameter $\lambda > 0$ is a trade-off between prediction accuracy and model complexity. The optimization solution Θ^* is the best set of parameters defining the optimal regression model. Several loss functions and regularization forms can be used in (6.1). For example, when squared loss is combined with squared norm regularization we can obtain a closed form solution. In other cases, gradient descent optimization methods need to be applied to find an approximation. As this is a typical formulation of regression models, abundant explanations can be found in any modern machine-learning book.

    In the following sections, we provide an in-depth analysis of the most relevant assumptions involved in instance-based regression methods. Representative algorithms are briefly described in each case.

6.3.1 Prime Instance Assumption

This approach assumes that the bag label is determined by only one instance in the bag, namely the primary or prime instance. The remaining instances are considered noisy observations of the prime instance. This assumption was proposed in the seminal work of Ray and Page [12] and has had a great impact on MIR works that followed. Inspiration was drawn from the standard MIL assumption for classification, which states that a single positive instance in a bag suffices for a positive bag label (Sect. 3.4.1).

6.3.1.1 Prime-MIR Algorithm

Formally, the prime-instance algorithm looks for the optimal regression model $f(x, \Theta)$ in (6.1) based on the set of prime instances $\{x_{1p}, \ldots, x_{mp}\}$, where x_{ip} is the prime instance in bag X_i. The general prime-instance regression model is defined as

$$\Theta^* = \arg\min_{\Theta} \sum_{i=1}^{m} L\left(y_i, f\left(x_{ip}, \Theta\right)\right) + \lambda R(\Theta). \tag{6.2}$$

In [10], the authors prove that the exhaustive search of the set of prime instances satisfying (6.2) has an NP-complete computational complexity. An approximating solution method is used in the form of an expectation-maximization (EM) algorithm. First, prime instances are selected at random from each bag. This initial guess is subsequently refined by iterating between expectation and maximization steps. In the maximization step, a new regression model is trained by using the current hypothesis of prime instances. In the expectation step, new candidates of prime instances are found by selecting the instance from each bag that has the lowest prediction error according to the current regression model. These steps are repeated until convergence.

The regression model $f(x, \Theta)$ obtained by means of (6.2) represents the hyperplane Θ that best approximates the prime instance outcomes, which in turn are supposed to be the best approximation of the bag labels. When a new bag is presented to the model, its prime instance needs to be located in order to evaluate the model and obtain the bag label. However, the model of Ray and Page [12] does not provide any information on which element is the prime instance. Although Cheung and Kwok [4] and Ray [10] identified problem domains in which it is possible to assume that the prime instance is the one with the largest output value, it is not possible to generalize this heuristic to other domains. Wang et al. [20] suggest a statistical solution by using the mean of the predictions of all instances in the new bag X_i, namely

$$\hat{y}_i = mean\left(f(x_{i1}), \ldots, f\left(x_{in_i}\right)\right). \tag{6.3}$$

To increase the prediction robustness against outliers, the median of the instance predictions can be more appropriate in some applications

$$\hat{y}_i = median\left(f(x_{i1}), \ldots, f\left(x_{in_i}\right)\right). \tag{6.4}$$

While the original proposal [10] was very simple and uses a non-regularized linear regression model, the general prime-instance model is more sophisticated. In particular, nonlinear models can also be applied, as for example neural networks [20]. Another improvement is proposed by Wang et al. [20]. Instead of initializing prime instances at random, the first selection can be based on predictions made by a simple MIR model constructed on the training data. Prime-instance regression algorithms have been used as benchmark in several studies [9, 19, 20].

6.3.1.2   Two Levels Regularization Framework

In Sect. 4.5, we described the MI-SVM method [2], an instance-based classification
SVM based on the standard MIL assumption. It selects a primary instance from each
bag and trains a standard SVM with these instances. In Sect. 5.2.2, we described the
MI kernel [7], a kernel defined over whole bags. It allows for an SVM to be used at
bag level in the classification of multi-instance data. Cheung and Kwok [4] translate
both ideas to the regression setting and connect them in a unified framework. A
general loss function that depends on both the training bags and training instances
is defined. This function is split into two parts. The first part considers the loss
between each bag label y_i and its prediction $f(X_i)$, using the hinge loss function
$\max(0, 1 - y_i f(X_i))$. The second part considers the loss between the prediction of
each bag $f(X_i)$ and those of its constituent instances $\{f(x_{ij}) | j = 1, \ldots, n_i\}$. It can
be defined in various ways. Cheung and Kwok present margin formulations for
the L1 loss $\ell(v_1, v_2) = |v_1 - v_2|$, the L2 loss $\ell(v_1, v_2) = (v_1 - v_2)^2$ and the ε-
insensitive loss $\ell(v_1, v_2; \varepsilon) = \max(0, |v_1 - v_2| - \varepsilon)$. The complete loss function is
defined as

$$V\left(\{X_i, y_i, f(X_i)\}_i, \{f(x_{ij})\}_{ij}\right) = \frac{1}{m} \sum_{i=1}^{m} \max(0, 1 - y_i f(X_i))$$
$$+ \frac{\lambda}{m} \sum_{i=1}^{m} \ell\left(f(X_i), \max_j f(x_{ij})\right), \quad (6.5)$$

where λ is a parameter that trades off the two components. Based on the fact that an
instance can also be considered as a bag of size one, they use the representer theorem
and the Constrained Concave–Convex Procedure (CCCP) to solve the problem as
a quadratic programming problem, which guarantees the convergence to a local
optimum. As the max operator is not a smooth function, the gradient is replaced by
a convenient sub-gradient in each iteration of the CCCP procedure.

   In regression problems, the loss functions has two parts as well. The first part
considers the loss between the value of each bag and its corresponding prediction.
As in ν-support vector regression [13], they use the ε-insensitive loss and an extra
$\nu\varepsilon$ term (where ν is a user-defined parameter) to penalize the value of ε. The second part considers the loss between the prediction of each bag and those of its
constituent instances. Following Ray and Page [12], they assume that there is one
primary instance in each bag that is responsible for the output of the bag, which is
set to the one with the highest output value. By introducing slack variables δ_i, ξ_i, ξ_i^*
the following optimization problem is presented:

$$\min_{w,b,\xi,\xi^*,\varepsilon,\delta} \frac{1}{2}\|w\|^2 + Cv\varepsilon + \frac{C}{m}\sum_i\xi_i + \frac{C}{m}\sum_i\xi_i^* + \frac{C\lambda}{m}\sum_i\delta_i$$

$$\begin{aligned}
s.t. \quad & f(X_i) - y_i \le \varepsilon + \xi_i, \\
& y_i - f(X_i) \le \varepsilon + \xi_i^*, \\
& -\delta_i \le f(X_i) - \max_j f(x_{ij}) \le \delta_i \\
& \xi_i, \xi_i^*, \delta_i, \varepsilon \ge 0.
\end{aligned} \tag{6.6}$$

Different loss functions for MI regression can be used. Both bags and instances directly participate in the optimization process.

6.3.1.3 Probabilistic Prime-MIR Algorithm

The above prime-instance methods make strong assumptions on the prime instances. The probabilistic method of Wang et al. [19] assumes that each instance has a certain probability to be the prime instance of the bag. Under this assumption, the bag label is treated as a random variable described by the mixture model

$$p(y_i|X_i) = \sum_{j=1}^{n_i} \pi_{ij} p(y_i|x_{ij}), \tag{6.7}$$

where π_{ij} is the prior probability that the jth instance is the prime instance of the ith bag. The value $p(y_i|x_{ij})$ is the label probability in case the jth instance is the prime instance. In the mixture model (6.7), the contribution of each instance to the bag label is proportional to its probability of being the prime instance. The label of the ith bag can be predicted as the expected value of the mixture model, which is the weighted sum of the label probabilities for individual instances

$$\hat{y}(X_i) = \sum_{j=1}^{n_i} \pi_{ij}(\boldsymbol{\theta}_g) f(x_{ij}, \mathbf{w}),$$

where the prior probability π_{ij} is a function of the model parameters $\boldsymbol{\theta}_g$ and $f(x_{ij}, \mathbf{w})$ is a regression function with parameters $\mathbf{w}$. The parametrized probabilities π_{ij} and $p(y_i|x_{ij})$ are learned from the data using the expectation maximization algorithm. Model parameters are randomly initialized at first. Later, expectation and maximization steps are alternated until convergence. In the expectation step, the algorithm evaluates the expected value of the log-likelihood of the training data with respect to the current estimate of the model parameters. In the maximization step, the algorithm updates these parameters to maximize the expectation. The framework allows for the prime instance probability to be modeled as appropriate to the application at hand. The method was successfully applied to two remote-sensing applications [19].

6.3.1.4   Prime Instance-Based Applications

The prime instance assumption has been used in several real-life applications. In [15], it was applied to the prediction of protein-ligand binding affinities to guide optimization in structure-based drug discovery. A bag corresponds to a protein-ligand pair and its instances are binding poses. The binding affinity of the ligand to a particular protein is to be predicted. The gradient boosting approach [6] is used, where an additive model $f(x) = \sum f_k(x)$ is constructed to minimize a squared loss function. In each boosting iteration, the instance with maximal output x_i^{max} is selected from the ith bag. It is based on the domain-specific assumption that the most plausible binding pose is that with the maximum predicted binding score. A new training set $R = \left\{ \left(x_i^{max}, r_i \right), i = 1, \ldots N \right\}$ is arranged from the N training bags, where $r_i = y_i - f\left(x_i^{max} \right)$ is the pseudo-residual from the bag label and the predicted output. This step effectively converts the initial MIR problem into a single-instance regression problem. A single-instance regression model $f_k(x)$ is trained on R and added to the boosting function $f(x)$ to decrease the value of the loss function.

Another application of the prime instance assumption has been in the prediction of polyp size in computed tomography images (CT) [8]. Polyps are precursors of cancer tumors and their dimension indicates cancer staging. A polyp is represented by a bag of polyp-like candidates extracted from a 3D CT scan. The polyp size y needs to be predicted. It is approximated by a hyperplane $w^T x$ described by the weight vector w. To make the size prediction, it is desirable to use the candidate whose segmentation is the closest to the actual layout of the polyp. Therefore, the authors assume that the primary instance is that whose estimated output $f(x) = w^T x$ differs the least from y, i.e., $\min |y - f(x)|$. Under this assumption, a ridge regression model is defined as

$$\min_{w} \sum_{j} \min_{i \in I_j} \left(y_j - w^T x_{ji} \right)^2 + \lambda \|w\|^2 ,$$

where I_j is the index set of instances belonging to the jth bag. Like the prime-instance algorithm described above, an EM approach is used to solve the optimization problem.

6.3.2   Collective Assumption

In Sect. 3.4.3, we described the collective MIL assumption for classification, which states that all instances in the bag contribute equally to the bag label. An extension of the collective assumption allows that each instance contributes independently, but not necessarily equally, to the class label of the bag. In this section, we consider a similar idea applied to the regression setting. The notion of a primary instance inside each bag is abandoned. Instead, all instances contribute equally to the bag label. We present an implementation of this assumption in Sect. 6.3.2.1. In the extended collective MIR assumption, not all instances have the same contribution to the bag label. Some instances are noisy and should be discarded, which is the idea behind the method described in Sect. 6.3.2.2. Alternatively, we can try to determine the weight that each instance has in the bag label formation. The algorithm described in Sect. 6.3.2.3 exploits that information to make its bag label predictions.

6.3.2.1 Instance-MIR Algorithm

The Instance-MIR algorithm is the regression counterpart of the wrapper classifier discussed in Sect. 4.2. Each instance x_{ij} from each bag X_i receives the label y_i of its bag. All instances are joined into a single-instance dataset $D = \{(x_{ij}, y_i), i = 1 \ldots m, j = 1 \ldots n_i\}$. To ensure that all bags are represented with the same importance in D, independently of their size, each bag is sampled with replacement and added to D the same number of times. An ordinary regression model f is trained on D. As in the collective assumption for classification (Sect. 3.4.3), the bag label probability is the expected outcome value of the instance population estimated by the sample mean (6.3). Alternatively, the median of the instance predictions (6.4) can be used in some applications to prevent outliers. The Instance-MIR algorithm has been used as benchmark in several studies [9, 11, 19, 20], showing competitive results on many datasets despite its simplicity.

6.3.2.2 Pruning-MIR Algorithm

The Instance-MIR algorithm, described in the previous section, uses all available training instances to construct the regression model. When bags contain many noisy instances, their inclusion can have a detrimental effect. On the other extreme, the Prime-MIR algorithm selects a single instance from each bag, which makes it highly probable that informative instances are discarded. The Pruning-MIR algorithm proposed in [20] is a compromise solution between these two extremes. The assumption is that each bag is generated by some random noise around a prime point in instance space. Bag labels are assumed to be generated by some function of the prime instances with added noise.

The algorithm aims to keep relevant instances from each bag, while removing those that seem noisy. It starts from the Instance-MIR solution. In each iteration, it discards a small fraction of the noisiest instances in each bag and trains a new predictor (using Instance-MIR) on the remaining instances. The noisiest instances in a bag are defined as those whose predictions are the farthest away from the median prediction over the non-pruned instances. In this way, noise is gradually removed and the quality of the training data is improved. The algorithm runs for as long as there is an improvement in prediction accuracy.

6.3.2.3   Weighted-MIR Algorithm

The weighted collective assumption states that each instance has a particular relevance or weight in the bag label generation. Under this assumption, the label $\hat{y}$ of a bag X_i can be calculated as the weighted aggregation of the prediction of bag instances, namely

$$\hat{y}(X_i) = \frac{\sum_j f\left(x_{ij}\right) w_{ij}}{\sum_j w_{ij}}, \tag{6.8}$$

where the denominator is present for normalization. However, expression (6.8) gives rise to problems. We need to determine both the instance weights w_{ij} and the regression model f.

Regression Based on Instance Weights

Wagstaff and Lane [16] develop a method to estimate instance weights in MIR under the assumption that each instance contributes independently to the bag label. Given a set of m bags $\{X_1, \ldots, X_m\}$ and their respective labels $Y = \{y_1, \ldots, y_m\}$, it is assumed that an exemplar p_i exists inside each bag X_i that can accurately predict the bag's true label, that is, $y_i = f(p_i)$. The exemplar can be described as a convex combination of instances, namely $p_i = \sum_j^{n_i} \psi_{ij} x_{ij}$, where $\psi_{ij} \geq 0$ and $\sum_j \psi_{ij} = 1$. Note that these two restrictions enforce p_i to fall within the convex hull of the points in X_i. The authors assume a linear regression $\hat{y}(p_i) = \Phi^T p_i$, where Φ is the vector of regression coefficients and p_i is a column vector. An optimization problem is defined according to the least squares objective dependent on $P = \{p_1, \ldots, p_m\}$, Y, Φ and the set of weight vectors $\Psi = \{\psi_1, \ldots, \psi_m\}$, $\psi_i = [\psi_{i1}, \ldots, \psi_{im}]^T$. The L_2 loss is used with regularization terms ε_1 and ε_2 for each ψ_i and Φ, respectively, yielding

$$\underset{\psi_1, \ldots, \psi_m, \Phi}{\arg \min} \sum_{i=1}^{m} \left[\left(y_i - \Phi^T X_i \psi_i\right)^2 + \varepsilon_1 \|\psi_i\|^2 \right] + \|\Phi\|^2$$

$$s.t. \ (\forall i, j)(\psi_{ij} \geq 0); \ (\forall i)(\sum_{j=1}^{n_i} \psi_{ij} = 1),$$

where the factor $X_i \psi_i$ represents the aggregation of the instances in the ith bag to one exemplar. This is a non-convex and difficult to optimize objective, because the minimization is with respect to both Φ and $\{\psi_i\}$ simultaneously. Wagstaff and Lane [16] propose an alternating projections solver, that alternates between two projection steps. First, the Φ values are fixed and each ψ_i is solved, which can be seen as a projection of Φ on the ψ_i space. Next, the ψ_i vectors are fixed and projected back onto the Φ space. The two steps are alternated until convergence.

Predicting Instance Weights

With the Wagstaff and Lane [16] optimization method we can obtain the coefficients Φ of the regression hyperplane as well as the instance weight vectors ψ_i for each training bag. Using the regression model Φ, we could compute the output of a new bag X_z as

$$\hat{y}(X_z) = \Phi^T X_z \psi_z,$$

where ψ_z is the weight vector representing the contribution of each instance in X_z to the label of X_z. Unfortunately, the method of Wagstaff and Lane [16] is unable to produce predictions. In their model, ψ_z is unknown, because the method can only find ψ_i for training bags. Pappas and Popescu-Belis [9] present a simple solution to this problem. They formulate another regression problem to predict instance weights of unlabeled bags as $\hat{\psi}_z = \Omega^T X_z$ where Ω are the coefficients of a linear regression model optimized over the weight vectors ψ_i of training bags. Assuming an ℓ_2-norm for the regularization with an ε_3 term, the optimization objective is

$$\arg\min_{\Omega} \sum_{i=1}^{m} \sum_{j=1}^{n_i} \left(\psi_{ij} - \Omega^T x_{ij} \right)^2 + \varepsilon_3 \|\Omega\|^2 .$$

Well-known least squares solving techniques can be used to solve this minimization task. The method allows to determine instance weights of an unlabeled bag and to predict its label. It was successfully applied to a sentiment analysis application [9]. In this case, a text is a bag of sentences and each sentence is modeled as a word vector. The desired prediction is a real-valued rating of the overall sentiment of the text with respect to a specific aspect.

6.4 Bag-Based Regression Methods

In bag-based regression methods the main learning process occurs at bag level. Like bag-based classifiers, regression methods that fall in this category can be further divided into two groups:

- **Bag-based regression methods that work in the original bag space**: these methods rely on a metric function defined over bags, which is used in a distance-based regression algorithm, e.g., a nearest neighbor algorithm. We refer to these methods as *original bag space regression methods* (original-BS methods, for short) and discuss them in more depth in Sect. 6.4.1.
- **Bag-based regression methods that work in a mapped space**: these methods transform the multi-instance data into a single-instance representation and train a single-instance regression algorithm in this transformed space. The same transformation is applied to an unseen bag and its outcome is predicted by the single-instance regression model learned in the mapped space. We refer to these methods as *mapped bag space regression methods* (mapped-BS methods, for short). They are discussed in Sect. 6.4.2.

6.4.1   Original Bag Space Methods

Any single-instance distance-based regression method can be upgraded to a MIR method by using an appropriate MIL metric. By virtue of this measure, the MIR model can be learned and used to make predictions in the original bag space.

The most popular algorithm in this category is RCitationKNN [1]. Its name makes reference to CitationKNN [18] for regression. The minimal Hausdorff distance (Sect. 3.5) is plugged into the CitationKNN algorithm. To obtain the prediction of a new bag, the closest neighbors (citers and references) are consulted and their outcomes averaged. The traditional KNN is also upgraded to MIL in [1].

As an alternative, a support vector regression model [14] can be transferred to the MIL setting by replacing its instance-level kernel by a bag-level kernel, for example the MI kernel [7].

6.4.2   Mapped Bag Space Methods

Mapping methods (Chap. 5) allow the transformation of bags into single-instance vectors. Once the MIL data has been mapped to a single-instance representation, any traditional classifier can be learned on the data. The same mapping methods can be used for regression and traditional regression models can be learned over the single-instance representations afterward. For example, in [21], the BARTMIP mapping is applied to MIR benchmark problems. Another illustrative example is the bioinformatic application described in [5] where the MILES mapping [3] is first applied and a support vector regression (SVR) model [14] is subsequently trained on the mapped data. We refer the interested reader to Sect. 5.3. Below, we discuss two mapping methods that are of particular interest, because they have been used as benchmarks in several studies on MIR [9, 19, 20].

6.4.2.1   Aggregate-MIR

The mapping step of the Aggregate-MIR algorithm [20] is similar to the average mapping described in Sect. 5.3.1. Each bag X_i is mapped to a single instance $(\bar{x}_i, y_i)$ where $\bar{x}_i$ is obtained by averaging all its instances, namely

$$\bar{x}_i = mean\left(\left\{x_{ij}, j = 1 \ldots n_i\right\}\right).$$

A single-instance set D is obtained after mapping all training bags. A traditional regression model is trained on it. To predict the label of a new bag X_i, we apply the mapping method to X_i and obtain the corresponding $\bar{x}_i$. The bag label is predicted as

$$\hat{y}(X_i) = f(\bar{x}_i).$$

The method can be more appropriate when the dataset has a low noise level and large bags. This simple method may be useful to initialize more advanced MIR methods.

6.4.2.2 Cluster-MIR

The Cluster-MIR algorithm [17] was set up for MIR problems with a structured instance space. The assumption is that instances in each bag are drawn from different underlying data distributions and that only one distribution is responsible for the bag label. The method can be considered as a generalization of Aggregate-MIR and is related to the stratified bag statistic mapping described in Sect. 5.3.1. The first step is to determine the space structure by the use of unsupervised learning. A soft clustering algorithm is applied over all instances of all training bags to identify k clusters. Training bags are mapped with respect to each cluster. A bag X is mapped with respect to a cluster θ as $\mathcal{M}(X, \theta) \mapsto \langle a_1, \ldots, a_d \rangle$, where $a_j = \sum_{i=1}^{m} r_{\theta i} x_{ij}$, x_{ij} is the value of the jth attribute in the ith instance of the bag X and $r_{\theta i}$ is the relevance of x_i with respect to the jth group. A total number k of single-instance datasets are obtained from the mapping of training bags with respect to each cluster. A regression model is constructed in each mapped dataset. The best regression model is selected based of the training data. At prediction time, a new bag is mapped with respect to the cluster corresponding to the selected regression model. Note that for $k = 1$, Cluster-MIR reduces to Aggregate-MIR.

6.5 Summarizing Comments

MIR is an important task within the MIL paradigm. Although the number of studies on MIR methods is small compared to the abundant literature on multi-instance classifiers, an increased interest on MIR is apparent in recent years. Current MIR methods can be categorized into two groups, instance-based methods and bag-based methods, much like the categories of classification methods. In a few cases, a traditional regression method is modified to the MIL setting. Mostly, the data is manipulated (e.g., an instance is selected, many instances are aggregated to a single instance per bag or bags are mapped to single vectors), such that traditional regression methods can be applied without modifications.

References

1. Amar, R., Dooly, D., Goldman, S., Zhang, Q.: Multiple-instance learning of real-valued data. In: Brodley, C., Danyluk, A. (eds.) Proceedings of the 18th International Confernce on Machine Learning (ICML 2001), pp. 3–10. Morgan Kaufmann Publishers, San Francisco (2001)
2. Andrews, S., Tsochantaridis, I., Hofmann, T.: Support vector machines for multiple-instance learning. In: Becker, S., Thrun, S., Obermayer, K. (eds.) Advances in Neural Information Processing Systems, pp. 561–568. MIT press, Cambridge (2002)

3. Chen, Y., Bi, J., Wang, J.: MILES: Multiple-instance learning via embedded instance selection. IEEE Trans. Pattern Anal. Mach. Intell. **28**, 1931–1947 (2006)
4. Cheung, P., Kwok, J.: A regularization framework for multiple-instance learning. In: Cohen, W., Moore, A. (eds.) Proceedings of the 23rd International Conference on Machine learning (ICML 2006), pp. 193–200. ACM, New York (2006)
5. EL-Manzalawy, Y., Dobbs, D., Honavar, V.: Predicting MHC-II Binding Affinity Using Multiple Instance Regression. IEEE/ACM Trans. Comput. Biol. Bioinf. **8**(4), 1067–1079 (2011)
6. Friedman, J.H.: Greedy function approximation: a gradient boosting machine. Ann. Stat. **29**(5), 1189–1232 (2001)
7. Gärtner, T., Flach, P.A., Kowalczyk, A., Smola, A.: Multi-instance kernels. In: Sammut, C., Hoffmann, A. (eds.) Proceedings of the 19th International Conference on Machine Learning (ICML 2002), pp. 179–186. Morgan Kaufmann Publishers, San Francisco (2002)
8. Lu, L., Bi, J., Wolf, M., Salganicoff, M.: Effective 3D object detection and regression using probabilistic segmentation features in CT images. In: Proceedings of the 2011 IEEE Conference on Computer Vision and Pattern Recognition (CVPR 2011), pp. 1049–1056. IEEE, Los Alamitos (2011)
9. Pappas, N., Popescu-Belis, A.: Explaining the stars: weighted multiple-instance learning for aspect-based sentiment analysis. In: Proceedings of the Conference on Empirical Methods in Natural Language Processing, pp. 455–466. The Associations for Computational Linguistics, Stroudsburg (2014)
10. Ray, S.: Learning from data with complex interactions and ambiguous labels. PhD Thesis, University of Wisconsin at Madison, United States of America (2005)
11. Ray, S., Craven, M.: Supervised versus multiple instance learning: an empirical comparison. In: De Raedt, L., Wrobel, S. (eds.) Proceedings of the 22nd International Conference on Machine Learning (ICML 2005), pp. 697–704. ACM, New York (2005)
12. Ray, S., Page, D.: Multiple instance regression. In: Brodley, C., Danyluk, A. (eds.) Proceedings of the 18th International Confernce on Machine Learning (ICML 2001), pp. 425–432. Morgan Kaufmann Publishers, San Francisco (2001)
13. Schölkopf, B., Smola, A.: Learning with Kernels: Support Vector Machines, Regularization, Optimization, and Beyond. MIT press, Cambridge (2002)
14. Shevade, S., Keerthi, S., Bhattacharyya, C., Murthy, K.: Improvements to the SMO algorithm for SVM regression. IEEE Trans. Neural Netw. **11**(5), 1188–1193 (2000)
15. Teramoto, R., Kashima, H.: Prediction of protein-ligand binding affinities using multiple instance learning. J Mol. Gr. Model. **29**(3), 492–497 (2010)
16. Wagstaff, K., Lane, T.: Salience assignment for multiple-instance regression. In: Proceedings of the ICML 2007 Workshop on Constrained Optimization and Structured Output Spaces, Citeseer (2007)
17. Wagstaff, K.L., Lane, T., Roper, A.: Multiple-instance regression with structured data. In: Bonchi, F., Berendt, B., Giannotti, F., Gunopulos, D., Turini, F., Zaniolo, C., Ramakrishnan, N., Wu, X. (eds.) Proceedings of the 2008 IEEE International Conference on Data Mining Workshops (ICDMW 08), pp. 291–300. IEEE, Los Alamitos (2008)
18. Wang, J., Zucker, J.: Solving the Multiple-Instance Problem: a Lazy Learning Approach. In: Langley, P. (ed.) Proceedings of the 17th International Conference on Machine Learning (ICML 2000), pp. 1119–1126. Morgan Kaufmann Publishers, San Francisco (2000)
19. Wang, Z., Lan, L., Vucetic, S.: Mixture model for multiple instance regression and applications in remote sensing. IEEE Trans. Geosci. Remote Sens. **50**(6), 2226–2237 (2012)
20. Wang, Z., Radosavljevic, V., Han, B., Obradovic, Z., Vucetic, S.: Aerosol optical depth prediction from satellite observations by multiple instance regression. In: Apte, C., Park, H., Wang, K., Zaki, M. (eds.) Proceedings of the 2008 SIAM International Conference on Data Mining, pp. 165–176. SIAM, Philadelphia (2008)
21. Zhang, M., Zhou, Z.: Multi-instance clustering with applications to multi-instance prediction. Appl. Intell. **31**(1), 47–68 (2009)

Chapter 7
Unsupervised Multiple Instance Learning

Abstract Unsupervised MIL is a descriptive task where the learning process is carried out without information about the labels of bags. This is a common setting when it is hard or costly to obtain labeled data or when the objective is to find inherent or unknown relations in data. As for supervised learning techniques studied in this book, unsupervised MIL is more complex than traditional single-instance unsupervised learning due to the inherent ambiguity in MIL. In this chapter, we consider the two main tasks in unsupervised learning that have been addressed from the MIL perspective. The first is *cluster analysis*, where the learning process consists of building groups in which similar examples are put together and less similar examples are separated (Sect. 7.1). The second task is *association rule mining*, where the learning process consists of obtaining rules that show unknown relationships in data (Sect. 7.2).

7.1 Multiple Instance Cluster Analysis

This section sets up the basis for studying multiple instance cluster analysis. Section 7.1.1 introduces cluster analysis, listing the basic concepts as well as a taxonomy in the traditional single-instance scenario. Section 7.1.2 details the more relevant conditions considered in multi-instance clustering. Common measures to evaluate cluster analysis techniques are described in Sect. 7.1.3. Sections 7.1.4.1, 7.1.4.2, 7.1.4.3, 7.1.4.4 and 7.1.4.5 present an overview of the most significant multi-instance clustering methods. Finally, Sect. 7.1.5 is devoted to the use of clustering as a preprocessing step before the application of other data mining techniques (e.g., a classifier).

7.1.1 Introduction to Cluster Analysis

Cluster analysis or clustering tries to group a given collection of unlabeled patterns into different subsets containing similar patterns. These groups are called clusters.

© Springer International Publishing AG 2016

F. Herrera et al., *Multiple Instance Learning*, DOI 10.1007/978-3-319-47759-6_7

They are collections of data objects that are similar to others within the cluster and dissimilar to objects in other clusters. A clustering method should produce clusters with high intraclass similarity and low interclass similarity.

Clustering has become a very interesting tool to guide the discovery of previously unknown groups in many research areas including data mining, statistics, machine learning, spatial database technology, information retrieval, web search, biology, and marketing. Moreover, as a result of the large dimensionality of data nowadays, clustering is often used in a preprocessing phase to facilitate the solution of other tasks. Cluster analysis is consequently a highly active topic in data mining research. The variety of data representation techniques, proximity measures, and ways to group data has produced a rich assortment of clustering methods. The main characteristics and categories are commented on in this section.

7.1.1.1   General Scheme

Most cluster analysis methods rely on (dis)similarities between patterns. In a single-instance setting, let $X = \{x_1, \ldots, x_j, \ldots, x_N\}$ be the set of data objects, where each pattern is represented in a d-dimensional space, that is, $x_i = \{x_{i1}, x_{i2}, \ldots, x_{id}\}$, for $i \in [1, N]$. The main steps of dissimilarity-based clustering are the following [9]:

1. Choose a pattern proximity measure. This is usually a distance function defined on pairs of patterns.
2. Compute the dissimilarity between pattern pairs. The dissimilarity metric usually satisfies the properties, for $k, l \in [1, N]$:

   - $dissimilarity(x_k, x_l) \geq 0$,
   - $dissimilarity(x_k, x_k) = 0$,
   - $dissimilarity(x_k, x_l) = dissimilarity(x_l, x_k)$.

3. Select the desired type of clustering. As described below, example types are hierarchical, partitioning or density based clustering.
4. Choose a criterion to evaluate the clusters, e.g., homogeneity and/or separation of the clusters.
5. Apply the selected algorithm on the data to obtain the clusters.

7.1.1.2   Clustering Taxonomy

As this task has been extensively studied in traditional single-instance learning [19], different categorizations of clustering can be found in the literature [9, 10]. It is however difficult to provide a categorization of clustering methods without overlap, because many methods have features from several categories. In order to present a relatively organized picture of clustering methods, we detail one of the most common categorizations used in single-instance clustering. In the following sections, this grouping is respected to categorize the multi-instance clustering techniques. The

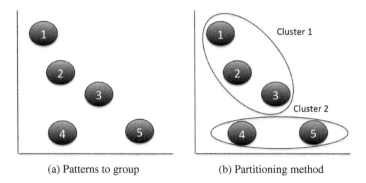

(a) Patterns to group   (b) Partitioning method

Fig. 7.1 Partitioning clustering method

major fundamental clustering methods can be classified in six groups [10], namely: partitioning methods, hierarchical methods, density based methods, grid-based methods, model-based methods, and maximum margin based methods.

- **Partitioning methods**: these methods attempt to provide a conventional partition of N objects into k disjunct clusters, such that each object belongs to exactly one cluster. An iterative process is used to add objects to clusters or exchange them between clusters. The existence of a function F is assumed that evaluates the quality of clusters and allows to optimize the constructed partitions. A general partitioning algorithm involves the following steps [8]:

1. Construct an initial partition of the data into k clusters and compute the value of F. The algorithms are usually very sensitive to the selection of the initial partition.
2. Iteratively change the partition to optimize the value of F as much as possible, maintaining the value of k. Empty or new clusters cannot appear. Algorithms differ from each other in the way they modify the partition and their definition of F.
3. If no further optimization of F is possible, the method halts and yields the current partition as the final result.

  An example partitioning method is described in Fig. 7.1. The input patterns are shown in Fig. 7.1a and the desired clusters in Fig. 7.1b. Partitioning methods work well for the detection of sphere-shaped clusters in small to medium size databases.
- **Hierarchical methods**: the objects are grouped in a sequence of partitions, going from singleton clusters to one cluster containing all individuals or the other way around. Two main types are distinguished:

  - *Agglomerative (bottom-up)*: in the first step, each object is considered as a separate cluster. These clusters are fused together into increasingly larger clusters during the analysis. In the final step, all objects are combined into a trivial cluster.

   – *Divisive (top-down)*: the opposite strategy is followed. The clustering process
     starts with all objects in a single cluster, which is divided into two parts in the
     first step. Each of them is further subdivided in the following steps until every
     cluster contains a single object.

Neither type allows corrections. If two objects are clustered together or separated
at the beginning of the analysis, their mutual relationships cannot be changed,
even when at a different hierarchical level relocation would improve the results.
The classificatory ability of the human brain seems to be closer to the divisive
approaches, whereas computerized realizations are much simpler for the agglomerative strategies. Figure 7.2 shows an example of hierarchical clustering. The input
patterns are shown in Fig. 7.1a. Figure 7.2b represents the process of agglomerative
and divisive algorithms.

- **Density based methods**: these methods assume that the objects that belong to
  each cluster are drawn from a specific probability distribution [4]. Their aim is
  to identify the clusters and their distribution parameters. In general, objects in a
  high density region are considered to belong to the same cluster. These methods
  are designed to discover clusters of arbitrary shape. However, they do not perform
  well when the density of the data space is low.
- **Grid based methods**: these algorithms attempt to divide the space into a finite
  number of cells that form a grid structure on which all clustering operations are
  performed. The main advantage of this approach is its fast processing time [10],
  which is independent of the number of data objects and only depends on the number
  of cells in each dimension of the quantized space. Due to its efficiency, grid-based
  methods can be integrated with other clustering methods, such as density-based
  methods and hierarchical methods.
- **Model-based methods**: the grouping between the given data and some mathematical models is optimized [7]. Unlike conventional clustering, which identifies
  groups of objects, model-based clustering methods also find characteristic descriptions for each group that represent concepts or classes. The problem of determining
  the number of components and the component probability distributions can be formulated as statistical model selection problems.

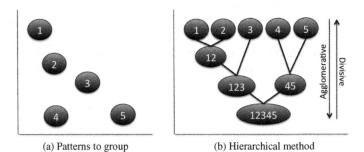

     (a) Patterns to group   (b) Hierarchical method

Fig. 7.2 Hierarchical clustering method

- **Maximum margin based methods**: the data is grouped based on maximum margin hyperplanes. Xu et al. [18], motivated by the success of large margin methods in supervised learning, proposed a method for clustering extending the theory of SVMs to unsupervised learning. While large margin supervised learning methods are usually formulated as convex optimization problems, large margin unsupervised learning is more complex and leads to non-convex integer programs. Most maximum margin clustering methods rely on reformulating and relaxing the non-convex optimization problem to deal with the high computation cost or sensitivity to the choice of kernel function.

7.1.2   Multiple Instance Clustering Requirements

Multiple Instance Clustering (MI-clustering) splits up a set of unlabeled objects into a number of more or less homogeneous subgroups on the basis of a similarity measure. In this sense, the clustering algorithms rely to a great extent on the definition of the similarity metric. Normally, it is subjectively selected based on its ability to obtain relevant clusters. Once a proximity measure has been chosen, a clustering criterion function converts its task in an optimization problem. The clusters are created such that the similarity between objects within a subgroup is larger than the similarity between objects belonging to different subgroups.

In this context, the inherent ambiguity of MIL, where each observation (bag) consists of several unlabeled instances with a particular relationship between them, renders the task of distributing objects into clusters more difficult. MI-Clustering has its own characteristics and the similarity measures used in single-instance clustering may not be appropriate, since instances in a bag usually exhibit different functionalities. For example, in drug activity prediction, only one or a few of the conformations describing a molecule would be responsible for its qualification. Similarly, only one or few of the regions describing an image is useful in the object identification task. These particularities should be taken into account in the similarity definition in MI-Clustering. To clarify this point, Fig. 7.3 shows three bags representing images. Each image is a bag and each instance in that bag corresponds to a particular region. If these images depict animals, the aim would be to group them according to the portrayed animal. Let us suppose that two of these bags contain a tiger (concretely, bag 1 whose instances are represented by pink squares and bag 2 whose instances are represented by orange circles) and the other bag contains an elephant (bag 3, green triangles). In this scenario, the ideal division of clusters would be one cluster composed of bags 1 and 2 and the other one composed of bag 3. This is where the natural ambiguity of MI-Clustering, about which portion of the image contains the clustering concept (tiger or elephant in this case) and which portion may be irrelevant, comes in. In this example, bags 2 and 3 could share an identical background and only differ in that one contains a tiger and the other contains an elephant. On the contrary, bags 1 and 2 could only share the tiger instance, while their backgrounds are completely different,

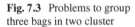

Fig. 7.3 Problems to group
three bags in two cluster

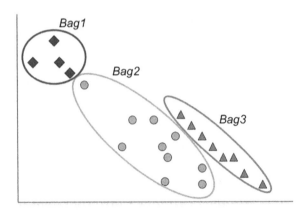

e.g., a snowy mountain compared to a green grassland. Depending on the selected
proximity distance (see Sect. 3.5), the clustering results can be very different.

This example highlights the fact that in MI-Clustering, the bags should not be
regarded as simple collections of independent instances. The characteristics and
relationships of the instances within bags should be carefully investigated. It is critical to identify the desired objects/concepts in each bag, such that the unsupervised
distance definitions can reveal the true distances between bags.

It is important to highlight that although this task has been extensively studied
in single-instance traditional learning, very few proposals have been developed in
MIL. In Sects. 7.1.4.1, 7.1.4.2, 7.1.4.3, 7.1.4.4 and 7.1.4.5, we examine each MI-
clustering method in detail, following the categorization specified in Sect. 7.1.1.
Some clustering algorithms integrate the ideas of several clustering methods, making
it difficult to classify a given algorithm to a unique category. We classify methods
according to the most relevant objective. For each algorithm, we also comment on
the experimental studies carried out by its developers.

7.1.3 Multiple Instance Clustering Evaluation Measures

There are different metrics to evaluate the clusters. They can be grouped into two
groups known as extrinsic and intrinsic measures. The former compare the clustering
against the real grouping. It is clear that these measures can only be applied when the
real grouping is available, that is, when the class of each pattern is known. Intrinsic
measures evaluate the goodness of a clustering by considering how well the clusters
are separated.

A considerable number of metrics can be found in literature. In this section, only the measures used in Sects. 7.1.4.1, 7.1.4.2, 7.1.4.3, 7.1.4.4 and 7.1.4.5 are included. For more details, other studies can be consulted [3, 10]. The definitions below are similar to those in single-instance clustering. However, as the objects in MI-Clustering are bags, the distance metric between patterns should be defined for sets (Sect. 3.5).

7.1.3.1   Extrinsic Measures

Each constructed cluster G_i is assigned the class label of the majority of the objects belonging to it. The dataset X is composed of N patterns $\{X_1, X_2, \ldots, X_N\}$ and each pattern is a bag of instances $X_i = \{x_{i1}, x_{i2}, \ldots, x_{in_i}\}$ composed of n_i instances.

- **Precision**: this measure evaluates the proportion of bags that were identified as a specific class and really belong to this specific class. It is defined as

$$Precision = \frac{\sum_{G_i \in G} |\{X_i | (G_i = argmax_{G_j \in G} Pr[G_j | X_i]) \wedge Class(X_i) = Class(G_i)\})|}{|X|}.$$

- **Recall**: this metric evaluates the proportion of bags that belong to a specific class and are correctly identified as such:

$$Recall = \frac{\sum_{G_i \in G} |\{X_i | (G_i = argmax_{G_j \in G} Pr[G_j | X_i]) \wedge Class(X_i) = Class(G_i)\})|}{|X_i | Class(X_i) = Class(G_i)|}.$$

- **F-measure**: this is the harmonic mean of the above two measures, given as

$$F = \frac{2 \cdot Recall \cdot Precision}{Precision + Recall}.$$

- **Entropy**: the quality evaluation is based on the impurity in the class labels of objects belonging to a cluster. It is given by

$$Entropy_{avg} = \frac{\sum_{G_i \in C} (|G_i| \cdot (- \sum_{Class_j} p_{j,i} log(p_{j,i})))}{|X|},$$

where $p_{j,i}$ is the relative frequency of the class label $Class_j$ in the cluster G_i.

7.1.3.2   Intrinsic Measures

The distance $d_{Bag}(X_1, X_2)$ between bags X_1 and X_2 is measured by an appropriate metric, like the ones listed in Sect. 3.5. The *silhouette coefficient* is a normalized summation-type index. Cluster cohesion is measured based on the distance between all points in the same cluster, while cluster separation is based on the nearest neighbor distance. The measure is computed as

$$Silhouette = \frac{1}{N} \sum_{G_k \in G} \sum_{X_i \in G_k} \frac{b(X_i, G_k) - a(X_i, G_k)}{max\{a(X_i, G_k), b(X_i, G_k)\}},$$

where

$$a(X_i, G_k) = \frac{1}{|G_k|} \sum_{X_j \in G_k} d_{Bag}(X_i, X_j)$$

and

$$b(X_i, G_k) = min_{G_l \in G \setminus G_k} \left[\frac{1}{|G_l|} \sum_{X_j \in G_l} d_{Bag}(X_i, X_j) \right].$$

7.1.4   Multiple Instance Clustering Methods

This section gives an overview of the most significant MI clustering methods grouped according to the taxonomy specified in Sect. 7.1.1.2.

7.1.4.1   Partitioning Method: BAMIC Algorithm

Partitioning is one of the simplest and most fundamental forms of cluster analysis. These methods organize the objects into several exclusive clusters. A general description can be found in Sect. 7.1.1. We describe the proposal of Zhang et al. [22], that adapts the classical k-medoids algorithm, BAMIC (BAg-level Multi-Instance Clustering) algorithm. Other works, such as Chen et al. [5], propose alternative distance measures to improve the performance of this method.

Description

BAMIC was developed by Zhang and Zhou [22] and modifies the popular k-medoids algorithm to partition the unlabeled training bags into k disjoint groups of bags. Bags are considered as atomic elements and the k-medoids algorithm is employed to construct groups based on the distances between them. The authors proposed a new bagwise distance called the average Hausdorff distance (see Sect. 3.5).

The main steps of BAMIC are listed in Algorithm 3. The first step arbitrarily selects k patterns to form the initial medoids, the representative bags for a cluster. In each iteration, each bag is assigned to the cluster with the closest medoid. The cluster medoids are recalculated by selecting the objects with the lowest value average dissimilarity measure. The iterative process continues until the quality of the resulting clustering cannot be improved by any replacement. This quality is measured by a cost function of the average dissimilarity between an object and the medoid of its cluster.

Algorithm 3 BAMIC Algorithm

Input: $X \leftarrow$ unlabeled multi-instance training set $\{X_1, X_2, \ldots, X_N\}$ $(X_i \subseteq \mathbb{X})$.
Input: $k \leftarrow$ cluster number.
Input: $Distance_{bag} \leftarrow$ distance between bags (see Sect. 3.5).
Output: $G \leftarrow$ clustered groups
Output: $C \leftarrow$ medoids of clustered groups
1: **for** $j \in \{1, 2, \ldots, k\}$ **do**
2:    $C_j \leftarrow$ Randomly select a training bag in X as the initial representative bag of each cluster
3: **end for**
4: **repeat**
5:   **for** $j \in \{1, 2, \ldots, k\}$ **do**
6:      $G_j = \{C_j\}$
7:   **end for**
8:   **for** $i \in \{1, 2, \ldots, N\}$ **do**
9:      $index = min_{j \in [1,k]} Distance_{bag}(X_i, C_j)$;
10:     $G_{index} = G_{index} \cup \{X_i\}$
11:   **end for**
12:   **for** $j \in \{1, 2, \ldots, k\}$ **do**
13:     $C_j = min_{X_i \in G_j}(\sum_{X_k \in G_j} Distance_{bag}(X_i, X_k)/|G_j|)$;
14:   **end for**
15: **until** the clustering results do not change;
16: $Groups = \{G_j | j \in [1, k]\}$
17: $Medoids = \{C_j | j \in [1, k]\}$;

Experimental Study

The experimental setting of [22] considers classic MIC datasets, Musk1 and Musk2 (Sect. 3.6). Versions of the BAMIC method using different measures of Hausdorff (maximum, minimum and average Hausdorff distance, see Sect. 3.5) are compared. To assess the efficacy of the method, the average purity and entropy is used. The experimental results show that the different distance metrics perform appropriately without significant differences between them.

7.1.4.2   Hierarchical Method: UC-kNN Algorithm

A hierarchical clustering method can be either agglomerative or divisive, depending on whether the hierarchical decomposition is formed in a bottom-up or top-down procedure (Sect. 7.1.1). We describe the UC-kNN (Unsupervised citation-kNN) algorithm [11], an agglomerative hierarchical method. Its authors define a new similarity metric based on mutual information.

Description

Henegar et al. [11] proposed the UC-kNN method by adapting the Citation-kNN method of Wang and Zucker (Sect. 5.2.1) to MI-Clustering. Two bags X_1 and X_2 composed of n_1 and n_2 instances measure their relationship as

$$D_{X_1 \to X_2} = 1 - S_{X_1 \to X_2} \left[\frac{1}{2\bar{n}_{12}} \sum_{i=1}^{\bar{n}_2} max_{j=1}^{\bar{n}_{12}} \overline{MI}(x_{1i}, x_{2j}) \right]. \tag{7.1}$$

The normalized pairwise mutual information $\overline{MI}(X_1, X_2)$ of two random variables X_1 and X_2 is defined as

$$\overline{MI}(X_1, X_2) = \frac{MI(X_1, X_2)}{max\{H(X_1), H(X_2)\}},$$

with $MI(X_1, X_2) = H(X_1) + H(X_2) - H(X_1, X_2)$. The value $H(X_1)$ is the entropy given by

$$H(X_1) = - \sum_{i=1}^{n_1} P(X_1 = x_{1i}) log_2 P(X_1 = x_{1i}).$$

Finally, $\bar{n}_{12}$ is the cardinality of n_{12}, computed as

$$n_{12} = \{x_{1i} \in X_1 \mid \exists x_{2j} \in X_2 : \overline{MI}(x_{1i}, x_{2j}) \geq T_{MI}\}.$$

The main steps of this algorithm are given in Algorithm 4. This method uses (7.1) and follows a nearest neighbor approach. A bag X_i is presumed a good reference for another bag X_j, if bag X_i is ranked among the k most closely related bags to bag X_j. At initialization, the first p most cited bags ($2 \leq p < m$) are assigned to each cluster as representative bags. Next, every other bag is grouped with its closest representative bag using a weighted voting procedure. Concretely, for each X_i different of the p representative bags, the closest representative bag X_j is located, minimizing the value

$$V_{G_s X_i} = rank(G_s, X_i) + \frac{1}{k} \sum_{j=1}^{k} rank(G_s, X_j),$$

Algorithm 4 UC-kNN Algorithm

Input: $X \leftarrow$ unlabeled multi-instance training bag set $\{X_1, X_2, \ldots, X_N\}$ $(X_i \subseteq \mathbb{X})$.
Input: $k \leftarrow$ number of nearest neighbor
Output: $G \leftarrow$ Clustered groups
1: Calculate the bag relationship matrix using (7.1)
2: **for** $(k \in \{1, 2, \ldots, N - 1\})$ **do**
3:   **for** $(j \in \{1, \ldots, N\})$ **do**
4:     $R_{X_j} \leftarrow \sum\limits_{X_i \in X} rank(X_j, X_i)$ **ssi** $rank(X_j, X_i) \leq k$
5:     $\mathcal{R} = \mathcal{R} \cup \{R_{X_j}\}$
6:   **end for**
7:   **for** $(p \in \{2, \ldots, m\})$ **do**   ▷ m is the number of clusters
8:     G_j $(j \in [1, \ldots, p]) \leftarrow$ the first p bags from $\mathcal{R}$ as cluster representative bag
9:     **for** $(X_i \in X$ and $X_i \notin G_j$ $(j \in [1, \ldots, p])$ **do**
10:       $X_j \leftarrow$ Find k best references for X_i
11:       $V_{G_s X_i}(s \in [1, \ldots, p]) \leftarrow rank(G_s, X_i) + \frac{1}{k}\sum\limits_{j=1}^{k} rank(G_j, X_j)$
12:       $G_j \leftarrow G_j \cup X_i$ ▷ X_i is assigned to closest cluster G_j
13:     **end for**
14:     Calculate silhouette index for the resulting partition of bags   ▷ Silhouette index is
      defined in Sect. 7.1.3
15:   **end for**
16: **end for**
17: Select the optimal partition of bags with maximum silhouette index, among those computed
    for each possible combination of values of k and p.
18: $Groups = \{G_j | j \in [1, m]\}$

---

where X_j belongs to the k nearest neighbors of bag X_i. For each pair of values (k, p), the method builds a partition $P_{(k,p)} = \{G_1 \cap \ldots \cap G_p\}$ of X into p distinct classes. An optimal partition can be selected by using a standard quality evaluation measure. The authors use the silhouette technique (Sect. 7.1.3).

Experimental Study

The experimental setting of [11] considers datasets related with pangenomic cDNA microarray expression. UC-kNN is compared to two other classic algorithms: an agglomerative hierarchical clustering and k-means partition clustering [12]. Both were modified for MIL by reducing the multi-instance model to a single-instance one and by relying on the symmetrical measure of the relationship between bags given by

$$D_{X_1 \rightarrow X_2} = \frac{1}{2}(D_{X_1 \rightarrow X_2} + D_{X_2 \rightarrow X_1}).$$

To evaluate the efficacy of the method, the silhouette index of the partitions is used (Silhouette index is defined in Sect. 7.1.3). The experimental results of UC-kNN are better than those of its competitors.

7.1.4.3   Density Based Method: COSMIC Algorithm

Partitioning and hierarchical methods are designed to find sphere-shaped clusters. They have difficulty finding clusters of arbitrary shape. Density based methods on the other hand model clusters as dense regions in the data space, separated by sparse regions. They can discover clusters of nonspherical shape. We describe the COS-MIC (COnceptual Specified Multi-Instance Clusters) algorithm [14], classified as a density-based clustering algorithm to find an arbitrary number of clusters and to distinguish noisy instances.

Description

Kriegel et al. [14] proposed the COSMIC algorithm, a method for deriving conceptually specified multi-instance clusters. It is based on the classic OPTICS algorithm [2] and consists of two steps. The first carries out a density based clustering and obtains the clustered set of all instances. The second step generates all concepts that contain at least a minimum support (*MinPts*). Some important notions have to be considered in any density-based method:

- **Core object**: an object that has at least *MinPts* bags in its ε-neighborhood, where ε is the size of neighborhood.
- **Core distance**: the smallest distance ε' between a bag X and one bag in its ε-neighborhood such that X would be a core object. In MI-Clustering, the definition of the core-distance is dependent on at least μ multi-instance objects instead of μ arbitrary instances.
- **Reachability distance**: for a bag X_1, this is the smallest distance such that X_1 is density-reachable from a core object. According to the definition of density-reachability, X_2 has to be a core object and X_1 must be in the neighborhood of X_2. Therefore, the reachability-distance from X_2 to X_1 is

$$max(core\text{-}distance(X_2), dist(X_1, X_2)).$$

If X_2 is not a core object with respect to ε and *MinPts*, the reachability distance to X_1 from X_2 is undefined. An object X_1 may be directly reachable from several core objects. Therefore, X_1 may have multiple reachability distances with respect to different core objects. The smallest reachability distance of X_1 is of particular interest, because it gives the shortest path for which X_1 is connected to a dense cluster.

The main steps of this method are listed in Algorithms 5 and 6. The first step of COSMIC, shown in Algorithm 5, computes an ordering of all objects and stores the core-distance and a suitable reachability distance for each object. COSMIC maintains a list called ControlList to generate the output ordering. Objects in ControlList are sorted by the reachability distance from their closest core objects, that is, by their smallest reachability distance. The procedure starts with an arbitrary input object as the current object X_i. It retrieves the ε-neighborhood of X_i, determines the core-distance and sets the reachability distance to undefined. The current object is then

---

Algorithm 5 COSMIC Algorithm - First Step

Input: $X \leftarrow$ unlabeled multi-instance training set $\{X_1, X_2, \ldots, X_N\}$ $(X_i \subseteq \mathbb{X})$.
Input: $\varepsilon \leftarrow$ radius parameter
Input: $MinPts \leftarrow$ the neighborhood density threshold
Output: $G_{ordered} \leftarrow$ cluster ordering of objects, coreDistance of objects and reachabilityDistance of objects.

```
 1: Mark all bags as not visited
 2: for (k ∈ {1, 2, . . . , N}) do
 3:    Select the bag X_k
 4:    if (X_k is not visited) then
 5:       N_ε(X_k) ← Obtain ε neighborhood
 6:       X_k ← visited
 7:       reachabilityDistance_{X_k} ← undefined
 8:       coreDistance_{X_k} ← coreDistance(X_k)
 9:       G_ordered ← X_k
10:       if (coreDistance_{X_k} ≠ undefined) then
11:          coreDistance_{X_k} ← coreDistance(X_k)
12:          for (each X_j ∈ N_ε(X_k) that is not visited) do
13:             dist_{X_j} ← max(coreDistance_{X_k}, distance(X_k, X_j))
14:             if (reachabilityDistance_{X_j} = undefined) then
15:                reachabilityDistance_{X_j} = dist_{X_j}
16:                ControlList ← X_j with reachabilityDistance_{X_j}
17:             else
18:                if (dist_{X_j} < reachabilityDistance_{X_j}) then
19:                   reachabilityDistance_{X_j} = dist_{X_j}
20:                   Update reachabilityDistance_{X_j} in ControlList
21:                end if
22:             end if
23:          end for
24:          for (X_i ∈ ControlList) do
25:             N_ε(X_i) ← Obtain ε neighborhood of X_i
26:             X_i ← processed
27:             coreDistance_{X_i} ← coreDistance(X_i)
28:             G_ordered ← X_i
29:             if (coreDistance_{X_i} ≠ undefined) then
30:                coreDistance_{X_k} ← coreDistance(X_k)
31:                for (each X_j ∈ N_ε(X_k) ∧ X_j is not visited) do
32:                   dist_{X_j} ← max(coreDistance_{X_k}, distance(X_k, X_j))
33:                   if (reachabilityDistance_{X_j} = undefined) then
34:                      reachabilityDistance_{X_j} = dist_{X_j}
35:                      ControlList ← X_j with reachabiliyDistance_{X_j}
36:                   else
37:                      if (dist_{X_j} < reachabilityDistance_{X_j}) then
38:                         reachabilityDistance_{X_j} = dist_{X_j}
39:                         Update reachabilityDistance_{X_j} in ControlList
40:                      end if
41:                   end if
42:                end for
43:             end if
44:          end for
45:       end if
46:    end if
47: end for
```

Algorithm 6 COSMIC Algorithm - Second Step

Input: $X \leftarrow$ unlabeled multi-instance training set $\{X_1, X_2, \ldots, X_N\}$ $(X_i \subseteq \mathbb{X})$.
Input: $\varepsilon' \leftarrow$ radius parameter
Input: $G_{ordered} \leftarrow$ cluster ordering of objects, coreDistance of objects and reachabilityDistance of objects.
Output: $G \leftarrow$ Clustered groups
                                                  ▷ Extracting clusters from $G_{ordered}$

1: $G_{id} \leftarrow$ NOISE
2: **for** $(X_i \in G_{ordered})$ **do**
3:      **if** $(reachabilityDistance(X_i) > \varepsilon')$ **then**
4:          **if** $(coreDistance(X_i) \leq \varepsilon')$ **then**
5:              $G_{id} \leftarrow nextID(G_{id})$
6:              $G_{id}(X_i) \leftarrow G_{id}$
7:          **else**
8:              $G_{id} \leftarrow NOISE$
9:          **end if**
10:    **else**
11:        $G_{id}(X_i) \leftarrow G_{id}$
12:    **end if**
13: **end for**

---

written to output. If X_i is not a core object, the method moves on to the next object in the ControlList (or the input data set, if ControlList is empty). If X_i is a core object, then for each object X_j in its ε-neighborhood, COSMIC updates its reachability distance from X_i and inserts X_j into ControlList if X_j has not yet been processed. The iteration continues until the input is fully consumed and ControlList is empty.

In the second step, shown in Algorithm 6, COSMIC uses the previously obtained cluster ordering and describes the cluster groups according to this information. After clustering the objects, COSMIC extracts the attributes that are useful for describing formal concepts from the resulting reachability plot and lists all concepts that can be found in the given dataset.

Experimental Study

The study of [14] considers drug activity prediction datasets, Musk1 and Musk2, identification protein datasets, Dobson and Doig and BRENDA, and a dataset on healthcare websites, WebKB. A description of any of these datasets is given in Sect. 3.6. COSMIC is compared with PAM [12] and OPTICS [2]. Both are single-instance clustering methods. To adapt them for MI-Clustering, the authors consider bags as atomic elements and use the minimum Hausdorff distance and sum of minimum distances (Sect. 3.5) as distance measure. To compare the methods, their precision and running time is used. The results show that COSMIC obtains a more precise clustering and scales well to larger data sets, obtaining a running time comparable to the other methods.

7.1.4.4   Maximum Margin Based Method: M3IC-MBM Algorithm

Maximum margin based clustering proposes a method for clustering based on finding maximum margin hyperplanes, that can separate the data from different classes in an unsupervised way. These models yield a non-convex integer optimization problem (see Sect. 7.1.1). We describe the M3IC-MBM (Maximum Margin Multiple Instance Clustering with Modified Bag Margin) method proposed by Zhang et al. [21], that tries to find the most representative instance by means of maximum margin. This method was later extended by Zhang et al. [23].

Description

Zhang et al. [21] proposed the M3IC-MBM algorithm, that combines the Constrained Concave-Convex Procedure (CCCP) and cutting plane methods. They formulate a Maximum Margin Multiple Instance Clustering (M3IC) problem based on Maximum Margin Clustering (MMC) [18], which aims to find the hyperplanes that maximize the margin differences on at least one instance per bag in an unsupervised way. Since M3IC problem results in a non-convex optimization problem, not possible to solve directly, the authors propose a relaxed definition of the optimization problem combining the constrained concave-convex procedure and the cutting plane method. Concretely, the optimization problem, where the large margin constraint is imposed on at least one instance per bag, is specified as

$$
min_{(\tilde{w}, \xi \geq 0)} \frac{1}{2} ||\tilde{w}||^2 + C\xi
$$
$$
s.t. i = 1, \dots, N; \forall c \in \Omega^{t_1},
$$
$$
\frac{1}{N} \tilde{w}^T \sum_{i=1}^{N} c_i \frac{\partial f(\tilde{w}, i)}{\partial \tilde{w}} \Big|_{(\tilde{w} = \tilde{w}^{(t)})} \geq \frac{1}{N} \sum_{i=1}^{N} c_i - \xi \tag{7.2}
$$
$$
\forall p, q \in \{1, 2, \dots, k\},
$$
$$
-l \leq \sum_{i=1}^{N} \sum_{x_{ij} s \in X_i} \frac{1}{n_i} \tilde{w}^T (x_{ij(p)} - x_{ij(q)}) \leq l.
$$

In this definition, k is the number of clusters and w_p is the weight vector associated to each cluster ($p \in [1, k]$). Ω^t is a subset of constraints obtained using an adaptation of the cutting plane algorithm [13]. The parameter l controls the cluster balance to avoid the trivially optimal solution. In the vector $x_{ij(p)}$, only the $(p-1)d$th to pdth elements are nonzero and set to the corresponding values in x_{ij}, where d is the dimension of x_{ij}. The most violated constraint vector is calculated as

$$
c_i^{t_0} = \begin{cases} 1 & \text{if } (\tilde{w}^{(t0)})^T \frac{\partial f(\tilde{w}, i)}{\partial \tilde{w}} \Big|_{\tilde{w} = \tilde{w}^{(t)}} \leq 1 \\ 0 & \text{otherwise.} \end{cases}
$$

Algorithm 7 M3IC-MBM Algorithm

Input: $X \leftarrow$ unlabeled multi-instance training set $\{X_1, X_2, \ldots, X_N\}$ ($X_i \subseteq \mathbb{X}$).
Input: $C \leftarrow$ regularization constant
Input: $\varepsilon_1 \leftarrow$ CCCP solution precision
Input: $\varepsilon_2 \leftarrow$ cutting plane solution precision
Input: $k \leftarrow$ cluster number
Input: $l \leftarrow$ cluster size balance
Output: $G \leftarrow$ Clustered groups
1: Construct $\tilde{B} = \{x_{ij}(r)\}$
2: Initialize $\tilde{w}^0, t = 0, \triangle J = 10^{-3}, J^{-1} = 10^{-3}$
3: **while** $\triangle J / J^{t-1} > \varepsilon_1$ **do**
4:     Derive problem (7.2)
5:     Set the constraint set $\Omega = \emptyset, \forall 1 \le i \le n, c_j(i) = 0, s = -1$
6:     **while** H^{ts} is true **do**
7:         $s = s + 1$
8:         Get $(\tilde{w}^{ts}, \xi^{ts})$ by solving (7.2) under Ω^{ts}
9:         Calculate the most violated bags, c_i^{ts}, by

$$c_i^{ts} = \begin{cases} 1, \text{ if } (\tilde{w}^{(ts)})^T \frac{\partial f(\tilde{w}, i)}{\partial \tilde{w}}|_{\tilde{w} = \tilde{w}^{(t)}} \le 1 \\ 0, \text{ otherwise} \end{cases}$$

and update the constraint set Ω^{ts} by $\Omega^{ts+1} = \Omega^{ts} \cup c^{ts}$
10:     **end while**
11:     $t = t + 1$
12:     $\tilde{w}^{(t)} = \tilde{w}^{(t-1)s}$
13:     $\triangle J = J^{t-1} - J^t$
14: **end while**
15: $\triangleright$ Cluster Assignment
16: **for** $X_i \in X$ **do**
17:     $G_p = argmax_p (\tilde{w}^{(t)})^T x_{ij^*(p)}$,
          where $j^* = argmax_{j \in X_i} (max_u (\tilde{w}^{(t)})^T x_{ij(u)} - mean_v ((\tilde{w}^{(t)})^T x_{ij(v)}))$
18: **end for**

The main steps of this method are given in Algorithm 7. It is characterized by an outer iteration using CCCP and an inner iteration using the cutting plane method. In this process, H^{ts} is used to denote the constraint

$$(1/n)(\tilde{w}^{ts})^T \sum_{i=1}^{n} c_i^{ts} (\partial f(\tilde{w}, i) / \partial \tilde{w}|_{\tilde{w} = \tilde{w}^{(t)}}) \le (1/n) \sum_{i=1}^{n} c_i^{ts} - (\phi^{(t_s)} + \varepsilon_2)$$

and $J^t = (1/2)||\tilde{w}^{(t)}||^2 + C\phi^{(t)}$.

Experimental Study

The study of [21] considers image classification data sets (Corel, SIVAL and natural scenes) and a text classification data set (Reuters). M3IC-MBM is compared with BAMIC (Sect. 7.1.4.1) using different Hausdorff distances and two classic methods of single-instance clustering: k-means [12] and CPM3C [24]. K-means and CPM3C are not designed to solve MI-Clustering, but were adapted as follows. These methods first cluster all instances. Next, for each bag, the cluster assignment is determined by the assignment that appears most frequently for the instances in that bag.

The accuracy, normalized mutual information and running time are used to compare the methods. The results show that the performance of M3IC-MBM is better than that of the other proposals. It obtains more accurate results than the conventional clustering methods. With respect to the running time, M3IC-MBM is faster than BAMIC and CPM3C and comparable to k-means.

7.1.4.5 Model Based Method: MIEM-Clustering Algorithm

We focus on probabilistic model based methods. These methods could be grouped in other taxonomic categories of Sect. 7.1.1, but, following other studies [6, 10], we consider it clearer to list them as a separate category.

Probabilistic model based methods are based on probability models, where objects are assumed to follow a finite mixture of probability distributions such that each component distribution represents a cluster. The cluster parameters can be estimated based on the data. It can be assumed that an unknown data category is a distribution over the data space, which can be mathematically represented using a probability density function (or distribution function).

We describe MIEM-Clustering (Multi-Instance EM Clustering) algorithm [15], an approach which derives multi-instance clusters based on EM clustering. The method groups the instances with ordinary EM clustering and uses a multinomial process to group bags of instances afterward.

Description

Kriegel et al. [15] proposed the MIEM-Clustering algorithm. It is a statistical clustering approach for MI objects. A bag is considered the result of selecting a concept several times and generating an instance with the corresponding process each time. Clusters of multi-instance objects are described as multinomial distributions over the concepts.

The main steps are described in Algorithm 8. Each cluster G_j is associated with a probability w_j. It is often assumed that $w_1, \ldots, w_k$ are provided as part of the problem setting and that $\sum_{j=1}^{k} w_j = 1$, which ensures that all objects are generated by the k clusters. The authors use a standard EM clustering algorithm on the union set of all multi-instance objects. A mixture model is determined, describing the instances of all bags. Assuming that each of the clusters within each mixture model corresponds to some valid concept, the algorithm can derive distributions for the bag clustering. Next, it is assumed that a bag containing n_i instances can be modeled as n_i draws from the instance mixture model. Each cluster of bags is described by a distribution over the instance clusters derived in the previous step and some prior probability. In the case of the standard MI assumption, it can be expected that there is at least one instance cluster that is very unlikely to appear in the multi-instance clusters corresponding to the negative bags.

Algorithm 8 MIEM Clustering Algorithm

Input: $X \leftarrow$ unlabeled multi-instance training set $\{X_1, X_2, \ldots, X_N\}$ $(X_i \subseteq \mathbb{X})$.
Input: $\sigma \leftarrow$ threshold for optimizing EM algorithm.
Output: $G \leftarrow$ Clustered groups
      ▷ Derive a Mixture Model for the instance set
1: **for** $X_i^E \in X$ **do**
2:     Select a multi-instance cluster G_j.
                            ▷ According to the prior distribution over the set of all clusters
3:     Derive the number of instances n within the multi-instance object.
                            ▷ According to some distribution depending on the chosen cluster
4:     **while** n times **do**
5:         Select some model component k_p within the mixture model of instances.
                            ▷ According to the multi-instance cluster specific distribution
6:         Generate an instance according to the distribution corresponding to component k_p.
7:     **end while**
8: **end for**
       ▷ Calculate a start partitioning
9: **for** $X_i^E \in X$ **do**
10:     $csv_j(X_i) = \sum_{x_{ih} \in X_i} Pr[k_p] * Pr[x_{ih}|k_p]$
11: **end for**
12: $G \leftarrow$ clustered groups by means of k-means using csv.
       ▷ Use the EM algorithm to optimize the initial partitioning
13: **while** $E(M) < \sigma$ **do**
14:     $E(M) = \sum_{X_i \in X} log \sum_{G_j \in M} Pr[G_j \in X_i]$
                            ▷ $Pr[G_j \in X_i]$ is calculated according to (7.3)
15:     Improve the distribution parameters of each cluster using from (7.4–7.6)
16: **end while**
17: $G \leftarrow$ clusters are grouped according to model obtained.

The EM algorithm starts with an initial set of parameters and iterates until the clustering cannot be improved, that is, until the clustering converges or the change is sufficiently small (less than a threshold). A mixture model is first derived describing concepts in the instance space. Next, the target distribution is initialized for each bag by a so-called k-dimensional confidence summary vector (csv). The classic k-means method is used to cluster the bags. In the final step, the distribution for each cluster of bags is optimized by means of an iterative process.

Let each cluster group G_j be described by a prior probability $Pr[G_j]$, a distribution $Pr[|X_i||G_j]$ over the number of instances in the bag X_i and a conditional probability describing the likelihood that a bag X_i belongs to G_j. The probability of an object X_j in the model M is calculated as

$$Pr[G_j|X_i] = \frac{1}{Pr[X_i]} \cdot Pr[G_j] \cdot Pr[|X_i||G_j] \cdot \prod_{x_{ih} \in X_i} \prod_{k \in MI} Pr[k|G_j]^{Pr[k|x_{ih}]}. \qquad (7.3)$$

In the expectation step, $E(M)$ can be calculated for a given set of distribution parameters and an instance model. To improve the distribution parameters, the authors propose to update the distribution parameters during the maximization step. If W_{C_j}

denotes the prior probability of a cluster of bags, they compute

$$W_{G_j} = Pr[G_j] = \frac{1}{|X|} \sum_{X_i \in X} Pr[G_j|X_i]. \tag{7.4}$$

To estimate the number of instances contained in a bag belonging to cluster C_j, the authors employ a binomial distribution determined by the parameter l_{C_j}. The parameters are updated according to

$$l_{G_j} = \frac{\sum\limits_{X_i \in X} Pr[G_j|X_i] \cdot |X_i|}{|X|} \cdot \frac{1}{MaxLength}, \tag{7.5}$$

where *MaxLength* is the maximum number of instances for any bag in the dataset. Finally, to estimate the relative number of instances drawn from concept k_p for bags belonging to cluster G_j, the updated parameter are derived under

$$P_{k_p,G_j} = Pr[k_p|G_j] = \frac{\sum\limits_{X_i \in X} (Pr[G_j|X_i] \cdot \sum_{u \in X_i} Pr[u|k_p])}{\sum\limits_{X_i \in X} Pr[G_j|X_i]}. \tag{7.6}$$

Experimental Study

The experiments of [15] are run on a protein identification problem using the Brenda dataset and a drug activity prediction problem using the Musk1 and Musk2 datasets. MIEM-Clustering is compared to the PAM algorithm [12], that is adapted to MI-Clustering by considering each bag as an atomic element and applying the maximum, minimum and average Hausdorff distances (Sect. 3.5). To measure the effectiveness, the authors use precision, F-measure and average entropy. It is shown that the performance of MIEM-Clustering is better than the other proposals according to the different metrics.

7.1.5 Multiple Instance Clustering as a Preprocessing Step for Classification

Cluster analysis can be used as a standalone tool to gain insight in the data distribution, to observe the characteristics of each cluster and to focus on a particular set of clusters for further analysis. In this section, we describe some proposals using clustering as a preprocessing step before constructing a prediction model.

Zhang and Chen [20] used MIL to solve region based image classification. This problem has a high dimensionality, since each image is divided into several semantic regions (instances). Before solving the problem with a one class SVM, a genetic algorithm based clustering method is used to reduce the search space to a few clusters that are relevant to the query region, that is, a few clusters whose centroids are the closest to that region. After clustering, the authors apply MIC to learn the region of interest based on relevance feedback from the user on the whole image.

With a similar purpose of creating a new lower dimensional space in MIC, Tax et al. [17] used a clustering method as a step in its classifier based on maximum diverse density idea. A simple clustering method, like k-means clustering, is utilized to obtain a fast preprocessing step. The Clustering Multi-instance learner is constructed to exploit the standard MI assumption. The concept is modeled by a spherical area in feature space, parametrized by a center and a radius. The center is selected from a collection of locations that is obtained by some clustering procedure on all instances of the positive bags. The distance to the concept center is used as the instance classifier.

From a different perspective, Zhou and Zhang [25] proposed to solve MIC problems by adapting the multi-instance to single-instance representation, on which single-instance methods can be applied. Concretely, they used a specific scheme of constructive induction based on Constructive Clustering based Ensemble. In this context, the clustering process is used to help change the representation. The instances contained in all bags are first collected. Since their labels are unknown, a clustering algorithm is employed to cluster the instances into d groups. Intuitively, since clustering can help find the inherent structure of a dataset, the clusters might implicitly encode some information on the distribution of the instances of different bags. The proposal tries to represent the bags based on the clustering results. In particular, d features are generated in such a way that if a bag has an instance in the ith cluster, then the value of the ith feature is set to 1. It is set to 0 otherwise. Each bag is represented by a d-dimensional binary feature vector, such that existing single-instance supervised classifiers can be employed to distinguish the bags. Various clustering results can be generated for a specific set of instances. The authors use classic k-means, but other traditional single-instance clustering method could be used as well. Alternatively, several classifiers based on different clustering results can be produced and combined in the prediction step.

7.2   Multiple Instance Association Rule Mining

Recently, association rule mining has been addressed from a multi-instance perspective [16]. As shown in other data mining techniques in the previous chapters, MIL is a very flexible learning setting that allows to solve many problems more efficiently than the single-instance paradigm. This section introduces the basis for multiple instance association rule mining. Section 7.2.1 provides a definition of association rule mining in the traditional scenario. Section 7.2.2 shows the most relevant requirements for multiple instance association rule mining and Sect. 7.2.3 presents the classic method Apriori which has been adapted to the MIL framework.

7.2.1 Association Rule Mining Introduction

Similar to clustering, association rule mining (ARM) is a descriptive task. Its aim is to extract strong relationships among sets of items within a pattern of potential interest. In general, ARM determines a pattern as interesting if it is highly frequent in the database.

With massive amounts of data continuously being collected and stored, many companies are becoming interested in mining such patterns from their databases. The discovery of interesting correlation relationships among huge amounts of business transaction records can help in many decision making processes, such as catalog design, cross marketing and customer shopping behavior analysis.

A typical example of frequent itemset mining is market basket analysis. In this problem, customer buying habits are analyzed by finding associations between the different items that customers frequently purchased together in the supermarket. For instance, a question could be that if a customer buys milk, how likely is he to also buy bread. This information can lead to an increase in sales by helping retailers develop marketing strategies.

Frequent itemset mining can be represented in the form of association rules, that show items that are frequently associated or purchased together. For example, the information that customers who purchase computers also tend to buy office software could be represented in the association rule: *IF computer THEN office software.* Association rules are similar to classification rules and are expressed as

IF Antecedent THEN Consequent

However, the main difference with respect to rule classification is that, in this case, the rule antecedent and consequent can be composed of any subset of items. The only requirement is that *Antecedent $\cap$ Consequent $= \emptyset$*. To simplify the descriptions, we denote the antecedent as A and the consequent as C. The rule is referred to $(A \rightarrow C)$.

ARM, given a transactional dataset, tries to find rules that describe unknown relations in the data. It detects when the occurrence of an item is associated with the occurrence of another item in the same transaction. More concretely, the ARM task aims to find, from the whole set of rules $\mathcal{R}$, any association rule R that satisfies a threshold α of interest specified by user, i.e.,

$$\text{ARM} = \{\forall R \in \mathcal{R} : quality(R) \geq \alpha\}$$

The level of interest of the rule is usually measured by means of rule support and confidence. They respectively reflect the usefulness and certainty of discovered rules. The support provides information on how frequently the item appears in the database. If $T = \{t_1, t_2, \ldots, t_m\}$ is the set of transactions, the support of a rule $(A \rightarrow C)$ is defined as the proportion of transactions that contains $A \cup C$,

$$Support_{ARM}(A \rightarrow C) = \frac{|\{t_i \in \mathsf{T} : \{A \cup C\} \subseteq t_i\}|}{|\mathsf{T}|}$$

The confidence gives information about of how often the rule is satisfied in the database. It is the proportion of transactions that contains A and C and is defined as

$$Confidence_{ARM}(A \rightarrow C) = \frac{Support_{ARM}(AUC)}{Support_{ARM}(A)}$$

Typically, association rules are considered interesting if they satisfy both a minimum support threshold and a minimum confidence threshold. These thresholds can be set by the user or domain experts.

7.2.2 Multiple Instance Association Rule Mining Requirements

Multiple Instance Association Rule Mining (MI-ARM) obtains rules to describe behaviors in multi-instance data. Below, an example is detailed to show its flexibility. Figure 7.4 shows a transactional database, where ten features are used to representing each transaction (see Fig. 7.4a). Let us consider attribute 1 (column 1) as an attribute that represents the height of a person and that can take on three possible values (*short* represented by striped white, *medium* represented by gray and *tall* represented by white). We can obtain a MIL representation with three bags, each one representing

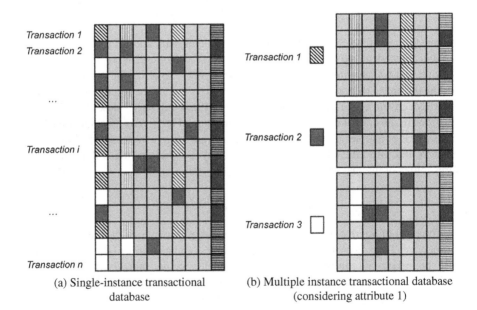

(a) Single-instance transactional database

(b) Multiple instance transactional database (considering attribute 1)

Fig. 7.4 Example of multiple instance association rule mining (I)

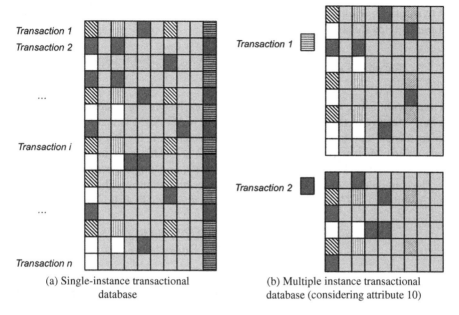

(a) Single-instance transactional database

(b) Multiple instance transactional database (considering attribute 10)

Fig. 7.5 Example of multiple instance association rule mining (II)

all transactions whose value of height is the same (see Fig. 7.4b). Bag 1 contains all transactions where attribute height is short, bag 2 the transactions where attribute height is medium and bag 3 the transactions where attribute height is tall. Figure 7.5 shows a different perspective of the dataset based on attribute 10, which represents the sex of a person. In Fig. 7.5a, the pink solid color represents women and the white striped color represents men. We can obtain a new perspective of the MIL dataset where the data are grouped by this attribute (Fig. 7.5b). Other attributes or general features could be used as well.

Consider the set of transactions $T = \{T_1, T_2, \ldots, T_m\}$. Each transaction $T_i \in T$ comprises n_i instances, $T_i = \{t_{i1}, t_{i2}, \ldots, t_{in_i}\}$. Each instance t_{ij} is a subset of the total set of items $I = \{i_1, i_2, \ldots, i_k\}$ in the dataset. The main definitions are:

- **Multiple instance association rule (MI-AR)**: this is an implication of the from $A \rightarrow C$, where A and C are subsets of items. The occurrence frequency of a MI-AR is defined as the number of transactions satisfied by the rule. Considering the standard MI assumption, a transaction T_i is satisfied if and only if at least one instance t_{ij} is satisfied by the rule.
- **Multiple instance association rule mining**: this procedure aims to find, from a multi-instance dataset, any MI-AR R in the full rule set $\mathscr{R}$ that satisfies specific user thresholds α of interest, i.e., MI-ARM $= \{\forall R \in \mathscr{R} : quality(R) \geq \alpha\}$.

MI-ARM considers the same quality measures as above to determine the interest of the rules. The main difference between ARM and MI-ARM lies with the concept of transactions and instances. The support of a rule $A \rightarrow C$ is defined as the number of transactions satisfied by rule, that is,

$$Support_{MI\text{-}ARM}(A \rightarrow C) = \frac{|\{T_i \in \mathbf{T} : (\exists t_{ij} \in T_i)(\{A \cup C\} \subseteq t_{ij})\}|}{|\mathbf{T}|}$$

A transaction T_i is satisfied if and only if at least one instance t_{ij} is satisfied by the rule. A major feature of the support quality measure in MI-ARM is that it is possible to obtain A and C that satisfy all the transactions on their own, but that do not satisfy any transactions when analyzed together, i.e., $A \cap C = \emptyset$. This assertion is not possible in classic ARM, since it considers each transaction as a single instance.

The confidence measure is defined as the proportion of the number of transactions that include A and C among all the transactions that include A. It is calculated as

$$Confidence_{MI\text{-}ARM}(A \rightarrow C) = \frac{Support_{MI\text{-}ARM}(A \cup C)}{Support_{MI\text{-}ARM}(A)}$$

Support and confidence are broadly conceived as the fitness quality measures in ARM and, consequently, a great variety of proposals make use of them by applying certain minimum thresholds. In Luna et al. [16] other definitions from the MIL perspective can be found, such as lift, conviction and leverage.

7.2.3 Apriori-MI Algorithm

Apriori [1] is one of the best-known algorithm in ARM. It uses prior knowledge of frequent itemset properties and carries out an iterative process. It first obtains the frequent patterns and then extracts the association rules that satisfy a minimum confidence value. Luna et al. [16] proposed Apriori-MI, an extension of the Apriori algorithm for solving problems in the MIL framework.

Description

The main steps of Apriori-MI are given in Algorithm 9. It implements an iterative approach known as a level-wise search, where k-itemsets are used to explore the next level of $(k + 1)$-itemsets. First, the set of frequent 1-itemsets is found by scanning the database to accumulate the count for each item and collecting those items that satisfy minimum support. The resulting set is denoted by $\mathscr{L}_1$. Next, $\mathscr{L}_1$ is used to find $\mathscr{L}_2$, the set of frequent 2-itemsets, which is used to find $\mathscr{L}_3$ and so on, until no more frequent k-itemsets can be found. It is not needed to evaluate the coverage for all the instances within each transaction. According to the standard MI assumption, once a specific instance is satisfied, it is not necessary to analyze them further and the algorithm can continue with the next transaction. A rule generation procedure of is used to obtain MI-ARs (see Algorithm 10).

Algorithm 9 Apriori-MI Algorithm

Input: α, minimum threshold for support
Input: $T \leftarrow$ multi-instance transactions set $\{T_1, T_2, \ldots, T_N\}$ $(T_i \subseteq \mathbb{X})$
Output: $\mathscr{L}$, the frequent k-itemsets
1: $k = 1$,
2: $\mathscr{L}_1 \leftarrow \{k - patterns(T)\}$,   ▷ *set of frequent 1-itemset*
3: $C \leftarrow \emptyset$ ▷ *set of candidate k-items*
4: $k \leftarrow 2$
5: **while** $\mathscr{L}_{k-1} \neq \emptyset$ **do**
6:     $C_k \leftarrow \{\{a\} \cup \{b\} | a \in \mathscr{L}_{k-1} \wedge b \in \mathscr{L}_{k-1} \wedge b \neq a \wedge \{\{a\} \cup \{b\}\} \notin \mathscr{L}_k\}$
7:     **for** $T_i \in T$ **do**   ▷ *For all transactions*
8:         **for** $(c|c \in C_k)$ **do**
9:             **if** $(\exists t_{i,j} \in T_i \wedge c \subseteq t_{ij})$ **then**
10:                 $count[c] \leftarrow count[c] + 1$
11:             **end if**
12:         **end for**
13:     **end for**
14:     $\mathscr{L}_k \leftarrow \{c | c \in C_k \wedge count[c] \geq \alpha\}$
15:     $k \leftarrow k + 1$
16: **end while**
17: $\mathscr{L} \leftarrow \bigcup_k \mathscr{L}_k$

Algorithm 10 Rule Generation Procedure

Input: $\mathscr{L}$, the frequent k-itemsets
Input: β, minimum threshold for confidence
Output: R, association rule
1: $R \leftarrow \emptyset$
2: **for** $(l \in \mathscr{L})$ s **do**
3:     **for** $(x \subset l$ such that $x \neq \emptyset$ and $x \neq l)$ **do**
4:         **if** $support(l)/support(x) \geq \beta$ **then**
5:             $R \leftarrow R \cap \{x \leftarrow (l - x)\}$
6:         **end if**
7:     **end for**
8: **end for**

Experimental Study

In [16], the idea is not to compare results of different algorithms, but rather to provide an overview of the use of MI-ARM as an unsupervised and descriptive task. Its utility is shown and compared with respect to classic ARM. Artificial and real-world datasets are used to show the validity of MI-ARM, describing the support and confidence of the obtained MI-ARs.

7.3 Summarizing Comments

In this chapter, unsupervised MIL is addressed. Two important tasks in this learning framework are discussed, cluster analysis and association rule mining. The most relevant concepts and definitions are introduced.

If we consider the last decades, it can be observed that unsupervised MIL has appeared more recently and is by far less investigated than traditional unsupervised learning. In this chapter, a survey of the existing methods is given. In the case of MI-Clustering, a field that has a few years of experience, different methods are reviewed including partitioning, hierarchical, density based, probabilistic model based and margin maximum based methods. In the case of MI-ARM, a very recent field, the single currently known method is described. For each algorithm, the experimental study of its developers is briefly reported. These experimental results indicate that each algorithm has its own advantages and disadvantages depending on the problem context. Unsupervised MIL is revealed as a promising area of future research.

References

1. Agrawal, R., Mannila, H., Srikant, R., Toivonen, H., Verkamo, A.I.: Fast discovery of association rules. In: Advances in Knowledge Discovery and Data Mining, pp. 307–328. American Association for Artificial Intelligence, Menlo Park (1996)
2. Ankerst, M., Breunig, M.M., Kriegel, H.P., Sander, J.: OPTICS: ordering points to identify the clustering structure. In: Delis, A., Faloutsos, C., Ghandeharizadeh, S. (eds.) Proceedings of the International Conference on Management of data (SIGMOD 1999), pp. 49–60. ACM, New York (1999)
3. Arbelaitz, O., Gurrutxaga, I., Muguerza, J., Pérez, J.M., Perona, I.: An extensive comparative study of cluster validity indices. Pattern Recogn. **46**(1), 243–256 (2013)
4. Banfield, J.D., Raftery, A.E.: Model-based Gaussian and non-Gaussian clustering. Biometrics **49**(3), 803–821 (1993)
5. Chen, Y., Wu, O.: Contextual Hausdorff dissimilarity for multi-instance clustering. In: Liu, Y. (ed.) Proceedings of the 9th International Conference on Fuzzy Systems and Knowledge Discovery (FSKD 2012), pp. 870–873. IEEE, Los Alamitos (2012)
6. Fraley, C., Raftery, A.E.: How many clusters? Which clustering method? Answers via model-based cluster analysis. Comput. J. **41**(8), 578–588 (1998)
7. Fraley, C., Raftery, A.E.: Model-based clustering, discriminant analysis, and density estimation. J Am. Stat. Assoc. **97**(458), 611–631 (2002)
8. Hartigan, J.A.: Clustering Algorithms. Wiley, New York (1975)
9. Hansen, P., Jaumard, B.: Cluster analysis and mathematical programming. Math. Program. **79**(1–3), 191–215 (1997)
10. Han, J., Kamber, M.: Data Mining: Concepts and Techniques. Morgan Kaufmann Publishers, Waltham (2001)
11. Henegar, C., Clément, K., Zucker, J.D.: Unsupervised multiple-instance learning for functional profiling of genomic data. In: Fürnkranz, J., Scheffer, T., Spiliopoulou, M. (eds.) Proceedings of the 17th European Conference on Machine Learning (ECML 2006), pp. 186–197. Springer, Heidelberg (2006)
12. Kaufman, L., Rousseuw, P.: Finding Groups in Data: An Introduction to Cluster Analysis. Wiley, New York (1990)

13. Kelley, J.E.: The cutting-plane method for solving convex programs. J. Soc. Ind. Appl. Math. **8**(4), 703–712 (1960)
14. Kriegel, H.P., Pryakhin, A., Schubert, M., Zimek, A.: COSMIC: conceptually specified multi-instance clusters. In: Clifton, C.W., Zhong, N., Liu, J., Wah, B.W., Wu, X. (eds.) Proceedings of the 6th International Conference on Data Mining (ICDM 2006), pp. 917–921. IEEE, Los Alamitos (2006)
15. Kriegel, H.P., Pryakhin, A., Schubert, M.: An EM-approach for clustering multi-instance objects. In: Ng, W.K., Kitsuregawa, M., Li, J. (eds.) Advances in Knowledge Discovery and Data Mining. Lecture Notes in Computer Science, vol. 3918, pp. 139–148. Springer, Berlin (2006)
16. Luna, J.M., Cano, A., Sakalauskas, K., Ventura, S.: Discovering useful patterns from multiple instance data. Inf. Sci. **357**, 23–38 (2016)
17. Tax, D.M., Hendriks, E., Valstar, M.F., Pantic, M.: The detection of concept frames using clustering multi-instance learning. In: Unay, D., Cataltepe, Z., Aksoy, S. (eds.) Proceedings of 20th the International Conference on Pattern Recognition (ICPR 2010), pp. 2917–2920. IEEE, Los Alamitos (2010)
18. Xu, L., Neufeld, J., Larson, B., Schuurmans, D.: Maximum margin clustering. In: Saul, L.K., Weiss, Y., Bottou, L. (eds.) Proceedings of the 18th Conference on Advances in Neural Information Processing Systems (NIPS 2004), pp. 1537–1544. MIT Press, Cambridge (2004)
19. Xu, D., Tian, Y.: A comprehensive survey of clustering algorithms. Ann. Data Sci. **2**, 165–193 (2015)
20. Zhang, C., Chen, X.: Region-based image clustering and retrieval using multiple instance learning. In: Leow, W.-K., Lew, M.S., Chua, T.-S., Ma, W.-Y., Chaisorn, L., Bakker, E.M. (eds.) Proceedings of the 4th International Conference on Image and Video Retrieval (CIVR), pp. 194–204. Springer, Berlin (2005)
21. Zhang, D., Wang, F., Si, L., Li, T.: Maximum margin multiple instance clustering with applications to image and text clustering. IEEE Trans. Neural Networks **22**(5), 739–751 (2011)
22. Zhang, M.L., Zhou, Z.H.: Multi-instance clustering with applications to multi-instance prediction. Appl. Intell. **31**(1), 47–68 (2009)
23. Zhang, T., Liu, S., Xu, C., Lu, H.: M4L: maximum margin multi-instance multi-cluster learning for scene modeling. Pattern Recogn. **46**(10), 2711–2723 (2013)
24. Zhao, B., Wang, F., Zhang, C.: Efficient maximum margin clustering via cutting plane algorithm. In: Ghosh, J., Lambert, D., Skillicorn, D., Srivastava, J. (eds.) Proceedings of the 8th International Conference on Data Mining (SIAM 2008), pp. 751–762. Society for Industrial and Applied Mathematics, Philadelphia (2008)
25. Zhou, Z.H., Zhang, M.L.: Solving multi-instance problems with classifier ensemble based on constructive clustering. Knowl. Inf. Syst. **11**(2), 155–170 (2007)

Chapter 8
Data Reduction

Abstract An increase in dataset dimensionality and size implies a large computational complexity and possible estimation errors. In this context, data reduction methods try to construct a new and more compact data subset. This subset should maintain the most representative information and remove redundant, irrelevant, and/or noisy information. The inherent uncertainty of MIL renders the data reduction process more difficult. Each positive bag is composed of several instances, of which only a part approximate the positive concept. Information on which instances are positive is not available. In this chapter, we first provide an introduction to data reduction. Next, two main strategies to reduce MIL data are considered. Section 8.2 describes the main concepts of feature selection as well as methods that try to reduce the number of features in MIL problems. Section 8.3 considers bag prototype selection and analyzes the corresponding multi-instance methods.

8.1 Introduction

Data reduction is a complex problem in any machine learning framework. Different techniques can be applied to obtain a reduced representation of the data, closely maintaining the original integrity. The reduced dataset should be more efficient to process and produce the same or similar analytical results.

As the dimensionality of a problem (number of features) increases, the well-known *curse of dimensionality* manifests itself. This concept was introduced by Bellman [1] to show that the number of samples required to estimate a function with a given level of accuracy grows exponentially with the problem dimension. For a given sample size, there is a maximum number of features above which the performance of an algorithm will degrade rather than improve. In fact, many data mining algorithms fail when the dimensionality is high, since data points become sparse and far apart from each other.

The large amount of data produced in any current application has resulted in datasets composed of thousands of objects represented by hundreds or even thousands of features. The dimensionality is a serious obstacle for the efficiency of most algorithms. Its reduction has become a necessary hot topic to ensure that algorithms

© Springer International Publishing AG 2016

F. Herrera et al., *Multiple Instance Learning*, DOI 10.1007/978-3-319-47759-6_8

can perform appropriately. Data reduction techniques have been studied extensively in many domains. Section 1.2 gave a brief introduction to data reduction, grouping these methods as follows:

- **Feature selection**: the dimensionality is reduced by removing irrelevant or redundant features [17]. The goal of feature selection is to find a minimum set of attributes, such that the resulting probability distribution of the output is as close as possible to the original distribution using all features. These methods facilitate the understanding of the extracted knowledge and increase the speed of the learning stage.
- **Instance selection**: the number of observations is reduced by removing less relevant or noisy instances [16]. In MIL, these methods can be divided into two categories, since data samples are bags composed of one or more instances. On the one hand, *bag prototype selection* aims to reduce the number of training samples. The removal of a bag implies the elimination of all instances contained in it. On the other hand, *instance prototype selection* reduces the number of instances inside each bag. The number of bags remains the same, while less representative instances within them are eliminated. Both methods reduce the size of the data and therefore the computational complexity.
- **Feature extraction**: this is an extension of feature selection that allows the modification of the internal values representing each attribute [15]. In feature extraction, apart from the removal of attributes, feature subsets can be merged or can contribute to the creation of artificial substitute features.
- **Instance generation**: this process extends instance selection by allowing the modification of samples [22]. These methods create or adjust artificial substitute examples that could better represent the decision boundaries in supervised learning.

In this chapter, data reduction in MIL is considered. We describe the two most common techniques, feature selection, and bag prototype selection. All included concepts and methods show the interaction of data reduction with classification.

8.2   Multiple Instance Methods for Feature Selection

Datasets may contain many irrelevant or redundant features. To give an example, if we focus on the identification of a particular illness in several patients, attributes such as the patient's telephone number or surname are likely to be irrelevant, unlike attributes such as age or blood pressure. Irrelevant features imply a huge amount of data that results in an increase in processing time of a learner and a reduction of its performance. Manually evaluating the features (e.g., by a domain expert) becomes intractable when the number of attributes is high and the data behavior is not well-known. Automatic feature selection methods have been extensively used to replace the original data volume by an alternative, more reduced representation.

In this section, we first give an introduction to feature selection, providing a brief background and the main taxonomy. We analyze the particularities of multi-instance feature selection and discuss the representative methods.

8.2.1   Introduction to Feature Selection

Feature Selection (FS) methods select a subset of features from the initial dataset according to certain criteria. These methods should remove noisy and irrelevant features and maintain only the most informative ones. In this way, the feature subset should be capable of producing results equal to or better than the full set. Reducing the feature set has several benefits, such as minimizing the computational cost of algorithms, improving the accuracy of the final result, and making the data mining results easier to understand.

FS can be defined as a search problem to find a subset of features optimizing a particular criterion. Formally, let A be the original feature set with cardinality M and B the subset of desired features ($B \subset A$) with cardinality m ($m << M$) [10]. FS tries to find an optimal subset B that minimizes the criterion function $\mathscr{F}$. The main steps of FS methods are the following [10]:

1. **The generation of different subsets**: the feature space is explored for the best subset.
2. **The evaluation of feature subsets**: an evaluation function is used to test the fitness of a feature subset. This function corresponds to the criteria that the FS method tries to fulfill.
3. **The stopping criterion**: a stopping criterion to halt the search needs to be specified.

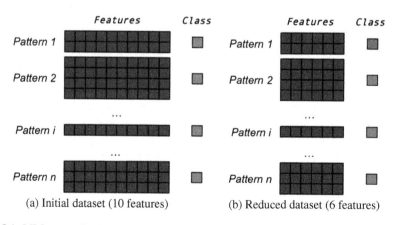

(a) Initial dataset (10 features)   (b) Reduced dataset (6 features)

Fig. 8.1 MI feature selection method

Figure 8.1 shows the process of feature selection in a MIL context. Figure 8.1a depicts the initial dataset, where the samples are composed of several instances, that is, several feature vectors. Figure 8.1b describes the dataset after application of FS, where the number of features describing each instance has been reduced. FS in MIL is more challenging than its counterpart in single-instance learning. In MIL, each observation is represented by a number of instances. Instance labels are not available and it is possible to find both positive and negative instances inside a positive bag. Different methods assume that positive bags consist of mainly positive instances. The negative instances in positive bags may limit the discriminative power of FS methods. As a consequence, determining the significance of each attribute becomes more difficult.

Before describing the most relevant proposals of FS in MIL, we specify the FS taxonomy. This categorization is probably the most known and employed in FS methods over the years [18]. It is based on how the methods combine the FS search with the construction of the classification model:

- **Filter methods**: features are selected based on a performance measure independent of the classification algorithm. In this case, FS is an independent preprocessing step before the application of a particular classifier. The optimal feature subset or a relevance ranking of the features is returned. The advantages are that these methods are computationally fast, scalable, and independent of the classifier. On the other hand, their main shortcomings are the fact that they ignore feature dependencies and interactions with the classifier.
- **Wrapper methods**: a learner is used to measure the quality of feature subsets without incorporating any information about the specific structure of the classification or regression function. These methods can be combined with any learner.
- **Embedded methods**: FS is performed during the modeling phase of the classifier. The FS method is embedded in the classifier. These methods have the advantage that they include the interaction with the classification model. They are often far less computationally intensive than wrapper methods. They directly return the final classifier.
- **Hybrid methods**: these algorithms combine the best properties of filter and wrapper methods. First, a filter method is used to reduce the dimension of the feature space and obtain several candidate feature subsets. Next, a wrapper is employed to find the best candidate subset among them.

FS has become an apparent need in many learning paradigms. Numerous studies show that the reduction can not only reduce computational complexity, but also improve validation results and enhance semantic interpretability. Below, we describe the most relevant FS methods in MIL. Table 8.1 provides an overview of the main contributions in this area grouped as filter, wrapper, embedded, and hybrid methods.

Table 8.1 Features selection methods in multi-instance learning

Filter methods	
ReliefF-MI algorithm [28]	
Reliability-based algorithm [9]	
Embedded methods	
Boosting based methods	*Kernel based methods*
MI-AdaBoost algorithm [27]	MILES algorithm [5]
MCMI-AdaBoost algorithm [32]	Ngiam et al. [20]
EBMIL algorithm [25]	MIO algorithm [14]
BEL algorithm [31]	MIL-MFS algorithm [11]
Online MIL adaboost algorithm [3]	FSPO algorithm [19]
Hybrid methods	
HyDR-MI algorithm [29]	

8.2.2   Filter Methods

To select a feature subset, these algorithms take advantage of general characteristics of the data, like distances or statistical dependencies between classes. They are faster than other approaches, because they act independently of the induction algorithm. However, they tend to select subsets with a high number of features. It is also difficult to fix an internal threshold above which a feature is important enough to be selected.

Two multi-instance FS methods can be listed in this group. ReliefF-MI [28] is based on the principles on the single-instance ReliefF algorithm [21]. The second included proposal describes a multi-instance FS algorithm based on information aggregation using a data reliability measure. Both methods assign a weight to each feature to determine its relevance and specify a threshold on these weights to determine the final feature subset. As any filter method, they can be used as a preprocessing step before the application of any classifier.

8.2.2.1   ReliefF-MI Algorithm

This method was proposed by Zafra et al. [28] and estimates the quality of features based on how well their values distinguish between bags that are near each other. A description of its main steps is given in Algorithm 11. First, bags are randomly selected from the training data. For each sampled bag R, its k nearest neighbors from the same class (nearest hits) are found as well as its k nearest neighbors of the opposite classes (nearest misses). Based on these neighbors, the weight of each feature is updated. These weights reflect the ability to distinguish class labels. A high weight indicates that this feature differs among bags from different classes and is the same in bags of the same class. Features are ranked by weight and those that exceed a user-specified threshold are selected to form the final subset. The calculation of the nearest neighbors and the definition of the $diff_{bag}$ function applied to the bags is carried out with different variants of Hausdorff distance. The authors of [28] also proposed the adapted Hausdorff distance (Sect. 3.5).

Experimental Study

The study of Zafra et al. [28] considers five benchmark real world datasets: Musk1, Musk2, Elephant, Tiger, and Fox. A description of any of these is given in Sect. 3.6. ReliefF-MI provides a reduced dataset in a preprocessing step independent of a classifier. To show the efficiency of the method, the reduced dataset is used in 17 multi-instance classification algorithms. The results are evaluated on both accuracy and execution time. They confirm the utility and efficiency of ReliefF-MI as a pre-processing step for all included algorithms. The classifiers statistically improve both their accuracy and execution time.

The experimental study also includes a comparison of different distance measures used by ReliefF-MI, namely the maximal, minimal, average, and adapted Hausdorff distances (Sect. 3.5). The results show that the adapted Hausdorff distance performs statistically best, obtaining a better dimensionality reduction, and better classifier accuracy. Its advantage lies with the different ways to measure the distance depending on the specific information available in each bag.

Algorithm 11 ReliefF-MI algorithm

Input: $X \leftarrow$ multi-instance training set $\{X_1, X_2, \ldots, X_N\}$ $(X_i \subseteq \mathbb{X})$
Input: $m \leftarrow$ number of times that the process is repeated
Input: $k \leftarrow$ number of nearest examples of the same and different class considered in the process.
Input: $\varepsilon \leftarrow$ threshold to determine if the feature is added to subset
Output: $selectedSubset$, the selected feature subset
1: $selectedSubset = \emptyset$
2: $W = 0$ ▷ Feature weight vector
3: **for** i from 1 to m **do**
4:     $R_i \leftarrow$ bag randomly selected from X
5:     $H_{R_i}^k \leftarrow findKNearestNeighborSameClass(R_i, X)$ ▷ Get k nearest hits
6:     **for** each class C $\neq$ Class (R_i) **do**
7:         $M_{R_i}^k \leftarrow findKNearestNeighborDifferentClass(R_i, X)$ ▷ Get k nearest misses
8:     **end for**
9:     **for** A from 1 to numberFeatures **do**
10:         $W[A] = W[A] + \dfrac{\sum_{j=1}^{k} diff_{bag}(A, R_i, H_{R_i}^j)}{m \cdot k} + \sum_{C \neq Class(R_i)} \left[\dfrac{\frac{P(C)}{1-P(Class(R_i))} \sum_{j=1}^{k} diff_{bag}(A, R_i, M_{R_i}^j(C))}{m \cdot k} \right]$
11:     **end for**
12: **end for**
13: **for** i from 1 to numberFeatures **do**
14:     **if** $W[i] > \varepsilon$ **then**
15:         selectedSubset $\leftarrow$ selectedSubset $\cup \{f_i\}$.
16:     **end if**
17: **end for**

8.2.2.2 Reliability Based Algorithm

Gan and Yin [9] proposed a method that ranks features based on the reliability measure of each attribute. The class labels are not used for evaluating features, such that this method can also be applied in unsupervised learning. Based on the OWA operator [24], a feature is considered reliable if its values are tightly grouped together. The main steps are shown in Algorithm 12. First, the reliability of each feature f_r for each example X_i using its k nearest neighbors $FR_{X_i,r}$ is determined. Second, the data reliability FR_r of each feature f_r is computed by combining the data reliability of all its values in all samples. From these values, the average data reliability of all features $FR_{average}$ can be derived. As a last step, the features whose FR_r is bigger than the average data reliability are selected. The calculation of the nearest neighbors is carried out using the minimum Hausdorff distance, such that the difference of feature f_r between two bags is equal to the minimum difference of feature f_r between instances from those bags.

This method as well as ReliefF-MI both use a k nearest neighbor approach to determine the relevance of each attribute. Both proposals use a Hausdorff distance to determine the distance between bags. This bag-wise similarity measure is very important in MIL, since it models the relevance and relationship of different instances inside one bag. Gan et al. [9] use the minimal Hausdorff distance, while Zafra et al. [28] uses the different variants presented in Sect. 3.5.

Experimental Study

The study of Gan and Yin [9] considers two datasets: Musk1 and Musk2 (Sect. 3.6). To show the efficiency of their method, the obtained reduced dataset is fed to four classifiers, whose accuracy is evaluated. The results show that the predictive accuracy of the learners was enhanced by using the reduced dataset. The experimental study also includes a comparative study using different values of the k parameter, which represents the number of neighbors. The results show that different values of this parameter scarcely affect the obtained results.

8.2.3 Embedded Methods

Embedded methods differ from other FS methods in the interaction of FS and learning. Wrapper and embedded methods are often confused. A wrapper method uses a learner to measure the quality of feature subsets without incorporating knowledge about the specific structure of the classification function. Embedded methods on the other hand cannot separate the learning and FS parts. These methods learn which features best contribute to the accuracy of the model while the model is being created.

In this section, we describe two embedded multi-instance FS methods, where FS is combined with the Adaboost or SVM methods. These models implicitly select important features and construct a classifier simultaneously.

Algorithm 12 Reliability based method

Input: $X \leftarrow$ multi-instance training set $\{X_1, X_2, \ldots, X_N\}$ $(X_i \subseteq \mathbb{X})$.
Input: $k \leftarrow$ number of neighbors
Input: $m \leftarrow$ number of features
Output: $selectedSubset$, the selected feature subset
1: $selectedSubset = \emptyset$
2: $FR_{average} = 0$
3: **for** r from 1 to m **do**
4:     $maxFeatureDiff \leftarrow$ maxFeatureDifference(X, r).   ▷ Calculate maximum difference of
    feature f_r between two bags in whole training set
5:     $FR_r = 0$
6:     **for** each $X_i \in X$ **do**
7:         $N_{X_i,r}^k = findKNearestNeighbor(X, k, X_i, r)$ ▷ k nearest neighbor of X_i considering
    feature f_r
8:         $D_{X_i,r}^k = averageFeatureDifference(N_{X_i,r}^k, k)$.   ▷ Average difference of feature f_r of
    bag X_i with its k nearest neighbor
9:         $FR_{X_i,r}^k = bagFeatureDataReliability(D_{X_i,r}^k, maxFeatureDiff)$.   ▷ Data reliability
    of feature f_r in bag X_i
10:         $FR_r = FR_r + FR_{X_i,r}^k$.   ▷ Data reliability of each feature by combining all examples
11:     **end for**
12:     $FR_{average} = FR_{average} + FR_r$
13: **end for**
14: $FR_{average} = FR_{average}/m$ ▷ Average data reliability
15: **for** r from 1 to m **do**
16:     **if** $FR_r > FR_{average}$ **then**
17:         selectedSubset $\leftarrow$ selectedSubset $\cup \{f_r\}$.
18:     **end if**
19: **end for**

8.2.3.1 Adaboost for Feature Selection

Boosting techniques have been extensively used for FS in the MIL scenario. The
key idea behind AdaBoost is that a strong classifier can be created by combining
many weak classifiers. These weak classifiers need only perform slightly better than
random guessing. Given a set of training samples, AdaBoost maintains a weight
w for each of them. The weights are initialized uniformly. At each iteration t, one
weak classifier is selected and the training samples are provided using weights w_t. A
weak classifier h_t is trained on these samples. The weights are updated to put more
emphasis on misclassified samples. Samples that are correctly classified by h_t get
lower weights, while misclassified samples are assigned higher weights. AdaBoost
focuses on samples with higher weights, which seem to be harder to predict correctly.
The process continues for T iterations. The final strong classifier is a combination
of the weak classifiers.

AdaBoost can be used to select the bag features and build the classifier simultaneously. The core idea is that each feature corresponds to a single weak classifier,
such that boosting can select some features out of the pool of all possible features
F. In each iteration t, the algorithm selects one new feature and adds it (with the
corresponding voting factor) to the ensemble. All features are evaluated and the best

one is selected to form the weak classifiers h_t. The sample weights are updated. In the last step, a strong classifier H is computed as a weighted linear combination of the weak classifiers. The number of iterations T is related to the number of dimensions with a sufficient differentiation ability in the whole feature vector. Algorithm 13 shows this process. Some differences with respect to the original AdaBoost method [7] are evident. In this schema, the sums of sample weights for positive and negative samples are always kept equal to 1/2. This maintains the balance between positive and negative bags. The weak classifier uses the weights in its real-valued prediction. The final strong classifier is a direct combination of the weak classifiers instead of a weighted combination.

Algorithm 13 AdaBoost feature selection Algorithm for MIL

Input: $X \leftarrow$ multi-instance training set $\{X_1, X_2, \ldots, X_N\}$ $(X_i \subseteq \mathbb{X})$
Output: H, the final strong classifier
1: Map X to a new bag-level feature space
2: $n^+ \leftarrow$ number of positive samples
3: $n^- \leftarrow$ number of negative samples
4: **if** $Class(X_i)$ is positive **then**   ▷ Initialize the weight vector
5:    $w(X_i) = \frac{1}{2}n^+$
6: **else**
7:    $w(X_i) = \frac{1}{2}n^-$
8: **end if**
9: **for** t from 1 to T **do**
10:    Train the weak classifier h_j for each feature j using $w(X_i)$
11:    Calculate the training error e_j of h_j,

$$e_j = \sum_i w(X_i)|h_j(X_i) - Class(X_i)|$$

12:    Choose $h_t = h_j$ with the lowest error and set $e_t = e_j$
13:    Update weights for positive examples

$$w_{t+1}(X_i) = \frac{w_t(X_i)\exp^{(-Class(X_i)\cdot h_t(X_i))}}{Z_{tp}}$$

14:    Update weights for negative examples

$$w_{t+1}(X_i) = \frac{w_t(X_i)\exp^{(-Class(X_i)\cdot h_t(X_i))}}{Z_{tn}}$$

   ▷ Z_{tp} and Z_{tn} are normalization factors to ensure that w_{t+1} is distribution and that the weight of positive and negative samples all sum up to 1/2
15: **end for**
16: $H(X) = sign[\sum_{t=1}^{T} h_t(X)]$

Depending on the employed weak classifiers, different proposals can be found regarding the weight distribution in their training phase and the way they are combined at the end of the algorithm. Different map-based algorithms are encountered.

As described in Sect. 5.3, these methods map each bag into a new feature vector and thereby transforms the multi-instance data to a single-instance representation. The MIL problem is converted to a standard single-instance problem, usually with a higher dimensionality such that it is convenient to perform a FS step. Any traditional single-instance FS method can be applied. We list proposals using AdaBoost with a linear weak classifier for selecting the bag features obtained by mapping and building the final classifier simultaneously (Algorithm 13).

The MI-AdaBoost algorithm was proposed by Yuan et al. [27]. It uses AdaBoost to select the bag features mapped by a certain set of instance prototypes. It considers two types of instance prototypes: instances from positive bags and the clustering centers of the instances from negative bags. The minimum Hausdorff distance is used to measure the distance between bags.

Zhu et al. [32] proposed the MCMI-AdaBoost method, an algorithm that uses AdaBoost to select the bag features by computing the Hausdorff distance to define a similarity measure between two bags. The bags are mapped to a new bag feature space based on this similarity. An AdaBoost algorithm is proposed to build a two-level classifier converting the multi-class classification problem to a series of two-class classification problems. The output of the first level indicates the possibility that a bag belongs to one class. The second level performs a two-class classification between the two classes with the highest possibility.

Based on their previous work, Yuan et al. developed the existence-based MIL called EBMIL in [25]. This method is able to select different feature modalities for each concept under MIL settings. As a step prior to AdaBoost, a mapping is applied based on points in the instance-level feature space, that hold potential information on the positive and opposite concepts. Positive instance prototypes and opposite instance prototypes are considered. The former are all the instances from positive bags, while the latter are the clustering centers of instances from negative bags.

More recently, Zhang et al. [31] proposed a boosted exemplar learning (BEL) approach for the computer vision field. Based on the learned exemplar, M candidate exemplars are obtained. Each action bag (e.g., an action in a video clip) is described as an M-dimensional vector of its similarity with the M exemplars. The AdaBoost algorithm integrates the FS and action modeling.

Ciliberto et al. [3] follow the philosophy of AdaBoost to design their online MIL algorithm. They include a mechanism for online FS based on Algorithm 13. In an online context, it is likely that useful and descriptive features (and hence potential centers for new weak classifiers) will not be available from the start, but may become available in a later stage. In the problem studied in [3], the object to be learned can rotate, revealing its previously hidden parts.

Experimental Study

The studies of Yuan et al. [25, 27] consider the Corel and Musk datasets (Sect. 3.6) to evaluate their proposals. The mean average precision and computation time are used as evaluation measures. The experimental results show that MI-AdaBoost [27] is much more efficient than the 1-norm SVM [5] and MI-Boosting [7]. Concretely, for the Corel dataset, MI-AdaBoost performs better than MI-Boosting, while its results are comparable with the 1-norm SVM. In the Musk datasets, MI-AdaBoost performs better than both MI-Boosting and 1-norm SVM. The EBMIL algorithm [25] achieves promising experimental results on the Corel dataset compared with four other feature reduction methods, confirming its effectiveness.

Other models based on AdaBoost for feature selection described in this section are applied to solve particular problems, such as the study of Zhu et al. [32] that shows that their approach, the MCMI-AdaBoost method, is an effective solution for the lung cancer classification problem. In order to evaluate its performance, they compare the accuracy of their method with four other proposals, including classic algorithms such as Citation-kNN and an SVM based algorithm. The study of Zhang et al. [31] considers two available datasets of video action recognition, the KTH human motion dataset and Weizmann human action dataset. To demonstrate the validity and effectiveness of their BEL algorithm, they compare its results with four other MIL classification methods based on the accuracy. The results show that the BEL algorithm outperforms its competitors.

8.2.3.2   SVM for Feature Selection

SVMs have also been widely used for interweaving FS and classifier construction. They allow the incorporation of feature weighting in their kernel function to combine different features. The performance of these methods can be improved by providing information about the features during model generation.

Ngiam et al. [20] incorporate feature weighting into the kernel function based on the idea that different features work well with different concepts. In their proposal, the weight learning is carried out by a simple greedy algorithm (Algorithm 14). In order to obtain the final classifier, each concept is considered independently using an SVM with extended Gaussian kernels over the χ^2 distance:

$$K(X_i, X_j) = \sum_{f \in F} \frac{1}{\mu_f} \chi^2(f(X_i), f(X_j)),$$

where μ_f is the average χ^2 distance for a particular feature, used to normalize the distances across different features.

There are others kernel-based methods that carry out FS using an SVM model to select important features and construct a classifier simultaneously. These methods transform MIL into a FS problem by embedding bags into a new feature space. According to the specific mapping function used in the transformation, the final purpose of a method can change. The MILES method of Chen et al. [5] (Sect. 5.3.4) falls in this category. MILES maps the bags via an instance similarity measure. It uses each instance as a candidate target point, such that the induced space has a high dimensionality. The authors use a $1-$norm SVM to select relevant features and build classifiers at the same time. At its core, this approach identifies relevant instances in the new bag feature space, since each feature is induced by an instance.

Algorithm 14 Greedy FS

Input: $X \leftarrow$ multi-instance training set $\{X_1, X_2, \ldots, X_N\}$ $(X_i \subseteq \mathbb{X})$, $Class(X_i) = 0$ for the
  negative examples and $Class(X_i) = 1$ for the positive examples
Input: $F \leftarrow$ all features
Output: $selected Subset$, feature subset
1: **repeat**
2:    **for** each feature $f \in F$ **do**
3:        Compute error rate if f is removed
4:    **end for**
5:    Remove the feature which results in the highest improvement
6: **until** removing any feature results in worse performance
7: **repeat**
8:    **for** each feature $f \in F$ **do**
9:        Compute error rate if f is added
10:        Compute error rate if f is removed
11:    **end for**
12:    $selected Subset \leftarrow$ Add feature which give best improvement
13: **until** local optimum is reached

The Multiple Instance Online (MIO) method proposed by Li et al. [14] is an online MI learning algorithm that has an efficient online update procedure. Similar to MILES, it maps each bag to a feature space defined by all instances and then performs joint FS and classification by using the 1-norm SVM.

The MIL-MFS (Multiple-Instance Learning with Multiple Feature Selection) algorithm was proposed by Jhuo et al. [11] and uses multiple kernel learning. The authors use a similarity based feature representation, where each instance may be mapped into diverse feature spaces. It iteratively selects the fusing of multiple features for classifier training.

More recently, Mao et al. [19] proposed the FSPO (Feature Selection method for multivariate Performance measures Optimization) algorithm. They propose a generalized sparse regularizer for FS, based on which a unified FS framework is presented for general loss functions. Specifically, they propose a two-layer cutting plane algorithm including group feature generation and selection to solve this problem effectively and efficiently. Multiple kernel learning is proposed to deal with the exponential size of constraints induced by multivariate losses.

Experimental Study

The study of Jhuo et al. [11] considers the Corel dataset (Sect. 3.6). They compare their proposal, the MIL-MFS algorithm, with four multi-instance classifiers based on SVM. Their results show that their method achieves the best accuracy among the included algorithms.

Considering a proposal of online MI learning, the study of Li et al. [14] utilizes synthetic datasets and the Musk datasets (Sect. 3.6) to compare their MIO algorithm with the MILES method. The experimental results show that their proposal outperforms MILES with a small number of passes. Moreover, the average error of nine multi-instance classifiers is used to validate the efficiency of MIO and the latter is shown to achieve competitive results.

Finally, a more recent study carried out by Mao et al. [19] considers the Corel and News datasets (Sect. 3.6). They compare their FSPO algorithm with four feature selection methods and evaluate the results using the F1 score measure [19]. Comparing with various feature selection methods, the FSPO algorithm is shown to be superior to the others.

8.2.4 Hybrid Method: HyDR-MI Algorithm

Hybrid FS methods combine the advantages of filter and wrapper methods. To determine the important properties of the feature space, a filter method assigns a score to each attribute. Features with very low scores are considered to be irrelevant and can be discarded. The reduced or ranked feature set is provided to a wrapper method, whose purpose is to select the best feature subset for a particular MIL algorithm.

Algorithm 15 HyDR-MI algorithm

Input: $X \leftarrow$ multi-instance training set $\{X_1, X_2, \ldots, X_N\}$ ($X_i \subseteq \mathbb{X}$)
Output: subsetFeature, the most relevant feature subset
       ▷ ReliefF-MI Method
1: subsetFeature $\leftarrow$ obtained with method ReliefF-MI
       ▷ Genetic Algorithm
2: $P_0 \leftarrow$ initial population, generated randomly
3: $P_0 \leftarrow$ evaluation of P_0 using a classification method
4: $t \leftarrow 0$
5: **repeat**
6:    $P_{parent} \leftarrow$ selectionParents (P_t)
7:    $P_{offspring} \leftarrow$ genetic operators crossover and mutation over P_{parent}
8:    $P_{offspring} \leftarrow$ evaluation of $P_{offspring}$ using a classification method
9:    $P_{t+1} \leftarrow$ update population using P_t and $P_{offspring}$
10:    $t \leftarrow t + 1$
11: **until** $t <$ maxGenerations
12: subsetFeature $\leftarrow$ the best individual obtained in genetic algorithm

---

Adhering to this setup, Zafra et al. [29] developed HyDR-MI (Hybrid Dimensionality Reduction method for Multiple Instance learning), as shown in Algorithm 15. This method consists of a filter component based on the ReliefF-MI algorithm [28] and a wrapper component based on a genetic algorithm [23] that optimizes the search for the best feature subset from a reduced set of features obtained by filter. This combination benefits both sides. On the one hand, the main restriction of the ReliefF-MI algorithm is the necessity of setting a threshold which determines how many top scored features should be selected. It evaluates each feature individually and cannot handle the problem of feature redundancy appropriately. The genetic algorithm assists the search for the best feature subset and thereby solves these issues. It uses the performance of a classifier as a fitness function and optimizes the FS by finding the most suitable subset for that classifier. On the other hand, the main limitation of a genetic algorithm is its computation time. ReliefF-MI helps to reduce the search space to achieve better results in less time.

Experimental Study

The study of Zafra et al. [29] considers five benchmark datasets: Musk1, Musk2, Elephant, Tiger, and Fox (Sect. 3.6). To show the efficiency of HyDR-MI compared to ReliefF-MI [28], the results of 17 multi-instance classification algorithms are compared based on the accuracy.

The results show the potential of HyDR-MI statistically improving the predictive performance of many classifiers compared to ReliefF-MI. This is achieved by the possibility to decide how many of the top ranked features are useful for each particular algorithm and the possibility to discard redundant attributes.

8.3   Multiple Instance Methods for Bag Prototype Selection

The second data reduction technique that we consider in this chapter is bag prototype selection. In Sect. 8.3.1, we introduce this concept. Section 8.3.2 describes several multi-instance methods implementing this procedure.

8.3.1   *Introduction to Bag Prototype Selection*

Bag prototype selection (BPS) methods reduce the dataset by selecting a subset of samples. The aim is to eliminate noisy and irrelevant bags and preserve only the most informative ones.

As multi-instance samples are bags composed of one or more instances, a different interpretation can be raised compared to the concept of instance selection in single-instance learning. BPS carries out a bag selection. From this perspective, the aim would be similar to traditional instance selection, that is, reducing the number of observations in the dataset. The distinctive feature is that the removal of a bag implies the elimination of all instances contained in it. An instance selection within each bag can be considered as well. This setting would eliminate individual instances, but it does not reflect the traditional aim of instance selection, which is the reduction of the number of data samples. The number of instances inside bags would be lower, but the total number of bags would be maintained.

Nevertheless, instance prototype selection has always concerned MIC algorithm developers. According to the standard MI assumption, negative bags contain only negative instances, while positive bags contain both positive and negative ones. Instance label ambiguity lies with the positive bags. Mislabeling negative instances in positive bags can limit the performance of multi-instance classifiers. Many methods have focused on selecting a subset of instances from positive bags to learn the

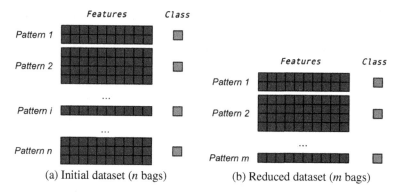

(a) Initial dataset (n bags)   (b) Reduced dataset (m bags)

Fig. 8.2 MI bag selection method

classifier. For example, the EM-DD algorithm [30] chooses one instance that is most consistent with the current hypothesis in each positive bag to predict the label for a new bag. DD-SVM [4] depends on the DD concept to identify instance prototypes. Those instances corresponding to local maximizers of the DD function are chosen as instance prototypes, after which an SVM with a Gaussian kernel is learned in the embedded space. MILD [13] performs the instance selection based on a conditional probability model. The instance having the highest ability to distinguish between positive and negative training bags is chosen from each positive bag as an instance prototype. The method learns a standard SVM with a Gaussian kernel using bag-level features. MILIS [8] achieves the initial instance selection by modeling the distribution of the negative population with a Gaussian-kernel-based kernel density estimator. It depends on an iterative optimization framework to update instance prototypes and learn a linear SVM.

Many algorithms can be included here, as several aim to locate the most relevant instance(s) inside of a bag, as related in previous chapters. In this section, we focus on BPS that tries to reduce the number of training bags. These methods have emerged recently in MIL and have a similar finality as single-instance instance selection methods. Figure 8.2 visualizes the BPS process. Figure 8.2a shows the initial dataset, where each sample is composed of several instances. The preprocessed dataset is shown in Fig. 8.2b. The number of bags has been reduced with respect to the initial dataset.

BPS can be defined as a search problem to find a subset of bags which optimizes a particular criterion. Formally, let T be the original dataset with n bags and S a subset of m bags ($m \ll n$) [10]. BPS tries to find the optimal subset S that does not contain superfluous bags and with which the performance obtained by the classifier is similar to or better than that with the original set T.

Following a similar taxonomy as for FS (Sect. 8.2.1), different BPS methods can be divided in filter, wrapper, and embedded categories. To the best of our knowledge, only filter proposals have been presented for BPS. A summary of these methods is shown in Table 8.2.

Table 8.2 Bag prototype
selection methods in
multi-instance learning

Bag prototype selection methods
Filter methods
MICLONE algorithm [26]
MILNS algorithm [26]
MILSUP algorithm [26]

8.3.2 Filter Methods

Three proposals designed by Yuan et al. [26] can be classified as filter methods.
Their MILCLONE, MILNS, and MILSUP methods are respectively based on clonal
selection theory [2], the negative selection principle [12], and self-regulation and
suppression mechanisms in natural immune systems [6]. The main features of these
methods are described below.

8.3.2.1 MICLONE Algorithm

The MICLONE method [26] is based on clonal selection theory [2]. This theory
explains the basic response of the adaptive immune system to an antigenic stimulus.
Only those cells capable of recognizing an antigen proliferate, while those that do
not are not selected. The main steps of MICLONE are shown in Algorithm 16.
The training set is composed of antigens (training bags). One antigen is provided
to the algorithm at a time, until all have gone through the entire process. After the
initialization of memory cells, memory cell identification, generation of candidate
memory cell and memory cell introduction, the output is a set of memory cells, and
corresponding to bag prototypes. In more detail, the first stage initializes memory
cells, where some antigens are selected to form the memory pool. Second, memory
cell identification is carried out and candidate memory cell are generated. For a given
antigen X, its closest (most stimulated) antigen with the same class is chosen as its bag
prototype (memory cell) from the pool. A stimulation function, which can determine
the closest bag, needs to be defined. The authors use the minimum Hausdorff distance.
In the memory cell introduction stage, developed candidate memory cell are added
to the existing set. The most stimulated memory cell is removed from the pool, if the
affinity between the candidate memory cell and its parental instance from the most
stimulated cell is less than the product of the affinity threshold AT_{CLONE} and the
user-specified threshold ATS_{CLONE}. The former is calculated as

$$AT_{CLONE} = \frac{\sum_{i=1}^{n-1} \sum_{j=i+1}^{n} affinity(X_i, X_j)}{\frac{n(n-1)}{2}},$$

where n is the number of training antigens, X_i and X_j are the ith and jth training antigen and $affinity(X_i, X_j)$ returns the minimal Hausdorff distance between two bags.

8.3.2.2 MILNS Algorithm

MILNS [26] is based on the negative selection algorithm [12]. These methods describe the negative representation of information when negative examples are not available. For example, in many anomaly detection applications, only positive (normal) examples are available for training, while negative (abnormal) examples are not. The positive examples are used to obtain some representative negative examples known as detectors.

The main steps of this method are described in Algorithm 17. All positive bags are regarded as self samples (self cells) and all negative bags as the set of candidate detectors (antibodies) from which negative example prototypes will be selected. Given a candidate detector, the method scans the set of self samples for the one with the lowest affinity with the candidate detector. If the affinity approximated by means of the minimum Hausdorff distance is greater than the product of the affinity threshold AT_{NS} and the threshold ATS_{NS} provided by the user, the candidate detector is considered as a negative example prototype. The affinity threshold is the average affinity value over all self examples, which is calculated as

$$AT_{NS} = \frac{\sum_{i=1}^{n-1} \sum_{j=i+1}^{n} affinity(X_i, X_j)}{\frac{n(n-1)}{2}},$$

where n is the number of self samples, X_i and X_j are the ith and jth self samples and $affinity(X_i, X_j)$ returns the minimal Hausdorff distance between these two.

Algorithm 16 MICLONE Algorithm

Input: $X \leftarrow$ multi-instance training set $\{X_1, X_2, \ldots, X_N\}$ $(X_i \subseteq \mathbb{X})$, $Class(X_i) \in \{0, 1\}$
Output: $subsetBags \leftarrow$ more relevant bag subset.
1: memory = initializeRandomRepertoire()
2: **for** $X_i \in$ memory **do**
3:     best = memoryCellIdentification($Class(X_i)$)
4:     fit = generationCandidateMemoryCell(best, X_i)
5:     Add fit to memory cell
6:     **if** $affinity(fit, closest_{best}) < (AT_{CLONE} \cdot ATS_{CLONE})$ **then**   ▷ $closest_{best}$ its the closest bag with the same class as X_i
7:         Eliminate best of memory cell
8:     **end if**
9: **end for**

8.3.2.3   MILSUP Algorithm

MILSUP [26] is based on an immune inspired suppressive algorithm [6]. It is inspired by the self-regulation and suppression mechanisms in the biological immune system. According to the self-regulation mechanism, those cells unable to neutralize danger tend to disappear from the organism (or be suppressed). By analogy, data not relevant to the classifier is eliminated from the training set.

The main steps of MILSUP are described in Algorithm 18. The affinity approximation between two bags is given by means of the minimal Hausdorff distance. The dataset is divided into two subsets, the first one representing the lymphocytes in the organism (training set) and the second one a set of pathogens (suppression set). The algorithm sets out with the idea that the system's model must identify the best subset of lymphocytes in order to recognize pathogens. Specifically, each pathogen in the suppression set is classified according to the closest lymphocytes in the training set. Those lymphocytes able to recognize pathogens are retained, while others are eliminated. The recognition ability is determined by comparing the label of the closest lymphocyte with that of the corresponding pathogen. If their labels are the same, the lymphocyte is considered to have the ability to recognize the corresponding pathogen, otherwise it is not.

Experimental Study

The study of Yuan et al. [26] considers five datasets: Musk1, Musk2, Elephant, Tiger, and Fox (Sect. 3.6). The experimental study includes a comparison between the three proposals (MILSUP, MICLONE, and MILNS). The reduced datasets provided by these methods are used by 20 classifiers for the Elephant, Tiger, and Fox datasets and by 12 classification algorithms for the Musk1 and Musk2 datasets. The accuracy and computation time are used as evaluation measures. The results show that MICLONE and MILNS are competitive with each other in terms of their effect on the classification accuracy. They are superior to MILSUP. All methods considerably reduce the computation time of the classifiers.

Algorithm 17 MILNS Algorithm

Input: $X \leftarrow$ multi-instance training set $\{X_1, X_2, \ldots, X_N\}$ $(X_i \subseteq \mathbb{X})$
Output: $subset\,Bags \leftarrow$ more relevant bag subset.
1: $self \leftarrow$ set of all positive bags
2: $detector \leftarrow$ set of all negative bags
3: $P \leftarrow \emptyset$ ▷ P is the set of bag prototypes
4: **for** $X_d \in dectector$ **do**
5:     $X_p \leftarrow argmin_{X_s \in Self} affinity(X_s, X_d)$
6:     **if** $affinity(X_p, X_d) > AT_{NS} \cdot AT S_{NS}$ **then**
7:         Add X_p to P
8:     **end if**
9: **end for**

Algorithm 18 MILSUP algorithm

Input: $X \leftarrow$ multi-instance training set $\{X_1, X_2, \ldots, X_n\}$, $(X_i \subseteq \mathbb{X})$, $Class(X_i) \in \{0, 1\}$
Input: Fraction $f \in [0, 1]$
Output: $bagSubset$, most relevant bag subset
1: $WBCs \leftarrow$ randomly assign $f \cdot n$ examples
2: $Pathogens \leftarrow$ examples not assigned to WBCs
3: **for** $X \in WBCs$ **do** $\triangleright$ Set a survival signal for every WBC and initialize it to be false
4:    $Survival_X = false$
5: **end for**
6: **for** $X_p \in Pathogens$ **do**
7:    $Nearest_{WBC} \leftarrow argmin_{w \in WBCs} affinity(X_p, X_w)$
8:    **if** $Class(Nearest_{WBC}) = Class(X_p)$ **then**
9:       $Survival_{Nearest_{WBC}} = true$
10:    **end if**
11: **end for**
12: Eliminate those bags of $WBCs$ with the survival signal set to false
13: Add to $bagSubset$ those bags of $WBCs$ with survival signal set to true

8.4 Summarizing Comments

Data reduction in MIL is a critical challenge. The inherent data ambiguity, where instances in a positive bag may or may not approximate the positive concept, adds more complexity to the problem. In this chapter, we considered two important tasks to reduce the computational complexity and improve the performance of the subsequent learner: FS and BPS. In case of FS, different methods are described adhering to the well-known taxonomy based on filter, wrapper, and embedded methods. A similar study is carried out for BPS, which is the more recently addressed task.

References

1. Bellman, R.: Dynamic Programming and Lagrange Multipliers. Princeton University Press, Princeton (1957)
2. Burnet, S.F.M.: The Clonal Selection Theory of Acquired Immunity. Vanderbilt University Press, Nashville (1959)
3. Ciliberto, C., Smeraldi, F., Natale, L., Metta, G.: Online multiple instance learning applied to hand detection in a humanoid robot. In: De Luca, A. (ed.) Proceedings of the IEEE International Conference on Intelligent Robots and Systems (IROS 2011), pp. 1526–1532. IEEE, San Francisco (2011)
4. Chen, Y., Wang, J.Z.: Image categorization by learning and reasoning with regions. J. Mach. Learn. Res. **5**, 803–821 (2004)
5. Chen, Y., Bi, J., Wang, J.Z.: MILES: multiple-instance learning via embedded instance selection. IEEE Trans. Pattern Anal. **28**(12), 1931–1947 (2006)
6. Figueredo, G.P., Ebecken, N.F., Augusto, D.A., Barbosa, H.J.: An immune-inspired instance selection mechanism for supervised classification. Memet. Comput. **4**(2), 135–147 (2012)
7. Friedman, J., Hastie, T., Tibshirani, R.: Additive logistic regression: a statistical view of boosting (with discussion and a rejoinder by the authors). Ann. Stat. **28**(2), 337–407 (2000)

8. Fu, Z., Robles-Kelly, A., Zhou, J.: MILIS: multiple instance learning with instance selection. IEEE Trans. Pattern Anal. **33**(5), 958–977 (2011)
9. Gan, R., Yin, J.: Feature selection in multi-instance learning. Neural Comput. Appl. **23**(3–4), 907–912 (2013)
10. García, S., Luengo, J., Sáez, J.A., López, V., Herrera, F.: A survey of discretization techniques: taxonomy and empirical analysis in supervised learning. IEEE Trans. Knowl. Data Eng. **25**(4), 734–750 (2013)
11. Jhuo, I.H., Lee, D.T.: Multiple-instance learning: multiple feature selection on instance representation. In: Proceedings of the 25th International Conference on Artificial Intelligence (AAAI 2011), pp. 1794–1795. Association for the Advancement of Artificial Intelligence, San Francisco (2011)
12. Ji, Z., Dasgupta, D.: V-detector: an efficient negative selection algorithm with "probably adequate" detector coverage. Inf. Sci. **179**(10), 1390–1406 (2009)
13. Li, W.J.: MILD: multiple-instance learning via disambiguation. IEEE Trans. Knowl. Data Eng. **22**(1), 76–89 (2010)
14. Li, M., Kwok, J.T., Lu, B.L.: Online multiple instance learning with no regret. In: Boykov, Y., Schmidt, F.R., Kahl, F., Lempitsky, V. (eds.) Proceedings of the International Conference on Computer Vision and Pattern Recognition (CVPR 2010), pp. 1395–1401. IEEE, Los Alamitos (2010)
15. Liu, H., Motoda, H.: Feature Extraction, Construction and Selection: A Data Mining Perspective. Kluwer, Boston (1998)
16. Liu, H., Motoda, H.: Instance selection and construction for data mining. Kluwer Academic Publisher, Norwell (2001)
17. Liu, H., Motoda, H.: Computational Methods of Feature Selection. CRC Press, Boca Raton (2007)
18. Liu, H., Yu, L.: Toward integrating feature selection algorithms for classification and clustering. IEEE Trans. Knowl. Data Eng. **17**(4), 491–502 (2005)
19. Mao, Q., Tsang, I.W.H.: A feature selection method for multivariate performance measures. IEEE Trans. Pattern Anal. **35**(9), 2051–2063 (2013)
20. Ngiam, J., Goh, H.: Learning global and regional features for photo annotation. In: Peters, C., Muller, H., Caputo, B., Gonzalo, J., Jones, G.J.F., Kalpathy-Cramer, J., Former, P., Giampiccolo, D. (eds.) Proceedings of 10th Workshop of Cross-Language Evaluation Forum for European Languages (CLEF 2009), pp. 287–290. Springer, Berlin (2009)
21. Robnikikonja, M., Kononenko, I.: Theoretical and empirical analysis of ReliefF and RReliefF. J. Mach. Learn. Res. **53**(1–2), 23–69 (2003)
22. Triguero, I., Derrac, J., García, S., Herrera, F.: A taxonomy and experimental study on prototype generation for nearest neighbor classification. IEEE Trans. Syst. Man Cybern. C **42**(1), 86–100 (2012)
23. Whitley, D.: A genetic algorithm tutorial. Stat. Comput. **4**(2), 65–85 (1994)
24. Yager, R.R.: On ordered weighted averaging aggregation operators in multicriteria decision making. IEEE Trans. Syst. Man Cybern. **18**(1), 183–190 (1988)
25. Yuan, X., Wang, M., Song, Y.: Concept-dependent image annotation via existence-based multiple-instance learning. In: Proceedings of the IEEE International Conference on Systems. Man and Cybernetics (SMC 2009), pp. 4112–4117. IEEE, Los Alamitos (2009)
26. Yuan, L., Liu, J., Tang, X.: Combining example selection with instance selection to speed up multiple-instance learning. Neurocomputing **129**, 504–515 (2014)
27. Yuan, X., Hua, X.S., Wang, M., Qi, G.J., Wu, X.Q.: A novel multiple instance learning approach for image retrieval based on adaboost feature selection. In: Yun-Qing, S., Liao, M., Hu, Y.H., Sheu, P., Ostermann, J. (eds.) Proceedings of the International Conference on Multimedia and Expo (ICME 2007), pp. 1491–1494. IEEE Service Center, Piscataway (2007)
28. Zafra, A., Pechenizkiy, M., Ventura, S.: ReliefF-MI: an extension of ReliefF to multiple instance learning. Neurocomputing **75**(1), 210–218 (2012)
29. Zafra, A., Pechenizkiy, M., Ventura, S.: HyDR-MI: a hybrid algorithm to reduce dimensionality in multiple instance learning. Inf. Sci. **222**, 282–301 (2013)

30. Zhang, Q., Goldman, S.: EM-DD: an improved multiple-instance learning technique. In: Becker, S., Thrun, S., Obermayer, K. (eds.) Proceedings of the 17th Conference on Advances in Neural Information Processing Systems (NIPS 1998), pp. 1073–1080. MIT Press, Cambridge (1998)
31. Zhang, T., Liu, J., Liu, S., Xu, C., Lu, H.: Boosted exemplar learning for action recognition and annotation. IEEE Trans. Circ. Syst. Video **21**(7), 853–866 (2011)
32. Zhu, L., Zhao, B., Gao, Y.: Multi-class multi-instance learning for lung cancer image classification based on bag feature selection. In: Wang, L., Jin, Y. (eds.) Proceedings of the 5th International Conference on Fuzzy Systems and Knowledge Discovery (FSKD 2008). Lecture Notes in Artificial Intelligence, pp. 487–492. Springer, Berlin (2008)

Chapter 9
Imbalanced Multi-instance Data

Abstract Class imbalance is widely studied in single-instance learning and refers to the situation where the data observations are unevenly distributed among the possible classes. This phenomenon can present itself in MIL as well. Section 9.1 presents a general introduction to the topic of class imbalance, list the types of solutions to deal with it, and the appropriate performance metrics. In Sect. 9.2, we recall a popular single-instance method addressing class imbalance. We provide a detailed specification of multi-instance class imbalance in Sect. 9.3 and discuss its solutions in Sect. 9.4 on resampling methods and in Sect. 9.5 on custom classification methods. Section 9.6 presents the experimental analysis accompanying this chapter. Some summarizing remarks are listed in Sect. 9.7.

9.1 Introduction

In the presence of class imbalance, the possible classes are unevenly represented in the dataset. Some classes may contain many observations, while others only have very few in comparison. The most common setting is that of a binary or two-class problem, where the instances of the majority class considerably outnumber those of the minority class. Elements of the minority class are usually labeled as positive and those of the majority class as negative. These names indicate that in most applications the minority class is the class of interest. In recent years, the focus of class imbalanced learning has widened to the general setting of multi-class classification, where the number of classes may exceed two. In this situation, there can be a mixture of majority, medium-sized, and minority classes, which automatically yields more challenging learning objectives. A large body of work has been done on the classification of imbalanced data in single-instance problems [18, 21, 26, 31]. Application areas in which class imbalance naturally presents itself include medical diagnosis [8, 19, 20, 22] and bioinformatics [41, 42, 44].

© Springer International Publishing AG 2016   191
F. Herrera et al., *Multiple Instance Learning*, DOI 10.1007/978-3-319-47759-6_9

9.1.1 Dealing with Class Imbalance

Traditional classifiers tend to lose some of their prediction strength in the presence of class imbalance, because they make the internal assumption of similar class distributions or misclassification costs. By definition, the former is violated for imbalanced data. The latter premise does not hold either, since a higher cost is usually associated with the misclassification of a positive element than with that of a negative observation. As a result, standard classifiers fail, for instance by predicting the majority label over-easily. Specific solutions to handle class imbalance have been proposed in the literature. We can divide these approaches into two general groups:

- **Data-level solutions**: this group consists of preprocessing methods known as *resampling* techniques. They modify the dataset before the application of a classifier, which means that they are independent of the latter. We distinguish between undersampling methods, that remove part of the majority class, oversampling methods, that add new minority elements, and hybrid methods, that combine the previous two approaches. A popular single-instance method, commonly used in comparative studies on class imbalance, is the SMOTE oversampling method [7]. It is described in detail in Sect. 9.2.
- **Customized approaches**: a second group of solutions handling class imbalance is found at the algorithm-level. These methods do not modify the data. We can make a further distinction between three diverse types of methods.
  - The first subgroup consists of cost-sensitive methods (e.g., [11, 43]). These algorithms assign different misclassification costs to the classes and aim to minimize the overall cost. In this way, relatively more focus can be put on the correct classification of minority class elements.
  - Second, we list the methods that focus on the construction of a classification model that is not hindered by the imbalance between classes. Based on imbalance-resistant heuristics, a learner is designed to tackle the imbalance problem.
  - Finally, a third subgroup is formed by custom ensemble techniques (e.g., [16]), that have already been used, possibly in combination with resampling methods, in the classification of single-instance imbalanced data.

Both types of approaches have been proposed in single-instance as well as multi-instance learning. The latter will be discussed in detail in Sect. 9.3.

With respect to multi-class imbalanced learning, decomposition strategies can be used to divide the multi-class problem in a set of binary ones, as done for single-instance methods in e.g., [14]. In that study, the one-versus-one and one-versus-all methods are used to derive binary prediction problems from the multi-class dataset. For each of them, a two-class preprocessing method is applied in conjunction with a classifier. The outcomes of all binary problems are aggregated to yield a single prediction value. Any binary solution can be combined with a decomposition scheme and aggregation method to perform a multi-class imbalanced classification. In single-instance learning, multi-class resampling methods as well as general classifiers to deal with multi-class imbalance without a decomposition step have also been proposed as well (e.g., [1, 39]).

9.1.2 Evaluation Measures in the Imbalanced Domain

The evaluation of classification performance in the class imbalanced domain warrants metrics that are not sensitive to the skewness in the class distributions. Among the measures listed in Sect. 1.4, the accuracy is the most commonly used in general studies. However, the research community agrees that it is not an appropriate measure to use in the presence of class imbalance, as it can lead to misleading results. As an example, consider a dataset with a 1000 observations, of which 900 belong to the negative class and the remaining 100 to the positive class. When a classifier predicts that each observation is negative, it attains an accuracy of 90 %. This is a high value and it does not in any way reflect the fact that the entire positive class has been misclassified. We conclude that this metric does not provide a faithful representation of the performance of the classifier.

As an alternative to the accuracy, we can use g, the geometric mean of the class-wise accuracies. The general definition is provided in Sect. 1.4. In a two-class setting, which is most common in studies on class imbalance, this reduces to

$$g = \sqrt{\text{TPR} \cdot \text{TNR}},$$

where TPR and TNR, respectively, correspond to the true positive and true negative rates of the classification. By computing the rate of correct predictions for each class separately, none of the classes can be ignored. In particular, in the above example, the value for g is zero, since all positive observations were misclassified. This clearly reflects the incapacity of the classifier.

A second measure that is commonly used in research on class imbalance, is the Area Under the ROC-curve (AUC, [3]), defined for two-class problems. A ROC-curve models the trade-off between true positive and false positive classifier predictions. It was originally defined for probabilistic classifiers, that use a threshold value θ on the positive class probability. When the estimated probability is higher than θ, the sample is classified as positive. In the other case, the negative class is predicted. By varying θ, different true positive and false positive rates are obtained. Each represents a point in ROC-space and together they form the ROC-curve. The area under it gathers the information represented by the curve in a single value. It can be computed by using the procedure described in [13]. A detailed description of ROC-curves and AUC computations can also be found in [33].

Fig. 9.1 Illustration of the
construction of one artificial
element in a single-instance
dataset by SMOTE, between
the seed x and a randomly
selected instance from
among its nearest neighbors
n_i in the minority class

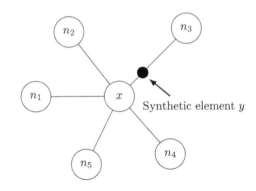

9.2 Single-Instance SMOTE

As noted above, one way to deal with class imbalance is to resample the dataset.
In single-instance learning, a popular resampling method is the Synthetic Minority
Oversampling Technique (SMOTE) proposed by Chawla et al. [7]. We recall this
algorithm here, as several multi-instance resampling proposals (Sect. 9.4) are based
on it.

SMOTE is an oversampling method, that increases the size of the minority class by
adding artificial new instances to it. Synthetic instances are constructed by selecting
one of the existing minority elements as seed and introducing a new instance at a
random position on the line segment connecting this seed element to one of its k
nearest minority class neighbors, as illustrated in Fig. 9.1. The pseudo-code of this
method can be found in Algorithm 19. We present the version that yields a perfectly
balanced dataset, that is, positive instances are created until their class reaches the
size of the negative class. This is the most commonly used setting, although the
amount of oversampling can also be controlled by a parameter, as presented in the
original proposal [7]. The value k is commonly set to 5. Step 8 of Algorithm 19
creates an artificial instance. Existing data samples are interpreted as vectors and a
new element is introduced at a random point on the line segment between them. The
user should take care to use an appropriate interpolation scheme for numeric and
categorical attributes.

9.3 Multi-instance Class Imbalance

We continue with a discussion on the presence of class imbalance in multi-instance
data. Compared to the single-instance setting, a very limited amount of work has
been done on multi-instance class imbalance. However, interest has been raised in
the past few years and it forms a promising area of future research.

Algorithm 19 SMOTE algorithm

Input: Imbalanced single-instance dataset T, with positive class P and negative class N. Number of neighbors k

Output: A perfectly balanced dataset T^*

1: $d \leftarrow |N| - |P|$ ▷ amount of artificial instances
2: $A \leftarrow \emptyset$ ▷ initialize set of artificial instances
3: **for** $i = 1, \ldots, d$ **do**
4:     $x \leftarrow$ random positive instance from T
5:     $\{n_1, n_2, \ldots, n_k\} \leftarrow k$ nearest neighbors of x in P
6:     $n \leftarrow$ random selection from $\{n_1, n_2, \ldots, n_k\}$
7:     $\alpha \leftarrow$ random value drawn from $[0, 1]$
8:     $y \leftarrow x + \alpha \cdot (n - x)$ ▷ generate a new instance by interpolation
9:     Label y as positive
10:     $A \leftarrow A \cup \{y\}$
11: **end for**
12: $T^* \leftarrow T \cup A$

9.3.1 Problem Description

The nature of class imbalance can be more complex in MIL than it is in single-instance learning. As argued by Wang et al. [35], the imbalance can occur at two different levels, namely that of the instances and that of the bags. Instance-level imbalance means that the number of positive instances in positive bags is relatively low compared to the number of negative instances they contain. In the standard MIL hypothesis, only one positive instance is required in a positive bag, such that imbalance at the level of instances can easily present itself. Imbalance can also occur at the bag-level, which is the direct generalization of class imbalance in single-instance learning and fits in the general description given in Sect. 9.1. It means that the number of positive bags is small compared to the number of negative bags.

The effects that these two types of imbalance have on multi-instance classifiers have been described by e.g., Mera et al. [23]. In the presence of instance-level imbalance, instance-based methods (Chap. 4) are likely to be biased toward the majority class, since the number of actual positive instances is low compared to actual negative instances. Mapping-based methods (Sect. 5.3) can also be hindered by this type of imbalance, when the mapping step is sensitive to instance imbalance. The example given in [23] to illustrate this situation is the averaging function: if the number of positive instances is relatively small in a bag, their information will be mostly lost when averaging over all instances. Bag-level imbalance results in a bias of bag-based classifiers (Sect. 5.2) toward the majority class.

The work of Wang et al. [35] showed that multi-instance imbalance is most pronounced at the level of the bags. Keeping this in mind, we define class imbalance for multi-instance problems at the bag-level. It is reflected in a (possibly considerably) larger number of bags of the majority class compared to the number of bags of the minority class. The degree of imbalance is measured by the so-called *imbalance ratio* (IR), which is defined as the ratio of the number of bags of the majority class over the number of bags of the minority class. Class imbalance results in more difficulty to recognize the minority class, leading to a high number of misclassifications of these bags. The study of [35] references the application of [37] concerning the object detection of mines based on sonar images. This is an imbalanced problem, since mines occur far less often than other objects (e.g., rocks).

9.3.2 Solutions for Multi-instance Class Imbalance

To date, we are not aware of any specific proposals to deal with multi-class imbalance in MIL. The existing solutions have been specifically proposed with binary problems in mind and have only been evaluated on this kind of data. However, the decomposition strategies discussed in Sect. 9.1 can be transferred from the single-instance to the multi-instance setting, in conjunction with any of the binary class imbalance solutions described below.

As noted above, compared to the amount of attention that the class imbalance problem has received in single-instance learning, its exploration in MIL has been very limited. Nevertheless, applications inherently prone to class imbalance also present themselves in this domain and custom methods able to deal with the intrinsic challenges of class imbalance are warranted. We discuss the recent developments in Sects. 9.4 and 9.5. As will be clear from Sect. 9.4, the study of multi-instance preprocessing techniques has so far been largely limited to extensions of the SMOTE method recalled in Sect. 9.2. In single-instance learning, this technique has been improved upon by many authors (e.g., [4, 5, 29]) and it is a valid question whether similar improvements can be made in MIL. Extensions of other single-instance solutions, like cost-sensitive support vector machines [32] or alternative ensemble techniques (e.g., [17, 38]), should be further explored as well.

9.4 Multi-instance Resampling Methods

In this section, we discuss the resampling methods that have been proposed to deal with multi-instance class imbalance. We recall the contributions of [23, 24, 35], which, to the best of our knowledge, form the complete set of multi-instance resampling methods dealing with class imbalance.

9.4.1 BagSMOTE, InstanceSMOTE, Bag_oversampling

Wang et al. [35] consider two approaches to deal with class imbalance in MIL: resampling on the one hand and cost-sensitive methods on the other. We describe their resampling methods here, the discussion of the cost-sensitive methods is postponed to Sect. 9.5. Two extensions of the SMOTE method of [7] are developed. Their first method is called BagSMOTE and creates synthetic minority bags. The procedure is presented in Algorithm 20. Each existing minority bag X leads to the creation of one new bag, that is also labeled with the minority class. For each instance $x \in X$, one of its nearest instances from within all minority bags is selected. A synthetic element is generated between x and its neighbor and added to the new bag.

Algorithm 20 BagSMOTE algorithm

Input: Imbalanced multi-instance dataset $\mathbf{T}$, number of neighbors k
Output: The oversampled dataset $\mathbf{T}^*$
1: $\mathbf{A} \leftarrow \emptyset$ ▷ initialize set of artificial bags
2: **for each** positive bag $X \in \mathbf{T}$ **do**
3:     $Y \leftarrow \emptyset$ ▷ initialize artificial bag
4:     **for each** instance $x \in X$ **do**
5:         $\{n_1, n_2, \ldots, n_k\} \leftarrow k$ nearest neighbors of x among all instances in all positive bags
6:         $n \leftarrow$ random selection from $\{n_1, n_2, \ldots, n_k\}$
7:         $\alpha \leftarrow$ random value drawn from $[0, 1]$
8:         $y \leftarrow x + \alpha \cdot (n - x)$ ▷ generate a new instance by interpolation
9:         $Y \leftarrow Y \cup y$
10:     **end for**
11:     Label Y as positive
12:     $\mathbf{A} \leftarrow \mathbf{A} \cup \{Y\}$
13: **end for**
14: $\mathbf{T}^* \leftarrow \mathbf{T} \cup \mathbf{A}$

The second method is called InstanceSMOTE and is presented in Algorithm 21. It modifies the multi-instance dataset to a single-instance dataset by assigning all instances to the class to which their parent bag belongs. The single-instance SMOTE method is applied to this transformed dataset. Afterwards, the dataset is changed back to its original multi-instance form, by assigning synthetic instances to the same bag from which the corresponding seed was drawn. Clearly, the largest difference between the BagSMOTE and InstanceSMOTE methods is that the first one creates new bags, while the second one inserts new instances in already existing bags.

In their experiments, Wang et al. also include a third alternative, that randomly duplicates minority bags to obtain a better balance between the classes. This method is referred to as Bag_oversampling. The experimental study shows that the BagSMOTE method yields the best results among the three proposals. The more intricate oversampling procedure in BagSMOTE has a better performance than the random procedure in Bag_oversampling. However, Bag_oversampling outperforms InstanceSMOTE, which supports the statement of the authors that multi-instance class imbalance occurs at the level of the bags and that there is where a solution should be applied.

Algorithm 21 InstanceSMOTE algorithm

Input: Imbalanced multi-instance dataset **T**, number of neighbors k
Output: The oversampled dataset **T***
1: $T \leftarrow \{(x, class(X)) \mid x \in X, X \in \mathbf{T}\}$ ▷ transformation to single-instance data
2: $T^* \leftarrow$ output of Algorithm 19 on T with value k. Store parent bag of seed instance for each
    artificial element.
3: $\mathbf{T}^* \leftarrow \emptyset$
4: **for each** parent bag $X \in \mathbf{T}$ **do**   ▷ transformation to multi-instance data
5:     $X^* \leftarrow$ set of all instances $x \in T^*$, either original or artificial, linked to this parent bag
6:     Label X^* with the class of X
7:     $\mathbf{T}^* \leftarrow \mathbf{T}^* \cup \{X^*\}$
8: **end for**

9.4.2 B-Instances

Mera et al. [24] proposed a preprocessing method to improve the classification of imbalanced multi-instance data by means of an enriched representation of the positive class. In their later work [23], they refer to this method as B-Instances. By means of kernel density estimation [25], they construct a function which estimates the degree to which an instance can be considered as negative. This measure is used to locate likely and unlikely positive elements within positive bags and use them in resampling procedures. The method consists of three main steps:

1. **Oversampling within positive bags**: the set T^+ is constructed containing the most positive (least negative) instance from every positive bag. In their experiments, the authors increase T^+ to include the second most positive instance from each positive bag as well, to improve the performance of the method. When T^+ has been determined, SMOTE is applied to oversample instances within the positive bags. The elements from T^+ are used as seeds. A synthetic instance is generated at a random position on the line segment connecting the seed with one of its k nearest neighbors in the entire dataset. The constructed instance is added to the bag which contained the seed element.
2. **Undersampling within positive bags**: undersampling is applied to the positive bags. To this end, the least positive (most negative) instance in each positive bag is located and added to the set T^-. For every element $x \in T^-$, its k nearest neighbors from among all data instances are determined. When the majority of these neighbors originate from negative bags, x is interpreted as a borderline element and it is decided to remove it.
3. **Undersampling within negative bags**: the third stage consists of removing instances from negative bags, using a similar procedure as in the undersampling of the positive bags. For each instance in a negative bag, its k nearest neighbors in the entire dataset are determined. When the majority of its neighbors belong to positive bags, the instance is a borderline element in the negative bag and is removed.

In the experimental study of [24], their B-Instances preprocessing method was combined with several classifiers and was shown to improve their performance on imbalanced multi-instance datasets. However, no comparison was offered with the methods of [35].

9.4.3 B-Bags

The proposal of [23] uses kernel density estimation as well. It is largely based on the standard MIL hypothesis, in that the method creates new positive bags that contain only one positive instance. The method is called B-Bags. Based on the kernel density estimation procedure, B-Bags aims to determine the most positive instance in the positive bags. It is a bag oversampling method and creates a total number of n new positive bags. For the construction of a synthetic positive bag, the following steps are performed:

1. **Positive instance**: one artificial positive instance is constructed and added to the new bag. Two random positive training bags are selected and, within each of them, the most positive instance is determined based on kernel density estimation. The new instance is obtained via linear interpolation between these two elements.
2. **Negative instances**: the remainder of the bag is filled with negative instances, until the size of the new bag equals the average size of the training bags. The construction of these negative instances also uses the two positive bags selected in the previous step. The most negative instance is determined in the first one. Random negative instances are selected in the second bag and artificial instances are generated by means of interpolation.

Mera et al. stress that the difference with the BagSMOTE algorithm from [35] is that their oversampling step is more informative, because it determines the most positive instances within the positive bags and uses these to generate new positive instances. The experiments of [23] compare B-Bags with their earlier proposal B-Instances and with BagSMOTE, in combination with several multi-instance classifiers, on nine datasets. B-Bags has the highest AUC in four out of the nine datasets and the highest g value in five.

9.5 Customized Multi-instance Approaches

In this section, we discuss the second type of solutions to deal with class imbalance, namely those at the algorithm-level. These are multi-instance classifiers that incorporate some imbalance-resistant heuristics in their internal workings.

9.5.1 Cost-Sensitive Boosting Models

Apart from their preprocessing techniques discussed in Sect. 9.4, cost-sensitive multi-instance classification procedures are introduced by Wang et al. [35, 36] as well. Their algorithms are based on the AdaBoost.M1 boosting scheme [15]. In single-instance learning, this is an iterative method, which trains a classifier in each iteration and reweighs instances based on their classification outcome, to ensure that misclassified elements receive more attention in the next iteration. Its weight update formula is

$$D_{t+1}(i) = \frac{D_t(i)K_t(x_i, y_i)}{Z_t},$$

with

$$K_t(x_i, y_i) = \exp(-\alpha_t y_i h_t(x_i)). \tag{9.1}$$

In these expressions, t is the iteration number and Z_t a normalization factor to ensure that D_{t+1} is a probability distribution. The function h_t refers to a single-instance classifier and $\alpha_t \in \mathbb{R}$ to the coefficient that represents the weight of h_t in the final classification aggregation. As AdaBoost.M1 was proposed as a single-instance learning method, (x_i, y_i) refers to an instance x_i and its outcome y_i. AdaBoost.M1 does not distinguish between classes in these weight update formulas. The cost-sensitive boosting methods proposed in [35, 36] do make this distinction, by introducing class-dependent costs in (9.1). A cost is defined for each class, that is, the methods use one cost value for the positive class and one for the negative class. The ratio of these two values is set in favor of the minority class. As a result, relatively more effort is taken to correctly classify minority bags. The authors note that the real ratio between the class-wise misclassification costs is generally not available. They advise to use the imbalance ratio as cost ratio, as this value can be easily derived from the data. They propose four versions of their algorithm, differing in the places where the cost factors are introduced. Their proposals are similar to the single-instance cost-sensitive boosting algorithms from [30]. The methods are called Ab1, Ab2, Ab3, and Ab4 and there weight update formulas are

Ab1: $\quad K_t(X_i, y_i) = \exp(-C_i \alpha_t y_i h_t(X_i))$
Ab2: $\quad K_t(X_i, y_i) = C_i \exp(-\alpha_t y_i h_t(X_i))$
Ab3: $\quad K_t(X_i, y_i) = C_i \exp(-C_i \alpha_t y_i h_t(X_i))$
Ab4: $\quad K_t(X_i, y_i) = C_i^2 \exp(-C_i^2 \alpha_t y_i h_t(X_i))$

In these formulas, X_i refers to a bag and y_i to its outcome. The function h_t corresponds to a multi-instance classifier. The value C_i is the cost associated with the bag X_i. It can take on only two values, either the cost for the positive class or that of the negative class, depending on the bag-label. Bags of the same class are automatically associated with the same cost.

The cost-sensitive boosting schemes are experimentally shown to outperform BagSMOTE in [35]. Based on their experimental work in [36], Wang et al. put Ab3 forward as best performing version among their proposed cost-sensitive boosting algorithms.

9.5.2 Fuzzy Rough Multi-instance Classifiers

In the recent contribution of Vluymans et al. [34], an algorithm-level solution to multi-instance class imbalance was proposed as an extension of the single-instance classifier from [27] that was developed for two-class imbalanced data. Two classifier families, one instance-based and one bag-based are developed. Both use fuzzy rough set theory [12], a mathematical concept that models vague and incomplete information.

To classify a new bag, these methods determine its membership degree to the fuzzy rough lower approximation of the two classes. This value is a number between 0 and 1. For a bag X and a class C, it expresses the degree to which the similarity of a training bag B with X implies the affinity of B with class C. When X has a high membership to the fuzzy rough lower approximation of C, training bags similar to X are likely to belong to class C. This information is used in the prediction step. An unseen bag is assigned to the class for which its membership degree to the lower approximation is highest.

The two classifier families in [34] differ from each other in the way they compute the lower approximation values for a bag. The instance-based methods first determine these values for the instances in the bag. These computations rely on a definition of similarity between instances, an affinity degree of instances with bags and of instances with classes. In a second phase, the instance-based values are aggregated to the bag level. The bag-based algorithms on the other hand directly derive the information from the bag as a whole, using an appropriate metric to measure the similarity between bags and the affinity of bags with classes.

Within the two families, classifiers differ from each other in the way they measure instance or bag similarity as well as in their aggregation procedures. The best performing representatives of the two families, referred to as FRI (Fuzzy Rough Instance-based multi-instance classifier) and FRB (Fuzzy Rough Bag-based multi-instance classifier) in [34], are experimentally shown to outperform the cost-sensitive boosting methods described in Sect. 9.5.1 as well as BagSMOTE in combination with the MITI classifier [6].

9.6 Experimental Analysis

In this section, we present an experimental comparison of methods dealing with multi-instance class imbalance. These experiments are performed on datasets coming from various application areas. We include both resampling methods and custom multi-instance classifiers. The experimental setup is specified in Sects. 9.6.1 and 9.6.2 presents the results.

Table 9.1 Description of the class imbalanced multi-instance datasets used in this comparison

Dataset	# Bags	# Inst	# Feat	IR
Bonds	160	3558	16	3.57
Chains	152	4630	24	4.63
Corel1	2000	7947	9	19
Corel2	2000	7947	9	19
Thio	193	26611	8	6.72
WIR-2	113	3423	298	4.38
WIR-5	113	3423	303	3.71

9.6.1   Setup

The datasets used in this experimental study are described in Table 9.1. We list the total number of bags and instances as well as the number of features. The degree of class imbalance is represented by the IR of the dataset. These datasets originate from different application domains. We use the same versions and partitions as in the experimental study of [34]. Bonds and Chains are bioinformatics datasets that originally appeared in [28] and were also used in the previous chapters. In this section, we use the imbalanced versions of [36]. Thio (Thioredoxin) is a bioinformatics dataset as well, while the two Corel datasets correspond to image recognition problems and were used in e.g., [9]. Finally, the two WIR datasets relate to the web index recommendation problem and were originally introduced in [45].

We use the fivefold cross validation procedure described in Sect. 1.4. In the comparison, we include the BagSMOTE (B-SMT), Bag_Oversampling (B-Over), and B-Bags resampling methods as well as all custom classifiers discussed in Sect. 9.5. We use the parameter settings recommended by the authors of the original proposals. BagSMOTE, Bag_Oversampling, and B-Bags are combined with the tree-based classifier MITI [6]. This classifier is used internally in the cost-sensitive boosting methods from Sect. 9.5.1 as well. We evaluate the performance of the classifiers by means of the AUC and g metrics.

9.6.2   Results and Discussion

In this section, we list the full results of the selected algorithms on all datasets and interpret them accordingly. We divide the main discussion in two parts, related to the evaluation by the AUC and the g value respectively. We also compare the performance of the resampling methods in combination with three different classifiers.

Table 9.2 Experimental AUC results for all methods

Dataset	B-SMT	B-Over	B-Bags	Ab1	Ab2	Ab3	Ab4	FRI	FRB
Bonds	0.7371	0.7680	0.6800	0.6857	0.7183	**0.8373**	0.7297	0.7345	0.6435
Chains	0.6692	0.6797	0.5726	0.6446	0.6970	0.7855	0.7736	**0.7913**	0.6081
Corel1	0.7797	0.6016	0.8074	0.7512	0.6931	0.8746	0.7960	**0.8751**	0.7469
Corel2	0.7392	0.6005	0.7437	0.7703	0.5197	0.7490	0.7131	**0.8444**	0.8211
Thio	0.5298	0.6169	0.4979	0.6571	0.5000	0.6437	0.6304	**0.7076**	0.6414
WIR-2	0.7893	0.7580	0.7547	0.8196	0.6674	0.8043	0.7384	0.8323	**0.8665**
WIR-5	0.6538	0.7011	0.7067	0.6695	0.5440	0.7278	0.7125	**0.8984**	0.8783
Mean	0.6997	0.6751	0.6804	0.7140	0.6199	0.7746	0.7277	**0.8120**	0.7437

9.6.2.1 Evaluation by AUC

The AUC values are listed in Table 9.2. For each dataset, we print the results of the best performing method in bold. The table shows that, on average, the FRI method from [34] attains the highest result. Furthermore, this method dominates the table by yielding the highest AUC value in five out of seven datasets. In the remaining two datasets, either Ab3 or FRB yield the best result.

Among the resampling methods, BagSMOTE gives the highest average value. It outperforms Bag_Oversampling, which was demonstrated in the original proposal [35] as well. Contrary to the observations in [23], B-Bags does not clearly outperform BagSMOTE. The former yields a higher AUC value than the latter in only three out of the seven datasets.

With respect to the custom learners for imbalanced multi-instance data, the first matter that is evident from Table 9.2 is that they generally provide better classification results than the resampling methods. Only the boosting method Ab2 is excluded from this observation, yielding an average AUC value considerably inferior to those of the three resampling algorithms. Our experiments confirm the finding of [36], that Ab3 is the best performing alternative for the cost-sensitive learners. Comparing the two methods from [34], FRI can be preferred over FRB. As noted above, FRI also stands out as best performing overall method when the classification performance is evaluated by the AUC.

The results of Table 9.2 are visually presented in Fig. 9.2. We have selected the two oversampling methods BagSMOTE and B-Bags and the classification methods Ab3 and FRI and plot their performance on all datasets.

9.6.2.2 Evaluation by *g*

The results for this evaluation can be found in Table 9.3 and Fig. 9.3. The conclusions are less clear-cut than for the AUC evaluation. The FRI method still yields the highest average result, but is the best performing algorithm in only two out of the

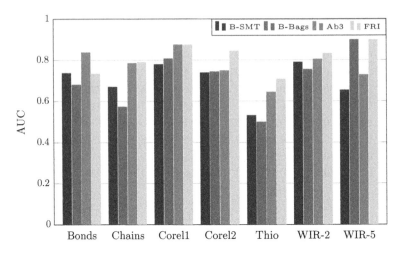

Fig. 9.2   Classification results of the four selected methods, measured with the AUC

Table 9.3   Experimental g results for all methods

Dataset	B-SMT	B-Over	B-Bags	Ab1	Ab2	Ab3	Ab4	FRI	FRB
Bonds	0.7026	0.7494	0.6197	0.4074	0.4743	**0.7715**	0.4071	0.6296	0.6583
Chains	0.5988	0.6228	0.4216	0.0000	0.2711	**0.7465**	0.0000	0.4163	0.4820
Corel1	0.7766	0.4808	**0.8074**	0.1995	0.2819	0.5358	0.0000	0.7846	0.6079
Corel2	0.7325	0.4876	0.7429	0.4527	0.0000	0.2115	0.0000	**0.8016**	0.7526
Thio	0.2440	0.5127	0.1852	0.2673	0.0000	0.0000	0.0000	**0.6612**	0.5521
WIR-2	0.7809	0.7563	0.7477	0.7323	0.3018	0.5898	0.0000	0.7198	**0.8140**
WIR-5	0.5914	0.6577	0.6616	0.4082	0.2041	0.6665	0.0000	0.7551	**0.7879**
Mean	0.6324	0.6096	0.5980	0.3525	0.2190	0.5031	0.0582	**0.6812**	0.6650

seven datasets. Both Ab3 and FRB are each dominant in two datasets as well. The oversampling method B-Bags attains the best result in the seventh dataset.

As for the AUC, we can conclude that the best results are generally obtained by custom classifiers rather than oversampling methods. However, we do note that the cost-sensitive boosting methods do not perform well. Ab3 is still the best version among them, but it does not perform at the same level as the resampling methods or FRI and FRB. Among the resampling methods, BagSMOTE attains the highest average result, followed by Bag_Oversampling. B-Bags performs best in three out of seven datasets, a number that is not sufficient to support the conclusion of [23] stating that this method can be preferred over the others. Naturally, as we fixed the classification algorithm (MITI) executed after the resampling methods, these observations may differ when another classifier is selected, as presented in the next paragraph.

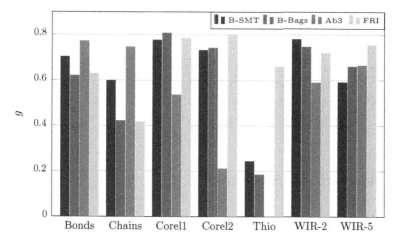

Fig. 9.3 Classification results of the four selected methods, measured with g

9.6.2.3 Resampling Methods

Resampling methods are performed in the preprocessing phase, which means that they are independent of the classification step. In particular, they can be combined with any multi-instance classifier and their effect on the performance of the latter may depend on the selected method. Some classifiers may benefit more from resampling than others.

In Table 9.4 we evaluate the performance of the three oversampling methods in conjunction with three different classifiers. The results for MITI were presented above. We also include the CitationKNN method from [40], using two references and four citers. The third method is the MILES algorithm with C4.5 from [9].

We compare the AUC and g values of these classifiers before (column 'None') and after preprocessing by any of the three resampling methods. The results for MITI were discussed above and we could put forward BagSMOTE as the preferred oversampling method for this classifier on this group of datasets. We also note the clear improvement in the two metrics of all resampling methods on the application of MITI without preprocessing. Clearly, this classifier greatly benefits from resampling. For CitationKNN, the AUC values of all resampling methods, as well as that of the classifier without preprocessing, are close together. For the evaluation by g on the other hand, the benefits of resampling are very clear. The highest g value is obtained by the simple Bag_Oversampling method. This method also yields the best results for MILES, for both evaluation metrics.

Table 9.4 Results of the resampling methods combined with different classifiers, taken as averages over the seven datasets

Classifier	AUC				g			
	None	B-SMT	B-Over	B-Bags	None	B-SMT	B-Over	B-Bags
MITI	0.5866	0.6997	0.6751	0.6804	0.4880	0.6324	0.6096	0.5980
CitationKNN	0.7082	0.7098	0.7084	0.7033	0.1430	0.2905	0.4238	0.2863
MILES	0.5702	0.5829	0.5937	0.5809	0.2666	0.2648	0.4154	0.2927

9.7   Summarizing Comments

In this chapter, we have discussed the phenomenon of class imbalance and the challenges it poses to both single-instance and multi-instance classification. The skewed distribution of the data observations among the classes inhibits the recognition of underrepresented classes. In single-instance learning, many solution methods to deal with class imbalance have been proposed over the past decades. A main distinction can be made between data-level and algorithm-level solutions. The former modify the dataset, e.g., by creating new minority class samples, and are independent of the classification step. The latter are custom classifiers, that use imbalance-resistant heuristics internally.

In MIL, comparatively less work has been done on this subject. We have described the existing methods in this chapter, including resampling methods and custom classifiers. We have compared these algorithms in an experimental study based on appropriate metrics for the setting of imbalanced classes. Our experiments indicate that, in imbalanced MIL, custom classifiers generally yield better results than resampling algorithms.

References

1. Abdi, L., Hashemi, S.: To combat multi-class imbalanced problems by means of over-sampling techniques. IEEE Trans. Knowl. Data Eng. **28**(1), 238–251 (2016)
2. Amores, J.: Multiple instance classification: review, taxonomy and comparative study. Artif. Intel. **201**, 81–105 (2013)
3. Bamber, D.: The area above the ordinal dominance graph and the area below the receiver operating characteristic graph. J. Math. Psychol. **12**(4), 387–415 (1975)
4. Barua, S., Islam, M., Yao, X., Murase, K.: MWMOTE-majority weighted minority oversampling technique for imbalanced data set learning. IEEE Trans. Knowl. Data Eng. **26**(2), 405–425 (2014)
5. Batista, G., Prati, R., Monard, M.: A study of the behavior of several methods for balancing machine learning training data. ACM Sigkdd Explor. Newsl. **6**(1), 20–29 (2004)
6. Blockeel, H., Page, D., Srinivasan, A.: Multi-instance tree learning. In: De Raedt, L., Wrobel, S. (eds.) Proceedings of the 22nd International Conference on Machine Learning (ICML 2005), pp. 57–64. ACM, New York (2005)

7. Chawla, N., Bowyer, K., Hall, L., Kegelmeyer, W.: SMOTE: synthetic minority over-sampling technique. J. Artif. Intel. Res. **16**(1), 321–357 (2002)
8. Chen, Y.: An empirical study of a hybrid imbalanced-class DT-RST classification procedure to elucidate therapeutic effects in uremia patients. Med. Biol. Eng. Comput. 1–19 (2016)
9. Chen, Y., Bi, J., Wang, J.Z.: MILES: multiple-instance learning via embedded instance selection. IEEE Trans. Pattern Anal. **28**(12), 1931–1947 (2006)
10. Dietterich, T.G., Lathrop, R.H., Lozano-Pérez, T.: Solving the multiple instance problem with axis-parallel rectangles. Artif. Intel. **89**(1–2), 31–71 (1997)
11. Domingos, P.: Metacost: a general method for making classifiers cost-sensitive. In: Proceedings of the 5th ACM SIGKDD International Conference on Knowledge Discovery and Data Mining, pp. 155–164. ACM, New York (1999)
12. Dubois, D., Prade, H.: Rough fuzzy sets and fuzzy rough sets. Int. J. Gen. Syst. **17**(2–3), 191–209 (1990)
13. Fawcett, T.: An introduction to ROC analysis. Pattern Recognit. Lett. **27**(8), 861–874 (2006)
14. Fernández, A., López, V., Galar, M., Del Jesus, M.J., Herrera, F.: Analysing the classification of imbalanced data-sets with multiple classes: binarization techniques and ad-hoc approaches. Knowl. based Syst. **42**, 97–110 (2013)
15. Freund, Y., Schapire, R.: Experiments with a new boosting algorithm. In: Saitta, L. (ed.) Proceedings of the 13th International Conference on Machine Learning (ICML 1996), pp. 148–156. Morgan Kaufmann Publishers, San Francisco (1996)
16. Galar, M., Fernández, A., Barrenechea, E., Bustince, H., Herrera, F.: A review on ensembles for the class imbalance problem: bagging-, boosting-, and hybrid-based approaches. IEEE Trans. Syst. Man Cybern. C **42**(4), 463–484 (2012)
17. Galar, M., Fernández, A., Barrenechea, E., Herrera, F.: EUSBoost: enhancing ensembles for highly imbalanced data-sets by evolutionary undersampling. Pattern Recognit. **46**(12), 3460–3471 (2013)
18. He, H., Garcia, E.: Learning from imbalanced data. IEEE Trans. Knowl. Data Eng. **21**(9), 1263–1284 (2009)
19. Kharbat, F., Bull, L., Odeh, M.: Mining breast cancer data with XCS. In: Proceedings of the 9th Annual Conference on Genetic and Evolutionary Computation (GECCO 2007), pp. 2066–2073. ACM, New York (2007)
20. Lee, Y., Hu, P., Cheng, T., Huang, T., Chuang, W.: A preclustering-based ensemble learning technique for acute appendicitis diagnoses. Artif. Intel. Med. **58**(2), 115–124 (2013)
21. López, V., Fernández, A., García, S., Palade, V., Herrera, F.: An insight into classification with imbalanced data: Empirical results and current trends on using data intrinsic characteristics. Inf. Sci. **250**, 113–141 (2013)
22. Mena, L., Gonzalez, J.: Machine learning for imbalanced datasets: application in medical diagnostic. In: Sutcliffe, G., Goebel, R. (eds.) Proceedings of the 19th International Florida Artificial Intelligence Research Society Conference (Flairs 2006), pp. 574–579. The AAAI Press, Menlo Park (2006)
23. Mera, C., Arrieta, J., Orozco-Alzate, M., Branch, J.: A bag oversampling approach for class imbalance in multiple instance learning. In: Parto, A., Kittler, J. (eds.) Progress in Pattern Recognition, Image Analysis, Computer Vision, and Applications, pp. 724–731. Springer, Switzerland (2015)
24. Mera, C., Orozco-Alzate, M., Branch, J.: Improving representation of the positive class in imbalanced multiple-instance learning. In: Campilho, A., Kamel, M. (eds.) Image Analysis and Recognition, pp. 266–273. Springer, Switzerland (2014)
25. Parzen, E.: On estimation of a probability density function and mode. Ann. Math. Stat. **33**(3), 1065–1076 (1962)
26. Prati, R., Batista, G., Silva, D.: Class imbalance revisited: a new experimental setup to assess the performance of treatment methods. Knowl. Inf. Syst. **45**(1), 247–270 (2015)
27. Ramentol, E., Vluymans, S., Verbiest, N., Caballero, Y., Bello, R., Cornelis, C., Herrera, F.: IFROWANN: imbalanced fuzzy-rough ordered weighted average nearest neighbor classification. IEEE Trans. Fuzzy Syst. **23**(5), 1622–1637 (2015)

28. Reutemann, P.: Development of a propositionalization toolbox. Master thesis, Albert Ludwigs University of Freiburg, Germany (2004)

29. Sáez, J.A., Luengo, J., Stefanowski, J., Herrera, F.: SMOTE-IPF: addressing the noisy and borderline examples problem in imbalanced classification by a re-sampling method with filtering. Inf. Sci. **291**, 184–203 (2015)

30. Sun, Y., Kamel, M., Wong, A., Wang, Y.: Cost-sensitive boosting for classification of imbalanced data. Pattern Recognit. **40**(12), 3358–3378 (2007)

31. Sun, Y., Wong, A., Kamel, M.: Classification of imbalanced data: a review. Int. J. Pattern Recognit. **23**(4), 687–719 (2009)

32. Veropoulos, K., Campbell, C., Cristianini, N.: Controlling the sensitivity of support vector machines. In: Dean, T. (ed.) Proceedings of the 16th International Joint Conference on AI, pp. 55–60. Morgan Kaufmann Publishers, San Francisco (1999)

33. Vluymans, S.: Instance selection for imbalanced data. Master thesis, Ghent University, Belgium (2014)

34. Vluymans, S., Sánchez Tarragó, D., Saeys, Y., Cornelis, C., Herrera, F.: Fuzzy rough classifiers for class imbalanced multi-instance data. Pattern Recognit. **53**, 36–45 (2016)

35. Wang, X., Liu, X., Japkowicz, N., Matwin, S.: Resampling and cost-sensitive methods for imbalanced multi-instance learning. In: Wei, D., Washio, T., Xiong, H., Karypis, G., Thuraisingham, B., Cook, D., Wu, X. (eds.) Proceedings of the 2013 IEEE 13th International Conference on Data Mining Workshops (ICDMW), pp. 808–816. IEEE, Los Alamitos (2013)

36. Wang, X., Matwin, S., Japkowicz, N., Liu, X.: Cost-sensitive boosting algorithms for imbalanced multi-instance datasets. In: Zaïne, O., Zilles, S. (eds.) Advances in Artificial Intelligence, pp. 174–186. Springer, Berlin (2013)

37. Wang, X., Shao, H., Japkowicz, N., Matwin, S., Liu, X., Bourque, A., Nguyen, B.: Using SVM with adaptively asymmetric misclassification costs for mine-like objects detection. In: Wani, M., Khoshgoftaar, T., Zhu, X., Seliya, N. (eds.) Proceedings of the 11th International Conference on Machine Learning and Applications (ICMLA 2012), pp. 78–82. IEEE, Los Alamitos (2012)

38. Wang, S., Yao, X.: Diversity analysis on imbalanced data sets by using ensemble models. In: Proceedings of the 2009 IEEE Symposium on Computational Intelligence and Data Mining (CIDM'09), pp. 324–331. IEEE, Los Alamitos (2009)

39. Wang, S., Yao, X.: Multiclass imbalance problems: Analysis and potential solutions. IEEE Trans. Syst. Man Cybern. B **42**(4), 1119–1130 (2012)

40. Wang, J., Zucker, J.: Solving multiple-instance problem: A lazy learning approach. In: Langley, P. (ed.) Proceedings of the 17th International Conference on Machine Learning (ICML 2000), pp. 1119–1125. Morgan Kaufmann Publishers, San Francisco (2000)

41. Yu, H., Ni, J., Zhao, J.: ACOSampling: an ant colony optimization-based undersampling method for classifying imbalanced DNA microarray data. Neurocomputing **101**, 309–318 (2013)

42. Yu, H., Hong, S., Yang, X., Ni, J., Dan, Y., Qin, B.: Recognition of multiple imbalanced cancer types based on DNA microarray data using ensemble classifiers. BioMed Res. Int. **2013**, 1–13 (2013)

43. Zadrozny, B., Langford, J., Abe, N.: Cost-sensitive learning by cost-proportionate example weighting. In: Wu, X., Tuzhilin, A., Shavlik, J. (eds.) Proceedings of the 3rd IEEE International Conference on Data Mining (ICDM 2003), pp. 435–442. IEEE, Los Alamitos (2003)

44. Zhao, X., Li, X., Chen, L., Aihara, K.: Protein classification with imbalanced data. Proteins Struct. Funct. Bioinform. **70**(4), 1125–1132 (2008)

45. Zhou, Z., Jiang, K., Li, M.: Multi-instance learning based web mining. Appl. Intel. **22**(2), 135–147 (2005)

Chapter 10
Multiple Instance Multiple Label Learning

Abstract As applications grow more complex, proper data representation becomes more relevant. Experience shows that a representation accurately reflecting existing relations and interactions in the data renders the learning task easier to solve. In this context, multiple instance multiple label learning (MIMLL) appears as a flexible learning framework. The combination of MIL and multi-label learning introduces a greater flexibility and ambiguity in the object representation by providing a natural formulation for representing complicated objects. This chapter provides a general introduction to MIMLL. First, a description and formal definition are presented in Sects. 10.1 and 10.2. The main applications are listed in Sect. 10.3. Appropriate evaluation metrics for MIMLL are described in Sect. 10.4. Section 10.5 presents an overview of the proposed methods and Sect. 10.7 describes some current advances. Finally, Sect. 10.6 describes the Yelp classification challenge.

10.1 Introduction

As described throughout this book, MIL is an alternative to traditional single-instance learning and represents a complicated object by a set of instances. Even though it allows to easily describe a complex concept, each observation is assumed to belong to only one class. However, there exist classification scenarios in which samples can belong to several classes. In such a situation, more flexibility needs to be introduced in the representation. In the framework of multiple label learning (MLL) [5], each observation can belong to several classes. Examples include images that belong to several classes simultaneously and text documents classified to several news categories.

In this chapter, MIMLL is described, combining the multi-instance and multi-label perspectives. It is a learning framework that introduces flexibility and ambiguity in the object representation of both the input and output spaces. An object is represented by a bag of instances and is allowed to have multiple class labels. MIMLL combines the MIL and MLL frameworks to formalize objects in real-world problems. For instance, in image classification, an image generally contains several naturally partitioned patches (instances) and the complete image can correspond to multiple semantic

© Springer International Publishing AG 2016

F. Herrera et al., *Multiple Instance Learning*, DOI 10.1007/978-3-319-47759-6_10

Fig. 10.1 Example of MIMLL problem

classes, such as clouds, grassland, and lions. In bioinformatics, a gene sequence generally encodes a number of segments (instances) and it may be associated with several functional classes, such as metabolism, transcription, and protein synthesis. In text categorization, each document usually consists of several sections or paragraphs (instances), while the document may be assigned to a set of predefined topics, such as sports and Olympic games. In Sect. 10.3, different application domains are described in more depth.

Compared to traditional learning frameworks, MIMLL is more convenient and natural for representing complex objects, because it adds a higher flexibility both in the input space and output space. Figure 10.1 shows an application of image annotation from the MIMLL perspective. Each image is composed of a bag of regions and is associated with multiple labels. The relationship between the image regions and labels is unknown. Concretely, the figure shows four different images where different concepts are considered, such as giraffe, elephant, zebra, water, and grassland. The combination of a multi-label object with a set of instances allows to obtain the relation between the input patterns and their semantic meaning more easily. In some cases, understanding why a particular object has a certain class label is even more important than simply making an accurate prediction. Under the MIMLL representation, we may discover that one object has $label_1$ because it contains $instance_1$ and another has $label_2$ because it contains $instance_2$, while the occurrence of both $instance_1$ and $instance_2$ triggers a more complex concept, such as a particular African region depending on the represented animals and landscape. In this context, MIMLL has demonstrated better performance to discover high-level concepts. For example, the concept of an African zone has a broad connotation and the images belonging to the Africa concept are varied and therefore not easy to classify. However, if we can exploit some low-level sub-concepts that are less ambiguous and easier to learn, such as water, grass, elephant, zebra, and giraffe, it is possible to induce the portrayed area of Africa much easier than by learning it directly.

10.2 Formal Definition

As a preliminary step to define MIMLL, we study its relationship with single-instance learning, multi-instance learning and multi-label learning, focusing on classification. The definitions of single-instance learning and MIL can be consulted in Chaps. 1 and 2. Figure 10.2 shows the differences among the different learning frameworks.

In single-instance learning, an instance x is a point in the instance space $\mathbb{X}$. It is commonly assumed that $\mathbb{X} \subseteq \mathbb{R}^d$, that is, each instance is described by a vector of d elements. The space $\mathbb{X}$ can be generalized to $\mathbb{X} \subseteq \mathscr{A}^d = \mathscr{A}_1 \times \cdots \times \mathscr{A}_d$ so that each instance is described by a d-dimensional vector where each attribute $\mathscr{A}_i (i = 1, \ldots, d)$ takes values from a finite or infinite set $\mathscr{V}_i$.

In MIC, a bag X is a set of n instances $\{x_1, \ldots, x_n\}$, $x_i \in \mathbb{X}$, $\forall i \in [1, \ldots n]$. Each bag can contain a distinct number of instances. In a training set $D = (\mathbf{X}, \mathbf{L})$,

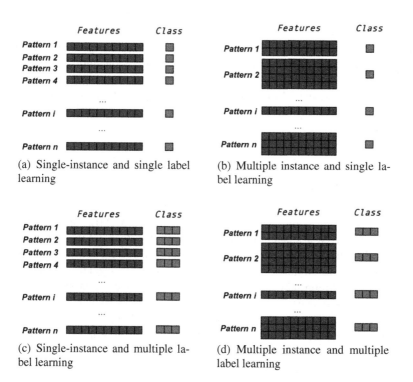

(a) Single-instance and single label learning

(b) Multiple instance and single label learning

(c) Single-instance and multiple label learning

(d) Multiple instance and multiple label learning

Fig. 10.2 Learning frameworks

$\mathbf{X} = \langle X_1, \ldots, X_m \rangle$ is a set of m bags and $\mathbf{L} = \langle \ell_1, \ldots, \ell_m \rangle$ is a set of class labels. Each bag X_i is assigned a class label $\ell_i \in \mathbb{L}$ for all $i = 1, \ldots, m$. The classes of instances inside the bags are not known. The objective is to find a function $f_{MIC} : \mathbb{N}^X \to L \in \mathbb{L}$, that allows us to predict class labels of new bags as accurately as possible. This problem can be seen as multi-instance single label learning.

On the other hand, MLL describes each object by one instance associated with several class labels. In a classification problem, we have a training set $D = (\mathbf{X}, \mathbf{L})$, where $\mathbf{X} = \langle x_1, \ldots, x_m \rangle$ is a set of m instances and $\mathbf{L} = \langle L_1, \ldots, L_m \rangle$ is a set of m class label sets. Each instance x_i is assigned a set of class labels $L_i = \langle \ell_{i1}, \ldots, \ell_{ik_i} \rangle$, with $\ell_{ij} \in \mathbb{L}$, $\forall j \in [1, \ldots, k_i]$. The objective is to find a function $f_{MLL} : \mathbb{X} \to L \subseteq \mathbb{L}$ that assigns a combination of labels to each instance. This problem can be seen as single-instance multi-label learning.

Based on the previous definitions and according to the formulation given by Zhou et al. [39], the task of MIMLL would consist of learning a function $f_{MIML} : \mathbb{N}^X \to L \subseteq \mathbb{L}$ from a set of MIML training examples $\{(X_i, L_i)|1 \leq i \leq m\}$, where $X_i \subseteq X$ is a bag of n_i instances $X_i = \langle x_{i1}, x_{i2}, \ldots, x_{in_i} \rangle$ and $L_i \subseteq L$ is a set of k_i labels $L_i = \langle \ell_{i1}, \ell_{i2}, \ldots, \ell_{ik_i} \rangle$ associated with X_i.

10.3   Applications

There are many real-world problems which can be properly formalized under MIMLL, since their complex objects involve a representation ambiguity in the input space (an object can have many input descriptions) and output space (an object can belong to many classes). Most of them are based on applications studied in Sect. 2.4, although each object is now represented not only by a set of instances but also by a set of labels.

10.3.1   Image Classification

Image classification is one of the most widely studied MIMLL applications. The purpose is to, given a image, identify the objects or categories that are portrayed. Traditional studies have used global image features to solve this task. Such features cannot characterize an image well, since it is usually composed of several complex objects. MIMLL represents an image as a bag of instances, where each instance corresponds to an image region. These image regional features can better characterize complex contents. On the other hand, assigning a single label to an image may be impractical in real applications. MIMLL achieves a more appropriate representation by associating multiple labels with an image. The learning aim is to uncover the unknown relationship between the regions and class labels. The learned relationship can be used to classify unlabeled images.

Region-based image classification of natural scene images has been addressed in several works [1, 4, 14, 33–37]. These studies employ 2000 images and five categories (desert, mountains, sea, sunset, and trees). This task has become a benchmark for image annotation. The classification objective is to predict which categories the complete image represents. Only 22% of the images in the dataset belong to more than one class. The average number of labels per image is 1.24 ± 0.44. Each image is represented as a bag of nine 15-dimensional instances (image patches).

Other works like [19, 22] use the classic Corel dataset containing 5000 images. The whole set consists of 50 groups, such as beach, aircraft, and tiger. Each group contains 100 similar images and every image is annotated with one to five categories. The total number of keywords in the Corel dataset is 371.

10.3.2 Video and Audio Concept Detection

With the rapid development of storage devices, networks and compression techniques, large collections of digital videos are available. Automatic video annotation has emerged as an interesting topic in the multimedia research community to facilitate the annotation of videos with concepts describing the information in the video content at the semantic level. These concepts can be used to index or browse the video.

Traditional studies represent one video clip with a flat feature vector. However, video data usually has a natural hierarchical structure. A video can be represented by a hierarchy including, from large to small: shot, frame, and region within the frame. Moreover, a video clip is generally relevant to multiple concepts. MIMLL represents each shot as a bag of instances in which each instance corresponds to a key-frame of the video. The relation between instances plays an important role, for example when the number of key-frames containing the concept needs to be determined in order to predict whether the shot is associated with that particular concept.

Xu et al. [29] work with 170 h of TV news videos from 13 different programs in English, Arabic, and Chinese to detect the presence or absence of 10 predetermined benchmark concepts in each shot. These concepts are walking, running, explosion fire, maps, flag US, building, waterscape waterfront, mountain, prisoner, sports, and car.

The automatic recognition of bird species from audio files has been dealt with in MIMLL as well. Habitat loss, declining biodiversity, and climate change require the development of better tools to monitor birds, including their ranges, diversity, and phenology. Birds are a good indicator of ecosystem health and diversity, because they are relatively easy to detect, may provide information about other organisms (plants, insects...) and respond quickly to environmental change. However, monitoring bird populations and activity is an intensive task. Machine learning tools can be used instead to estimate species presence/absence, abundance, gender, age, and other individual characteristics. In MIMLL, each audio record is a bag of instances and each instance is a segment of the spectrogram corresponding to syllables of bird sounds described by a feature vector of acoustic properties. The labels are the species present in the recording.

Briggs et al. [3] and Pham et al. [17] work with more than 10 terabytes of audio recordings of birds using unattended omnidirectional microphones. These microphones pick up all sounds in the environment, particularly wind and stream noise. There are often several birds vocalizing at once. The goal is to detect the presence or absence of 13 different species of birds. Each recording contains between one and five species, with 2.144 species on average.

10.3.3   Text Categorization

Another application domain of MIMLL is text categorization. Traditional studies represent a whole document by means of a word bag. However, a document usually consists of several separated semantic parts (paragraphs). Different topics evolve along these parts. MIMLL represents each document as a bag of instances, where each instance corresponds to a paragraph in the document or a text segment enclosed in a sliding window of a particular size. Different labels are assigned to each document.

Several works deal with fragment-based text classification [1, 14, 31, 34–36]. Although all of them are based on the classic Reuters-21578 text collection, a benchmark for text categorization, different configurations have been used to represent documents in the MIMLL framework. The original dataset contains 10788 and 10 classes, but the most commonly used dataset contains 2000 documents and the aim is to categorize them in seven different categories. Documents with multiple labels comprise around 15 % of the dataset and the average number of labels per document is 1.15 ± 0.37.

10.3.4   Bioinformatics

Common bioinformatics tasks are the understanding of gene functions, interactions and networks. Nature often brings several domains together to form multi-domain and multi-functional proteins. Each domain may fulfill its own function independently or together with its neighbors. With the rapid growth of the number of sequenced genomes, the vast majority of proteins can only be annotated computationally. A gene sequence generally encodes a number of segments, each one of which can be expressed as an instance in MIMLL. The gene sequence itself may be associated with several functional classes, such as metabolism, transcription, and protein synthesis.

Several works carry out the automated annotation of protein functions [26, 28]. They use a complete proteome on seven real-world organisms, containing 379 proteins (bags) with a total of 320 gene ontology terms (classes) given by the Gene Ontology Consortium. From the MIMLL perspective, each protein is represented as a bag of instances, where each instance corresponds to a domain and is labeled with a group of gene ontology molecular function terms. The average number of instances (domains) per bag (protein) is 3.20 ± 1.21 and the average number of labels per example (protein) is 3.14 ± 3.33.

Li et al. [13] carry out the automated annotation of embryo images (concretely, studies of Drosophila embryogenesis). They use six different ranges to classify the gene expressions captured in the images with anatomical and development ontology terms. Each image contains only one individual embryo represented by a bag. The image is divided in several patches using a 128-dimensional vector to represent each patch.

10.4 Evaluation Metrics

MIMLL algorithms make multi-label predictions. Their performance is evaluated with multi-label metrics that also have to consider that the dataset consists of bags of instances.

Similar to MLL [5], *example-based metrics* are calculated separately for each bag and averaged over samples, while the *label-based metrics* are computed independently for each label before averaging. Two different strategies can be applied, namely *macro-averaging* and *micro-averaging*. In the former, the metric is calculated individually for each label and the result is divided by the number of labels. For the latter, the hit and miss counts for each label are first aggregated and the metric is computed only once after that. The metrics can also be grouped according to the result provided by classifier. In *binary bipartition*, a vector of 0s and 1s, indicating which of the labels are relevant to each sample, is obtained. In *label ranking*, a label list ranked according to some relevance measure is returned.

In this section, we describe five popular measures. These are example-based metrics to evaluate bipartitions. With respect to notation, D is a MIML dataset, $D = (X, L)$, where X is a set of n bags $X = \{X_1, \ldots, X_n\}$. Each bag $X_i = \{x_{i1}, \ldots, x_{in_i}\}$ is composed of n_i instances and $L = \{L_1, \ldots, L_n\}$ is a set of n label sets, where each label set $L_i = \{\ell_{i1}, \ldots, \ell_{ik}\}$ is composed of k labels. The function $h(X_i)$ returns a set of labels of X_i. The $|\cdot|$ operator counts the number of elements in a set.

- **Hamming loss**: this metric counts the number of incorrect example-label pairs,

$$Hloss = \frac{1}{n} \sum_{i=1}^{n} \frac{1}{l} |h(X_i) \triangle L_i|,$$

where $\triangle$ denotes the symmetric difference between the two sets L_i, the real label set of the ith bag, and $h(X_i)$, the predicted one. There are l labels in total. The Hamming loss, which should be minimized, is an indicator of the errors of the classifier proportional to the label set length. It results in different assessments for the same amount of errors depending on the label set lengths of the dataset.

- **Accuracy**: the ratio between the number of correctly predicted labels and the total number of active labels, both in the real label set and the predicted one, is evaluated. Like all example-based metrics, the accuracy is computed for each instance and then averaged, namely

$$Accuracy = \frac{1}{n} \sum_{i=1}^{n} \frac{|L_i \cap h(X_i)|}{|L_i \cup h(X_i)|}.$$

- **Precision**: this measure computes the ratio of the number of correctly predicted labels and the total number of predicted labels. It can be interpreted as the percentage of predicted labels that are truly relevant for the bag. It is calculated as

$$Precision = \frac{1}{n} \sum_{i=1}^{n} \frac{|L_i \cap h(X_i)|}{|h(X_i)|}.$$

- **Recall**: the ratio of the number of correctly predicted labels and the total number of real labels is evaluated. Recall can be interpreted as the percentage of correctly predicted labels among all truly relevant labels, that is,

$$Recall = \frac{1}{n} \sum_{i=1}^{n} \frac{|L_i \cap h(X_i)|}{|L_i|}.$$

- **F1 score**: this metric, also known as the F-measure, is based on the precision and recall statistics. The mean F1 score is obtained by averaging the F1 scores of the individual labels. It is a weighted measure of how many relevant labels are predicted and how many of the predicted labels are relevant. It is computed as

$$F1Score = \frac{1}{n} \sum_{i=1}^{n} \frac{2 \cdot |h(X_i) \cap L_i|}{|h(X_i)| \cap |L_i|}.$$

10.5   Multi-instance Multi-label Learning Methods

MIMLL methods are classified according to the general grouping proposed by Zhou et al. [39]. A distinction is made between algorithms that solve the problem by degeneration or those that solve it by regularization. In degeneration methods, the problem is transformed to a MIL or MLL task. In regularization algorithms on the other hand, the problem is addressed directly using the MIML representation.

10.5.1 Methods Based on Problem Degeneration

These methods use an intuitive way to tackle the problem by identifying its equivalent in traditional supervised learning (that is, single-instance and single label learning, SISL) via problem reduction. Both MIL and MLL are degenerate versions of MIMLL. They are used as a bridge to solve the MIML problem. Based on this idea, two different paradigms have been proposed.

- **MIL as a bridge**: these models transform the MIMLL task, which learns a function $f_{MIML} : \mathbb{N}^{\mathbb{X}} \rightarrow 2^{\mathbb{L}}$, to a MIC task learning a function $f_{MIC} : \mathbb{N}^{\mathbb{X}} x \mathbb{L} \rightarrow \{-1, +1\}$. For any $\ell \in L_i$, $f_{MIC}(X_i, \ell) = +1$ if $\ell \in L_i$ and -1 otherwise. The labels L^* for a new example X^* can be determined as $L^* = \{\ell \mid sign[f_{MIC}(X^*, \ell)] = +1\}$. As an illustration, Fig. 10.3 shows the transformation of a MIML problem with three labels into three different MIC problems with one label each. The resulting MIC task could be transformed into a traditional supervised learning task to learn a function $f_{SISL} : \mathbb{X} \rightarrow \mathbb{L} \in \{-1, +1\}$, under a constraint specifying how to derive $f_{MIC}(X_i, \ell)$ from $f_{SISL}(x_{ij}, \ell)(j = 1, \dots, n_i)$. For any $\ell \in L_i$, $f_{SISL}(x_{ij}, \ell) = +1$ if $\ell \in L_i$ and -1 otherwise. The constraint can be $f_{MIC}(X_i, \ell) = sign\left[\sum_{j=1}^{n_i} f_{SISL}(x_{ij}, \ell)\right]$, which is used to transform MIC tasks into traditional supervised learning tasks.

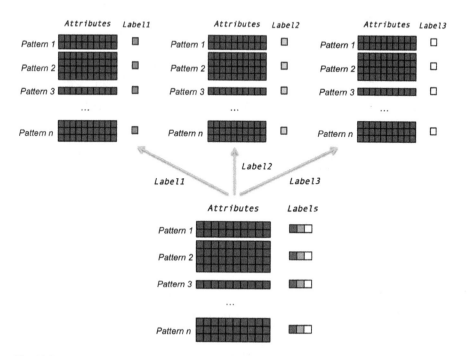

Fig. 10.3 Using MIL as bridge to solve MIMLL problem

- **MLL as a bridge**: these methods transform a MIMLL task into a MLL task, that learns a function $f_{MLL} : \mathbb{Z} \rightarrow 2^{\mathbb{L}}$. For any $z_i \in \mathbb{Z}$, $f_{MLL}(z_i) = f_{MIML}(X_i)$ if $z_i = \phi(X_i)$, $\phi : \mathbb{N}^{\mathbb{X}} \rightarrow \mathbb{Z}$. The labels for a new example X^* can be determined as $L^* = f_{MLL}(\phi(X^*))$. The mapping ϕ can be any that encodes bags as single vectors. As an example, Fig. 10.4 shows two possible transformations. In Fig. 10.3a, each instance in a bag is converted into an instance with the same labels, while Fig. 10.3b depicts the situation where each bag is converted to one instance using as function ϕ returning the closest instance to the bag centroid. In the latter case, each bag yields one pattern. The MLL task can be transformed into a traditional supervised learning task learning a function $f_{SISL} : \mathbb{Z} \times \mathbb{L} \rightarrow \{-1, +1\}$. For any $\ell \in L_i$, $f_{SISL}(z_i, \ell) = +1$ if $\ell \in L_i$ and -1 otherwise, such that $f_{MLL}(z_i) = \{\ell \mid f_{SISL}(z_i, \ell) = +1\}$.

Table 10.1 shows an overview of algorithms developed within this scheme. A distinction between them is made based on the degeneration scheme and on the algorithm type used to solve the problem.

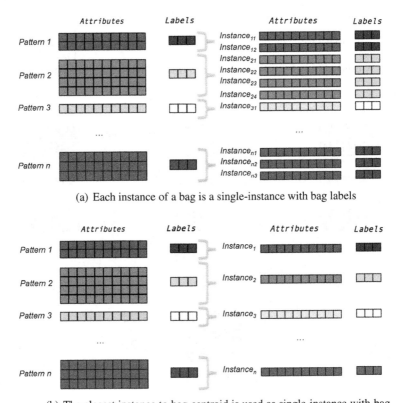

(a) Each instance of a bag is a single-instance with bag labels

(b) The closest instance to bag centroid is used as single-instance with bag labels

Fig. 10.4 Using MLL as bridge to solve MIMLL problem

Table 10.1 Models based on problem degeneration

Multi-label learning as brigde
Kernel-based methods
MIMLSVM [37]
MIMLSVM$^+$ [13]
E-MIMLSVM$^+$ [13]
SISL-MIML [10]
Ensemble methods
En-MIMLSVM [29]
Neural Networks-based Methods
CPNMIML [30]
Multi-instance learning as brigde
Ensemble methods
MIMLBOOST [37]

The first subgroup consists of *kernel-based methods*. Zhou et al. [37] published one of the pioneering works in this area. They proposed the MIMLSVM method, which solves a MIML problem by degenerating it into a single-instance multi-label problem through a clustering process. Li et al. [13] proposed two different approaches based on SVMs. The first one, MIMLSVM$^+$, employs a degeneration strategy that decomposes the learning of multiple labels into a series of binary classification tasks. An SVM is constructed for each of them. Their second method, E-MIMLSVM$^+$, extends MIMLSVM$^+$ by incorporating the term correlations via kernel-based multi-task learning techniques. An improved degeneration approach is defined by Nguyen et al. [10], where the authors propose an SISL-MIML algorithm based on SVM. They use quadratic and integer programming to solve the problem.

Ensemble methods are also encountered. Zhou et al. [37] were one of the first to propose a solution to the MIML problem by degenerating it into a multi-instance single-label problem. Their MIMLBOOST method reduces the problem by adding pseudo-labels to every instance. Xu et al. [29] proposed the En-MIMLSVM algorithm based on the MIMLSVM method. It is an ensemble that first samples several subsets from the majority class independently. It then trains multiple classifiers using these subsets and the minority class. All constructed classifiers are combined to obtain the final decision. With this methodology, En-MIMLSVM is able to deal with class imbalance.

With respect to *neural networks-based methods*, Yan et al. [30] proposed the CPN-MIML algorithm that combines probabilistic latent semantic analysis (PLSA) with the neural networks. Concretely, the PLSA model translates the MIML problem into a single-instance multi-label problem. A neural network method is used to solve it.

The main shortcoming of degeneration models is that they do not use any information about connections between instances and labels or correlations among labels. This information is lost during the reduction process, although it can help improve the performance of algorithms. On the one hand, compared to the MLL framework, MIMLL could capture the intrinsic causation of each individual label and directly model the latent semantic meaning of instances. On the other hand, in contrast with MIL methods that model individual labels independently, MIMLL can simultaneously model the labels as well as their interactions.

10.5.2   Methods Based on Problem Regularization

As stated above, the performance of degeneration algorithms may suffer from the information loss incurred during the reduction process. Ideally, the connections between instances and labels as well as the correlations among labels should be taken into account. This group of methods includes the remaining regulation frameworks that have been proposed to solve MIMLL problems. Table 10.2 shows an overview.

Table 10.2   Models based on problem regularization

Maximum margin-based methods
M3MIML [34]
MIMLwel [32]
Neural networks-based methods
MIMLRBF [35]
IMIMLRBF [14]
IMIMLRBF-GMBO [1]
MIMLNN [4]
Nearest neighbor-based methods
MIML-kNN [36]
Markov-MIML-kNN [25]
Kernel-based methods
D-MIMLSVM [38]
ML_MLML [24]
Ensemble methods
Peng et al. [19]
EnMIMLNN [26]
Other methologies
Yang et al. [31]
MIML-RE [23]
MIMLGP [6]
Pham et al. (I) [16]
Pham et al. (II) [17]

Following the same procedure as above, these algorithms are grouped according to the approach used to solve the MIMLL problem.

Maximum margin-based methods generally use a subset of the available instances in a given bag and maximize the margin between classes. The score of a bag with respect to each class is computed from the score-maximizing instance in the bag. One of the earliest works in this context was of Zhang et al. [34], who proposed a maximum margin method named Maximum Margin Method for Multi-Instance Multi-Label learning (M3MIML). This method directly considers the connections between instances and labels by defining a specific margin on each example. M3MIML assumes a linear model for each class, where the output for one class is set to the maximum prediction of all the MIML examples instances with respect to the corresponding linear model. Subsequently, the outputs for all possible classes are combined to define the margin of the MIML example within the classification system. Following a similar theory, Yang et al. [32] proposed the MIMLwel approach, that assumes that highly relevant labels share some common instances and that the underlying class means of bags for each label have a large margin. In this proposal, a bag of instances is first mapped to a feature vector, where each element measures the degree of the bag associated with a group of similar instances. Afterward, sparse predictors are employed to learn the bag labels such that the class means of bags for each label are maximized.

Proposals based on *neural network methods* for tackling MIML problems have been developed as well. Zhang et al. [35] proposed the MIMLRBF algorithm, which uses a radial basis function (RBF). A k-medoids clustering step groups the examples of each class. The weights of the method are optimized by a sum-of-squares error function. An improved version of this model was proposed by Li et al. [14]. Their IMIMLRBF method applies an improved k-medoids clustering on the data that still performs appropriately in case of noise. Another improvement of MIMLRBF has recently been developed [1]. The authors proposed a hybrid search method to estimate the RBF neural network parameters (the weights, widths and centers of the hidden units) simultaneously. First, the Gases Brownian Motion optimization algorithm is used to determine the width and center of the network nodes. Next, the parameters are optimized by a gradient-based method. Chen et al. [4] also proposed a multi-instance multi-label algorithm based on neural networks, MIMLNN, based on the popular multi-layer perceptron and derived with the classic backpropagation algorithm.

Proposals based on *k-Nearest Neighbor* are also used to solve this type of problems. Zhang et al. [36] proposed the MIML-kNN algorithm based on the popular k-nearest neighbor technique. MIMLkNN makes predictions based on neighboring and citing examples. This algorithm was computationally optimized with MarkovMIML-kNN learning [25]. MarkovMIMLkNN is a nearest neighbor approach to learn correct labels based on neighbor information as well as on the affinities in a Markov chain. The Markov chain computes the class probability of each object, instead of determining the k-nearest neighbors of the unseen object and using maximum a posteriori probability to calculate its label.

With respect to *methods based on kernels*, Zhou et al. [38] proposed the D-MIMLSVM algorithm using SVMs. Its basic assumption is that the labels associated with the same examples are somehow related and that the bag classification performance depends on the information loss between the labels and the predictions on the bags as well as on the constituent instances. Recently, Tong et al. [24] proposed the ML_MLML algorithm. This method proceeds in three steps. First, instance correlations in a bag are described by constructing a graph. This graph is mapped to a vector in a high-dimensional space to represent the bag features. With this information, the multi-instance bag is transformed into a single-instance sample. Next, considering that predictions of different labels correspond to graphs in different scales, MK_MIML introduces multi-kernel fusion. It constructs multiple kernel functions according to different parameters and graphs in different scales. In the fusion step, a convex combination of the kernels is considered. Finally, the algorithm performs its classification by means of SVM.

Several proposals use *ensemble-based methods*. Peng et al. [19] proposed an ensemble method to combine the results of MIMLSVM$^+$ trained on different visual features. More recently, Wu et al. [26] proposed an ensemble MIML learning framework, EnMIMLNN. Concretely, three algorithms were developed by combining the advantage of three kinds of Hausdorff distance metrics and different voting-based methods.

The remaining frameworks to address the MIML problem are grouped together. Yang et al. [31] proposed the Dirichlet–Bernoulli Alignment (DBA) approach, a probabilistic generative model for multi-class, multi-label, and multi-instance corpora. DBA assumes a tree-structure in the data. Its model is similar to latent Dirichlet Allocation. In DBA, each pattern is modeled as a mixture over the set of predefined classes. An instance is then generated independently conditioned on a sampled class label. The label of a pattern is generated from a Bernoulli distribution conditioned on all the sampled labels used for generating its instances. From another perspective, Surdeanu et al. [23] proposed MIML-RE, a graphical model based on distant supervision for relation extraction. It models both multiple instances (by modeling the latent labels assigned to instances) and multiple labels (by providing a simple method to capture dependencies between labels). The proposal of Briggs et al. [2] presented a possible solution using label ranking. They proposed rank-loss support instance machines, that optimize a regularized rank-loss objective for each bag and can be instantiated with different aggregation models connecting instance-level and bag-level predictions. He et al. [6] proposed the MIMLGP algorithm based on a Gaussian process. The basic idea is to define a latent function with a Gaussian process prior in the instance space for every label and then output the probabilities over different labels for each sample based on the latent function values of its instances. In later work, MIMLGP was used to solve multi-label problems in visual mobile robot navigation [7]. Recently, models based on the maximum likelihood approach have been developed. Pham et al. [16] proposed a discriminative probabilistic model based on maximum likelihood to determine the model parameters and learn an instance-level classifier that accounts for novel instances. At the same time,

Pham et al. [17] proposed a graphical model based on these principles taking into account the inner structure of each class.

10.6 Case Study: Kaggle Yelp Challenge

The Yelp Restaurant Photo Classification recruitment competition[1] ran on Kaggle from December 2015 to April 2016 corresponding with round 6 of the Yelp dataset challenge. The Yelp Data Challenge is globally organized and consists of the classification of restaurants based on images that various Yelp users have posted. The idea is to use business images to automatically capture meta-data and be able to semantically infer coherent information regarding restaurants, which allows to improve recommendations to users.

Yelp has millions of photos uploaded from all around the world. Some examples are shown in Fig. 10.5. These pictures can provide valuable information and insights into the restaurants they are visually describing. A user may want to know if a restaurant is good for a romantic date, has live music, or serves alcohol. Currently, restaurant labels are manually selected by Yelp users when they submit a photo. They can give ratings and write reviews on businesses and services. While ratings are useful to communicate the overall experience, they do not convey the context which led a

Fig. 10.5 Restaurant photos of the Yelp dataset

---

[1]https://www.kaggle.com/c/yelp-restaurant-photo-classification.

Comment
We have the **best happy hours**, **the food is good**, and **service is even better**. When it is winter we become regulars

Categories	
Service	good
Food	good
Discounts	Happy hours
Ambience	0
Prices	0

Fig. 10.6 Relating categories with comments

reviewer to that experience. For example, Fig. 10.6 considers a comment about a restaurant given by a Yelp user: *"We have the best happy hours, the food is good, and service is even better. When it is winter we become regulars."* Together with the comment, the user gave the restaurant a 4 star rating. This comment allows to identify that the review talks about *food*, *service* and *deals/discounts* (happy hour). Food and service categories are easy to interpret. Deals and discounts categories correspond to offers during happy hour or specials run by the venue. Other categories, such as an ambiance category related to the look and feel of the restaurant or a price category are not considered in this comment.

This high-level categorization of reviews into relevant categories can help a user to understand the rating assigned by others. It can assist other Yelp users to make a personalized choice, especially when one does not have much time to peruse reviews. It can also be used to rank restaurants according to these categories.

This task can be viewed as a MIMLL problem in the image domain. Each restaurant has an arbitrary number of photos associated with it and can be assigned to multiple categories (many output labels).

10.6.1 Dataset of Round 6 Yelp Challenge

The full dataset is comprised of approximately 234000 images corresponding to 2000 restaurants. The number of images corresponding to each restaurant ranges from 1 to 2974, with roughly 117 images per restaurant on average. The test set contains 237152 images with information on around 10000 businesses. Each business can have nine self-explanatory attributes which are not evenly distributed. The frequency, identifier, and name of each individual label in the training set is presented in Table 10.3.

The goal is to predict class labels from photos uploaded by users. These labels are annotated by the Yelp community and are based on a real-life scrape of Yelp data. Labels can be incomplete or noisy. There are images in the dataset that include photographs of outdoor scenes and leisure photos not at all related to a restaurant. The attribute distribution across images is not uniform, as there are some attributes that occur more frequently than others. Duplicate information can occur as well, as

Table 10.3 Categories: names and frequencies

ID	Label	Relative frequency
0	Good for lunch	0.336
1	Good for dinner	0.497
2	Takes reservations	0.513
3	Outdoor seating	0.502
4	Restaurant is expensive	0.274
5	Has alcohol	0.625
6	Has table service	0.680
7	Ambience is classy	0.286
8	Good for kids	0.619

a consequence of users accidentally uploading the same photo of the same business more than once.

The images are of variable size, ranging from icon-size to 500×500, although almost all of them are larger than the required input size of 224×224. Figure 10.5 contains examples of restaurant pictures and food items. Approximately 70 % of the pictures of a restaurant are of food items, a good number of these being shots of various items kept on the table. This information can be used for obtaining information on suitability for lunch/dinner, alcohol, or table service. Other categories are more difficult to obtain.

10.6.2   Winners of Round 6 Yelp Challenge

355 Kagglers accepted the challenge of Yelp to predict multiple attribute labels for restaurants based on user-submitted photos. First place was awarded to Dmitrii Tsybulevskii. Thuyen Ngo came in second. We comment on their work below.

First Place, Dmitrii Tsybulevskii

Dmitrii Tsybulevskii took first place in this competition. In order to tackle the multi-label and multi-instance aspects of this problem, he used the *embedded space paradigm* (Sect. 5.3), where each bag is mapped to a single feature vector summarizing its relevant information. To deal with the multi-label component, he used Binary Relevance (BR) and Ensemble of Classifier Chains (ECC) with binary classification methods. His best performing model was the multi-output neural network. This network shares weights for the different label learning tasks and performs better than several BR or ECC neural networks with binary outputs, because it takes into account the multi-label aspect.

Second Place, Thuyen Ngo

Thuyen Ngo ranked in second place in this competition. He used a multilayer perceptron to handle the multiple label and multiple instance aspects at the same time.

For the multi-label part, he used 9 sigmoid units. To address the multi-instance task, he employed a procedure known as the *attention mechanism* in the neural network literature. The idea is to let the network learn by itself how to combine information from many instances. The model is trained using the business-level labels, such that each business represents a training sample. Standard cross entropy is used as the loss function. With limited labeled data, this approach would have badly overfitted the data, since it has more than 2M parameters. To remedy this, Thuyen Ngo used dropout for almost all layers and early stopping to mitigate overfitting.

10.7   Relevant Multi-instance Multi-label Learning Research Directions

As discussed in Sect. 3.5, the inherent features of MIL require a careful study of appropriate distance measures. When MIL is combined with MLL, this topic becomes even more important. Jin et al. [9] proposed an iterative algorithm for MIMLL distance metric learning. Their proposal first estimates the association between instances in a bag and the assigned class labels. Next, it learns a distance metric from the estimated association by means of discriminative analysis. Finally, the learned metric is used to update the association between instances and class labels, which is further used to improve the learning of the metric.

Another relevant area in any learning paradigm is the improvement of the algorithmic efficiency. This task is more pronounced in MIMLL because its hypothesis space expands dramatically, resulting in high complexity and limiting this type of applications. A few studies deal with this problem directly. Huang et al. [8] proposed the MIMLfast approach, which first constructs a low-dimensional subspace shared by all labels and then trains label-specific linear models to optimize the approximated ranking loss via stochastic gradient descent. Ren et al. [20] adapted MIMLfast to perform appropriately in specific classification problems with a small quantity of high-quality data. High-quality data are data where the number of training bags is much less than the number of features.

We also encounter studies that exploit the power of the MIMLL framework by combining it with others. In recent years, many learning methods have been proposed to work with multi-view data by considering the diversity of different views. These views may be obtained from multiple sources or different feature subsets. The learning task can be conducted with abundant information showing a better generalization ability than single-view learning. The combination of multi-view, multi-instance, and multi-label learning has shown a greater flexibility for representing objects. Nguyen et al. [11] proposed a Multimodal Multi-instance Multi-label Latent Dirichlet Allocation (M3LDA), where the model consists of a visual-label part, a textual-label part, and a label topic part that allows to work with discrete views. An extension of this work was carried out by Nguyen et al. [12], presenting the Multi-Instance Multi-Label Mixture (MIMLmix) algorithm, a more efficient model that allows to work with continuous views. Wu et al. [27] modeled the music emotion recognition as a multi-label multi-layer multi-instance multi-view learning problem. Music is formulated as a hierarchical multi-instance structure, where multiple emotion labels correspond to at least one of the instances with multiple views of each layer. To solve this problem, a Hierarchical Music Emotion Recognition model was proposed. Shen et al. [21] combined multi-task multi-label and multi-instance learning and they proposed MTML-MIL, an algorithm based on SVM to leverage both large-scale loosely tagged images and the inter-object correlations for achieving more effective training of a large number of inter-related object classifiers.

Finally, in recent years, we encounter studies that accomplish the specification of novelty detection in the MIMLL setting. Novelty detection is the task of classifying new or unknown data that are not labeled during training and play an important role in machine learning. It is a fundamental requirement of a good classification or identification system, since the test data sometimes contains information about objects that were not known at training time. Contrary to the common assumption in MIMLL that each instance in a bag belongs to one of the known classes, in novelty detection, bags may contain novel-class instances. The goal is to determine, for any given instance in a new bag, whether it belongs to a known class or to a new one. Several works in this line [15, 16, 18] show that novelty detection in the MIMLL setting captures many real-world phenomena and has many potential applications of recognition, such as handwritten digit recognition or letter recognition.

10.8 Summarizing Comments

In solving real-world problems, a good data representation is often more important than having a strong learning algorithm, since a good representation may capture more meaningful information and render the learning task easier to tackle. MIMLL appears as a natural and convenient framework for problems involving complex objects. It provides flexibility in both the input and output space. In this chapter, a description of MIMLL is presented, including a formal definition, applications, and main methods. The recent Yelp dataset challenge is recounted as an illustration of a real-world MIMLL application.

References

1. Abdechiri, M., Faez, K.: Efficacy of utilizing a hybrid algorithmic method in enhancing the functionality of multi-instance multi-label radial basis function neural networks. Appl. Soft Comput. **34**, 788–798 (2015)
2. Briggs, F., Fern, X.Z., Raich, R.: Rank-loss support instance machines for MIML instance annotation. In: Goethals, B. (ed.) Proceedings of the 18th ACM International Conference on Knowledge Discovery and Data Mining (SIGKDD 2012), pp. 534–542. ACM, New York (2012)

3. Briggs, F., Lakshminarayanan, B., Neal, L., Fern, X.Z., Raich, R., Hadley, S.J., Betts, M.G.: Acoustic classification of multiple simultaneous bird species: a multi-instance multi-label approach. J. Acoust. Soc Am. **131**(6), 4640–4650 (2012)
4. Chen, Z., Chi, Z., Fu, H., Feng, D.: Multi-instance multi-label image classification: a neural approach. Neurocomputing **99**, 298–306 (2013)
5. Gibaja, E., Ventura, S.: Multi-label learning: a review of the state of the art and ongoing research. Wiley Interdiscip. Rev. Data Min. Knowl. Discov. **4**(6), 411–444 (2014)
6. He, J., Gu, H., Wang, Z.: Bayesian multi-instance multi-label learning using Gaussian process prior. Mach. Learn. **88**(1), 273–295 (2012)
7. He, J., Gu, H., Wang, Z.: Multi-instance multi-label learning based on Gaussian process with application to visual mobile robot navigation. Inf. Sci. **190**, 162–177 (2012)
8. Huang, S.J., Zhou, Z.H.: Fast multi-instance multi-label learning. In: Proceedings of the 28th AAAI Conference on Artificial Intelligence (AAAI 2014), pp. 1868–1874. AAAI Press, Québec (2014)
9. Jin, R., Wang, S., Zhou, Z.H.: Learning a distance metric from multi-instance multi-label data. In: Flynn, P., Mortensen, E. (eds.) Proceedings of 20th International Conference on Computer Vision and Pattern Recognition (CVPR 2009), pp. 896–902. IEEE, Los Alamitos (2009)
10. Nguyen, N.: A new SVM approach to multi-instance multi-label learning. In: Webb, G.I., Liu, B., Zhang, C., Gunopulos, D., Wu, X. (eds.) Proceedings of the IEEE International Conference on Data Mining (ICDM 2010), pp. 384–392. Conference Publishing Services, Sydney (2010)
11. Nguyen, C.T., Zhan, D.C., Zhou, Z.H.: Multi-modal image annotation with multi-instance multi-label LDA. In: Rossi, F., Thrun, S. (eds.) Proceedings of the 23rd International Joint Conference on Artificial Intelligence (IJCAI 2013), pp. 1558–1564. AAAI Press, Québec (2013)
12. Nguyen, C.T., Wang, X., Liu, J., Zhou, Z.H.: Labeling complicated objects: multi-view multi-instance multi-label learning. In: Rossi, F., Thrun, S. (eds.) Proceedings of the 23rd International Joint Conference on Artificial Intelligence (IJCAI 2013), pp. 2013–2019. AAAI Press, Québec (2014)
13. Li, Y.X., Ji, S., Kumar, S., Ye, J., Zhou, Z.H.: Drosophila gene expression pattern annotation through multi-instance multi-label learning. IEEE ACM Trans. Comput. Biol. Bioinform. **9**(1), 98–112 (2012)
14. Li, C., Shi, G.: Weights optimization for multi-instance multi-label RBF neural networks using steepest descent method. Neural Comput. Appl. **22**(7), 1563–1569 (2013)
15. Lou, Q., Raich, R., Briggs, F., Fern, X.Z.: Novelty detection under multi-label multi-instance framework. In: Sanei, S., Smaragdis, P., Nandi, A., Ho, A., Larsen, J. (eds.) Proceedings of the International Workshop on Machine Learning for Signal Processing (MLSP), pp. 1–6. IEEE, Los Alamitos (2013)
16. Pham, A.T., Raich, R., Fern, X.Z., Arriaga, J.P.: Multi-instance multi-label learning in the presence of novel class instances. In: Bach, F., Blei, D. (eds.) Proceedings of the 32nd International Conference on Machine Learning (ICML 2015), vol. 3, pp. 2427–2435. Omnipress, Lille Grand Palais (2015)
17. Pham, A.T., Raich, R., Fern, X.Z.: Simultaneous instance annotation and clustering in multi-instance multi-label learning. In: Erdomu, D., Akcakaya, M., Kozat, S., Larsen, J. (eds.) Proceedings of the 25th International Workshop on Machine Learning for Signal Processing (MLSP 2015), pp. 1–6. IEEE, Los Alamitos (2015)
18. Pei, Y., Fern, X.Z.: Constrained instance clustering in multi-instance multi-label learning. Pattern Recogn. Lett. **37**, 107–114 (2014)
19. Peng, L., Xu, X., Wang, G.: An empirical study of automatic image annotation through multi-instance multi-label learning. In: Tan, T., Zhou, M., Wang, Y. (eds.) Proceedings of the IEEE Youth Conference on Information Computing and Telecommunications (YC-ICT 2010), pp. 275–278. Institute of Electrical and Electronics Engineers Inc, Beijing (2010)
20. Ren, D., Ma, L., Zhang, Y., Sunderraman, R., Fox, P.T., Laird, A.R., Turner, J.A., Turner, M.D.: Online biomedical publication classification using multi-instance multi-label algorithms with feature reduction. In: Wang, Y., Lu, J., Howard, N., Hu, X. (eds.) Proceedings of the 14th International Conference on Cognitive Informatics & Cognitive Computing (ICCI-CC 2015), pp. 234–241. IEEE, Los Alamitos (2015)

21. Shen, Y., Fan, J.P.: Multi-task multi-label multiple instance learning. J Zhejiang Univ. Sci. C **11**(11), 860–871 (2010)
22. Shen, Y., Peng, J., Feng, X., Fan, J.: Multi-label multi-instance learning with missing object tags. Multimed. Syst. **19**(1), 17–36 (2013)
23. Surdeanu, M., Tibshirani, J., Nallapati, R., Manning, C.D.: Multi-instance multi-label learning for relation extraction. In: Tsujii, J., Henderson, J., Pasca, M. (eds.) Proceedings of the Joint Conference on Empirical Methods in Natural Language Processing and Computational Natural Language Learning (EMNLP-CoNLL 2012), pp. 455–465. Association for Computational Linguistics, Stroudsburg (2012)
24. Tong-tong, C., Chan-juan, L., Hai-lin, Z., Shu-sen, Z., Ying, L., Xin-miao, D.: A multi-instance multi-label scene classification method based on multi-kernel fusion. In: Arai, K. (ed.) Proceedings of the Conference on Intelligent Systems (IntelliSys 2015), pp. 782–787. IEEE Service Center, Piscataway (2015)
25. Wu, Q., Ng, M.K., Ye, Y.: Markov-miml: a markov chain-based multi-instance multi-label learning algorithm. Knowl. Inf. Syst. **37**(1), 83–104 (2013)
26. Wu, J.S., Huang, S.J., Zhou, Z.H.: Genome-wide protein function prediction through multi-instance multi-label learning. IEEE ACM Trans. Comput. Biol. Bioinform. **11**(5), 891–902 (2014)
27. Wu, B., Zhong, E., Horner, A., Yang, Q.: Music emotion recognition by multi-label multi-layer multi-instance multi-view learning. In: Cai, Y., Tavanapong, W. (eds.) Proceedings of the 22nd International Conference on Multimedia (MM 2014), pp. 117–126. ACM, New York (2014)
28. Wu, J.S., Hu, H.F., Yan, S.C., Tang, L.H.: Multi-instance multilabel learning with weak-label for predicting protein function in electricigens. Biomed. Res. Int. **2015**, 1–9 (2015)
29. Xu, X.S., Xue, X., Zhou, Z.H.: Ensemble multi-instance multi-label learning approach for video annotation task. In: Sundaram, H., Feng, W.-C., Sebe, N. (eds.) Proceedings of the 19th ACM International Conference on Multimedia (MM 2011), pp. 1153–1156. ACM, New York (2011)
30. Yan, K., Li, Z., Zhang, C.: A New multi-instance multi-label learning approach for image and text classification. Multimed. Tools Appl. **75**(13), 7875–7890 (2015)
31. Yang, S.H., Zha, H., Hu, B.G.: Dirichlet-bernoulli alignment: a generative model for multi-class multi-label multi-instance corpora. In: Bengio, Y., Schuurmans, D., Lafferty, J.D., Williams, C.K.I., Culotta, A. (eds.) Proceedings of 22nd Conference on Advances in Neural Information Processing Systems (NIPS 2009), pp. 2143–2150. MIT Press, Cambridge (2009)
32. Yang, S.J., Jiang, Y., Zhou, Z.H.: Multi-instance multi-label learning with weak label. In: Rossi, F., Thrun, S. (eds.) Proceedings of the 23rd International Joint Conference on Artificial Intelligence (IJCAI 2013), pp. 1862–1868. AAAI Press, Beijing (2013)
33. Zhang, M.L., Zhou, Z.H.: Multi-label learning by instance differentiation. In: Holte, R.C., Howe, A. (eds.) Proceedings of 22nd Conference on Artificial Intelligence (AAAI 2007), pp. 669–674. AAAI Press, Vancouver (2007)
34. Zhang, M.L., Zhou, Z.H.: M3MIML: a maximum margin method for multi-instance multi-label learning. In: Giannotti, F., Gunopulos, D., Turini, F., Zaniolo, C., Ramakrishnan, N., Wu, X. (eds.) Proceedings of 8th IEEE International Conference on Data Mining (ICDM), pp. 688–697. IEEE, Los Alamitos (2008)
35. Zhang, M.L., Wang, Z.J.: MIMLRBF: RBF neural networks for multi-instance multi-label learning. Neurocomputing **72**(16), 3951–3956 (2009)
36. Zhang, M.L.: A k-nearest neighbor based multi-instance multi-label learning algorithm. In: Gregoire, E. (ed.) Proceedings of the 22nd IEEE International Conference on Tools with Artificial Intelligence (ICTAI 2010), vol. 2, pp. 207–212. IEEE, Los Alamitos (2010)
37. Zhou, Z.H., Zhang, M.L.: Multi-instance multi-label learning with application to scene classification. In: Schölkopf, B., Platt, J.C., Hoffman, T. (eds.) Proceedings of 19th Conference on Advances in Neural Information Processing Systems (NIPS 2006), pp. 1609–1616. MIT Press, Cambridge (2006)

38. Zhou, Z.H., Zhang, M.L., Huang, S.J., Li, Y.F.: MIML: a framework for learning with ambiguous objects. Cornell University Library, pp. 1–57 (2008). arXiv:0808.3231
39. Zhou, Z.H., Zhang, M.L., Huang, S.J., Li, Y.F.: Multi-instance multi-label learning. Artif. Intell. **176**(1), 2291–2320 (2012)

Glossary

Accuracy The percentage of correctly classified observations.

Attribute A descriptive property, commonly represented as a column in a dataset.

Bag An observation in multi-instance learning, represented as a set of instances.

Bag prototype selection A data reduction technique that decreases the number of training bags by eliminating noisy and irrelevant ones. It preserves the most informative bags.

Boosting A machine learning method that takes a basic learner and iteratively creates a set of classifiers that together make more accurate predictions than that the basic learner does on its own.

Class imbalance An uneven distribution of classes in a dataset.

Classification The prediction of a discrete output.

Clustering The division of a dataset in cohesive and well-separated groups.

Cost function A function estimating the cost involved in the predictions of a learning model in order to evaluate its performance.

Cross validation A commonly used validation technique to confidently evaluate the performance of an algorithm.

Data reduction The reduction of a dataset, e.g., by removing observations or features. The aim can be to improve the interpretability and/or computational complexity of a learner applied on the data.

Dataset A set of observations, usually represented as a matrix with observations in the rows and features in the columns.

Dimensionality The number of features in a dataset.

Ensemble model A set of learning models that join their predictions according to a given strategy.

Entropy A diversity measure of class labels in a set of observations. It is often used to guide the construction of learning models such as, for example, decision trees.

Expectation-maximization A two-step iterative method to estimate parameters in statistical models.

Example A single data element, commonly represented as a row in a dataset.

Exemplar See *example*.

Feature See *attribute*.

© Springer International Publishing AG 2016

F. Herrera et al., *Multiple Instance Learning*, DOI 10.1007/978-3-319-47759-6

Feature selection The selection of a subset of the available features in a dataset, typically to remove redundancy or noise and to speed up computations.

Input space The geometric space generated by the descriptive features.

Instance A vector of feature values, one element of a bag in multi-instance learning.

Instance prototype selection A data reduction technique that decreases the number of instances inside a bag by eliminating the less representative ones.

Instance space The geometric space in which instances are points.

Kernel function A function that allows to translate a representation space into a higher dimensional space where a solution can be found.

Label The value of a decision attribute (e.g., class) associated with an observation.

Loss function See *cost function*.

Multiple instance learning A learning framework in which each observation is a collection of feature vectors.

Multi-instance learning See *multiple instance learning*.

Multiple label learning A learning framework in which each observation is associated with multiple outcomes.

Multi-label learning See *multiple label learning*.

Multiple instance multiple label learning A learning framework where an observation is described by multiple instances and associated with multiple class labels.

Multi-instance multi-label learning See *multiple instance multiple label learning*.

Observation See *example*.

Outcome See *label*.

Outlier Unusual value, out of the expected range. This can be an entire observation or a single feature value.

Output space The geometric space generated by the outcome(s).

Overfitting The construction of an overly complex model that fits the training data (almost) perfectly, but has a poor generalization capacity.

Preprocessing A procedure applied before learning, in order to, among other things, ensure a suitable format of the data.

Probability distribution A function that assigns a probability value to each possible event.

Prototype An observation with representative characteristics.

Random variable A variable which takes values from a set of possibilities, each with an associated probability.

Regression The prediction of a continuous output.

Regularization A method to constrain a problem formulation to prevent overfitting.

Sample See *example*.

Semi-supervised learning A learning setting in which some observations are associated with an outcome, while others are not.

Single-instance learning The traditional learning setting, in which each observation is represented by one feature vector.

Supervised learning A learning setting in which each observation is associated with a known outcome.

Statistic A measure used to describe the data, e.g., the sample mean and variance.

Training data The data available to a learner, e.g., to base its prediction model on.

Test data The data that is unavailable at the learning stage, but used to evaluate the generalization performance of the learner.

Unsupervised learning A learning setting in which no outcome information is available for the observations.

Wrapper method An entity acting as an interface between two spaces or data structures.

Printed in the United States
By Bookmasters